FLYING TALES

FLYING TALES

by
Larry Van Pelt

2014

Flying Tales
Copyright © 2014 by Larry Van Pelt

Cover designed by Doug Van Pelt, HM Press

All rights reserved. No part of this publication may be reproduced, stored in a retrieval system or transmitted in any form or by any means – electronic, mechanical, photocopying, recording or otherwise – without the prior written permission of the publisher and copyright owners.

First Printing: 2011

ISBN: 978-1-312-30593-9

Published by HM Press
21102 Boggy Ford Road #4
Lago Vista, Texas 78645
For inquiries, contact dougvanpelt@gmail.com

U.S. trade bookstores and wholesalers: please contact HM Press at (512) 350-3556 or dougvanpelt@gmail.com

Ordering information:
Special discounts are available on quantity purchases by corporations, associations, educators and others. For details, visit the author's website: flying-tales.com

Other titles available on HM Press:
Desert High by Doug Van Pelt
Rock Stars on God, Vol. 2 by Doug Van Pelt

Printed in the United States of America

INTRODUCTION

I can clearly remember my very first flying experience. I was only three or four years old, but the image is emblazoned in my memory. My dad was in the Army and we were living in El Paso, Texas. Dad and mom had taken me out to watch a Ford Tri-Motor passenger airplane that was giving rides. For some reason my dad asked mom to take me for a ride on the big passenger airplane. I remember looking through the rectangular windows (unique to a Ford Tri-Motor) and watching the mountains of El Paso go by in that short 5 or 10 minute flight. Perhaps it was that short flight and the image that was planted in my mind that became the seed in my life that grew to a lifelong interest in flying.

Later, growing up on a farm I wondered how I would ever be able to live the dream I had nurtured for so many years. I discovered that the Air Force ROTC program would avail me that opportunity. What followed were many years of flying experiences; from pilot training, through fighter training, through combat, through the test pilot school, into several years of flight test, and (after retiring from the Air Force) many years of flying general aviation aircraft. A dream which began when I was three or four years old became a lifelong adventure.

Perhaps the most difficult aspect of flying is relating those adventures to family and friends, many of whom have never experienced the joy of flying themselves. Quite often we pilots give up trying to describe to non-aviators some of the vivid memories we have of moments in the air ... **UNTIL a grandchild asks about them**. That's what happened to me. A couple of years ago two of my grown up grandchildren asked me to tell them a "Flying Tale" ... which I was glad to attempt.

The response was most encouraging. They asked me to put more of those tales down on paper and send them to them. Thus began a two-year effort to relate some of the more memorable flying experiences I have had. For two years I sent a new "Flying Tale" out via e-mail every Sunday morning. This book contains all 100 of those "Tales."

All of these "Tales" are true. Where memory might have faded I might have embellished a bit. However the names and places are as accurate as I could remember them. Each story stands alone; hence the sequence is rather random ... to avoid getting bored with reading all about one particular airplane at once. Some of the "Tales" reveal embarrassing errors in judgment which I would not have shared in the past ... but at my age now it is time to fess up to the fact that all pilots are fallible, including myself. Perhaps someone can learn from my errors. I must also admit that reliving some of these adventures had me laughing so hard I had to stop my writing for a few minutes ... even if some of the humor was rather bizarre fighter pilot humor. There were also many melancholy moments relating flights with and about my wonderful wife Carolyn, who has been my ardent supporter through all the "Flying Tales" years.

My hope is that you will enjoy: the ups and the downs (excuse the pun), the harrowing and the humorous, the excesses and the escapes, while recognizing with me that it was God's grace and mercy that prevailed to get me through a lifetime of "Flying Tales."

LARRY VAN PELT

CONTENTS

Watch out for the Golden BB 1

Two, I said "fighting wing"... NOT "wingtip"
You almost hit my brother's barn! 4

Why does the windsock keep changing its mind? 7

New Guy checkout with squadron Top Gun 11

No emergencies allowed 14

I wonder what will happen when we hit that cloud? 17

Pull up ... So this is what it feels like to die 19

Who's flying that? 23

Oh no, I'm going to be cut in half by a Gatling gun 25

First solo ... boom the hermit 29

Squadron Commander gives New Guy the once over 31

Formation roll ... PULL-TWO! 36

My first combat 39

Dive bombing at night 43

Hi, Carolyn 46

Clearing the face mask at 35,000 feet
without losing consciousness 49

Last fighter flight from Itazuke 53

All those hits in one pass ?! 58

I've been hit ... uhh, disregard 62

Sir, I think I found the problem 66

Instructor vs. Rookie dive bombing challenge 70

FLAMEOUT !! Don't worry boss, I'll get you there 74

This is the worst formation flying I've ever seen 78

I didn't know an OV-10 could do that 81

Why do my eyes hurt? 84

Safety chase - you're too close 87

My first violation ... I wouldn't have hit that airliner 90

Double flameout – while taxiing? 93

Carolyn's first roll 96

You don't have to shout 99

Sorry about that bobble four ... Are you alright? 101

What's that thump, thump, thump? WOW ... that was low 104

You can fly close if you want, Fitz, but 107

Carolyn's first flight 110

Strafing record ... wow 112

Flameout in an F-104 "Zipper" 115

Oh no – I'm in a spin 118

Check ride – in a different aircraft 122

JD – Have you ever flown under a bridge? 125

Come on, Stick, let's takeoff – we're doing 200 knots 128

Sawing down telephone poles with a Gatling gun 131

Taking control from the IP 134

First solo cross-country 137

I'll never do that ... oops 140

Bloody cold 143

Dreamland 146

Get those Reveille Raiders 149

Get-home'itis 154

Watch out for the Chipmunks 159

How low can you go? 163

You're cleared to buzz 166

Goodbye Army tent city ... Goodbye Air Force wings 168

Oh no! I'll have to fly through the fireball 172

Clark tower ... I'll just stop here ... I can't see the taxiway 176

Butt Snapper fired ... what's next? 180

If that engine so much as coughs 183

Why did that fuel tank go over my wing? 186

Okay Two – Where are you? 189

700 mph at 50 feet ... cockpit fog 192

Worst airplane I ever flew 195

Shake, rattle, and roll 199

Get off the brakes ... Get off the brakes 202

Super Sabre vs. Spad 205

Uncontrolled flight 209

They're really shooting at someone 212

Sorry boss ... that was the worst landing I have ever made 215

Flat out in an F-4 at 100 feet 218

Oh – the engine quit 221

Don't worry ... you can't bomb that good 224

Check and double check 227

Just one more pass 230

F-4 ... cattle stampede 233

Bucking Bronco 236

Rudder limit 239

Now THAT'S a compressor stall 243

It's just a little thundercloud 247

Hustled by a B-58 250

The 60 second pattern 255

My first OUTSIDE loop 259

Formation with a bird 262

Electric and hydraulic failure 265

School's out 268

Van-Williams bridge 271

Runaway tank 275

Bulldozer 280

What were you doing ... strafing? 285

The ping pong paddle 288

Sidewinder vs. searchlight 292

Road cave-in 297

Grasshopper takeoff 301

Let it down ... Let it down 304

Trees walking 308

Dive bombing in a Spad 312

Happy New Year 316

B-52 vs. F-4 320

Most beautiful sight 324

First cluster bombs 327

Chopper pilot flying my jet 331

Swallowed gun door 335

Gunsight failure 339

Watch out for the Golden BB

OV-10 (Chu Lai Air Base, Vietnam)

One of my more memorable missions at Chu Lai occurred when flying an OV-10 (twin-engine observation plane). I took one of my bosses, a wing commander (lieutenant colonel) from the Australian Air Force, with me. Normally I flew solo. Being my boss, he got to fly in the front seat. Being an IP (instructor pilot), I flew in the back seat. When we got to the airplane, as I began my preflight inspection, I noticed there was something unusual on the airplane. Underneath the aircraft mounted on the belly centerline was this single steel rocket tube with no rocket in it. Normally we carried four rocket pods with seven rockets each ... two pods on each sponson. But here was one single tube on the belly centerline. I had never seen it before and thought *"That's really strange ... what's that on there for?"* The ground crew said they found it and just wanted to see if we could fly it ... just a little thing ... a steel tube about 3" in diameter and about 40 inches long, positioned right under the back seat of the airplane right underneath my ejection seat. I said *"No sweat."*

So we takeoff and go flying. It was just an orientation flight for the wing commander from Australia. He went with me because one of the areas that I was responsible for was in Laos, as well as Vietnam ... out well beyond where the good guys were ... out where there were only bad guys. Australians could not go into Laos. But I could take him over close to show him what the place looked like. So we flew over there and observed no enemy activity.

But while there he tells me he wants to fire the guns, which were armed for every flight. The OV-10 had four machine guns, two in each sponson. He had never fired the guns. I said *"Okay, but be sure to stay above 1500 feet because we're in bad guy territory, and even though we can't see them in the trees below I'm sure they'll be shooting at us."* But the confident Aussie retorted. *"It will take a lucky shot to hit us."* We always referred to the lucky shot as a **Golden BB**.

He was probably right, so I found a big rock in a mountain stream in the valley to use as a target. He rolls in, aims at the target, fires a few rounds, pulls up and turns around for another pass. He wanted to do it again. He liked firing those guns. There was no obvious visible evidence of enemy firing at us in the area, so I said okay and let him do two or three more passes. Each time, though, I noticed we were getting a little lower ... typical of an aggressive fighter pilot, pressing below the 1500 feet minimum altitude. On the last pass he (we) probably got down below 500 feet. I didn't think too much of his wisdom -- being out where we were ... where there was nothing but bad guys on the ground. There was really no place to evade if we got shot down out there. Of course the bad guys always knew when we were there because of the airplane noise, and they were always looking for a chance to shoot us down. They probably shot at us anyway hoping that their gunfire didn't give their position away. But not to worry ... the Golden BB was not to be ... and we survived.

After the strafing exercise I thought it best that we get back to some friendly territory where we did some more flying around in my area of operation in Vietnam and then returned back to land at Chu Lai. After we parked the airplane it was customary to get out and look around the airplane to make sure it was ready for its next flight. When I inspected after this flight I naturally wanted to look at that little steel rocket tube to see how it fared.

Lo and behold, there's a bullet hole right in the bottom of it! The bullet went through the lower skin of the tube and was stopped by the upper skin ... stopped only because it was a steel tube. If that rocket tube had been a normal thin aluminum tube there might have been a different result, as the bullet wouldn't have even slowed down in soft aluminum. I noticed that the bullet hole was right directly under where I was sitting. If the steel tube had not stopped the bullet it would have gone right up my spine. The proverbial Golden BB was there, and I had been hit by it !! ... but a mysterious rocket tube saved me.

I never found out where that rocket tube came from. And I don't know why it was on my airplane. It was never seen again.

Two, I said "fighting wing," NOT "wingtip" ... You almost hit my brother's barn!

F-105 (McConnell Air Force Base, Kansas)

Ken Mason and I had both just been selected to attend the prestigious Air Force Test Pilot School ... hotshot fighter pilots! For a few months, though, we had to bide our time flying singleseat F-105 Thunderchief fighters (the world's largest single engine airplane) out of an Air Force base near Wichita, Kansas.

Flying Tales

One day Ken and I had an opportunity to bring our careers to a crashing end. We were scheduled to go as a two ship flight to a gunnery range near Salina, Kansas and practice our bomb dropping, rocket firing, and strafing skills. These kinds of training flights are the best a fighter pilot can ask for, but this flight offered something even better!

You see, the gunnery range was only about 50 miles from my home town where my brother Jerry and his family lived on a farm near by. With a smile on my face and a twinkle in my eye I told Ken that when we finished on the gunnery range, we would just fly over there and I would show him the farm where I grew up. Most fighter pilots would quickly recognize this as a recipe for disaster ... so I did make some cautionary comments. I specifically told Ken that as we approached the farm to be sure and be in the "fighting wing" position, which would place his aircraft about 500 feet behind me and about 30 degrees off to the side, where he could maneuver with me and observe my position regardless of how violently I maneuvered and still keep a safe distance.

Well, the gunnery range practice went smilingly, and I signaled Ken to join up on me in close "wingtip" formation where we visually checked each other for any abnormalities. Finding none, I signaled him to move into "fighting wing" position and we proceeded at low level (about 500 feet above the ground) to a rendezvous with a memory ... and nearly a terrifying one at that.

We approached Jerry's farm in our awesome, silver Thunderchiefs at such a low altitude that I didn't see it until we were only about five miles away. I checked Ken's position and told him the "target" was in sight and I was going down to check it out. From that point on I concentrated my attention on the farm and began my descent to give Jerry a "good look" at his brother's F-105. As I approached the farm (at about 450 mph) I descended to about 100 feet and rolled rapidly into a steep right bank so I could look out the side of the canopy right down on Jerry. Oh, it was a perfect pass ... I went right between the shop and the silo! And when I looked down, there was Jerry standing outside the shop, waving.

HOWEVER, when I looked down at Jerry I also saw something that nearly stopped my heart ... KEN was flying CLOSE '**WINGTIP**' FORMATION on my right wing !! I almost drug him into the barn !!

Of course, he was concentrating on me (looking UP at my aircraft) and had no idea his aircraft was precariously close to extinction. Since I was at about 100 feet above the ground and he was below me as I banked to the right, his right wingtip must have been about 50 above the ground. The trees were about that tall! I was sure glad that I had flown BETWEEN the shop and the silo ... otherwise Ken's aircraft may have hit something very hard.

Fortunately Ken had always flown close formation with his wing overlapping the lead aircraft's wing. Hence, Ken's canopy was probably less than 10 feet from my right wingtip. I say fortunately, because if he had not been overlapping wingtips with me, he might have made a very angry fireball clear across my brother's farmyard ... and brought our Air Force careers to a literal crashing end!! Besides, I don't think Jerry would have appreciated that.

As we pulled up from that pass I judiciously gained a few hundred feet and then transmitted *"TWO, I SAID FIGHTING WING!"* (One usually does not shout on the radio. But this time, it just came naturally). Ken moved out and then we 'calmly' put on a demonstration of tactical fighter maneuvering before we departed to return back to base.

Many days later, when I visited Jerry, he asked me a strange question. He asked *"Do you always fly that close to each other?"* I don't remember what I told him.

Why does the windsock keep changing its mind?

Cessna 120 (Manhattan, Kansas)

There I was, a confident new pilot with at least ten or twelve hours total flying time, flying solo out beyond sight of the airport, just doing my thing ... learning how to keep my wings level, make turns, change airspeed ... all of those exciting (?) things that make flying such a challenging and rewarding experience.

I noticed the weather looked kind of strange though, even for Kansas in the Spring, so as I headed back to the field, I thought I would just impress my instructor with my situational awareness and enter the pattern in textbook fashion ... heading for the center of the field, observing the windsock, and then circling the field to set up a downwind leg for landing on the appropriate runway. You see, there were two runways at Manhattan municipal airport, one oriented North-South and the other oriented East-West. A wise pilot would first observe which way the wind was blowing by observing the windsock and then position himself on a downwind.

As I approached the airfield from the east I dutifully noted that the windsock was pointing to the north, so I concentrated in positioning myself on downwind for a landing to the south. Being careful to keep my altitude exact and make a precise turn to downwind (to impress my instructor, who I noted was in his jeep parked near the middle of the runway intersection ... I thought this was kind of strange, but didn't give it much thought, except to be sure I was very precise in my traffic pattern entry). After I had positioned myself very accurately on the proper downwind heading at the proper altitude and at the proper airspeed, I then had time to glance at the ground again and noticed that the proper heading was not producing the proper ground track.

I then stole a quick look at the windsock, and it was now pointing to the west! That's strange, I thought, but I now knew that I set up to land on the wrong runway (and oh dear, my instructor was watching from the ground). Oh well ... I decided that I was in position to just turn 90 degrees left onto a downwind to land on the east runway. This time I REALLY concentrated on positioning properly on heading and altitude and airspeed. After the necessary attention to these required details, I again looked back at the airfield and noticed that I was again drifting away from the desired ground track.

Another quick look at the windsock revealed that I had a determined adversary ... that darn windsock was now pointing south and it was sticking out very briskly. How could that windsock do this to me? He had never been this contrary before. I also noticed that my instructor was now standing out in the middle of the runway intersection jumping up and down and waving his arms. Since I was flying so precisely, I surmised that he must have another student in the pattern that I had not been aware of.

Well, I decided it was now time to enter the downwind leg to land to the north. After more time concentrating on setting up at the proper downwind heading, airspeed and altitude, I again took time to look out and observe my position with respect to the runway. Again, I had not flown parallel to the desired runway, and a quick look at the windsock revealed that that dastardly thing had again changed its mind. I also noticed that my instructor seemed to be directing all his attention towards me and waving quite dramatically. I guessed he was impatient and wanted to see one of my wonderful landings.

So, even though the windsock was now pointing down the runway I had just passed up, I decided that that windsock was out of commission and I was going to land to the north. I was getting tired of chasing that thing. I now concentrated on making a perfect approach to a perfect touchdown. But my attention had been diverted somewhat, and as I got closer to the runway my airplane (a Cessna 120 ... a two place taildragger) began to jump around like a colt being ridden for the first time. What an embarrassment ... me, mister smooth pilot, was being tossed around by a cantankerous young airplane. A quick glance showed me that the windsock was doing its thing and moving one direction and then the other. And there was my instructor, standing in the runway ahead of me motioning for me to put it down.

I soon realized I didn't have much choice. I thought maybe a wheel landing would impress him, but with the wind blowing from all directions, I just kind of created my own landing style. Well, the wing rolled up and then it rolled down and then I finally made contact with the runway and then bounced back up in the air, and then another contact and another bounce. After a few really wild bounces and some nose swaying back and forth with vigor, I finally came to a stop. And you know what? When I looked at that stupid windsock, it was pointing away from me and I think it was laughing.

I came to a stop pretty close to my instructor, actually. He kind of went limp for a few seconds, and then he came running over to my airplane and got in. I thought the door was going to fly off when he opened it. That's when I noticed that a lot of weeds and other debris were flying all over the field.

My instructor seemed calmer than when I had seen him from the air. He kind of sighed and said he was glad I made it. He wouldn't let me taxi the airplane back in though. He said something about a frontal passage (whatever that is) with gusts of 30 to 40 knots just as I was landing. Up until then, I had thought 30 knot winds were normal for flying. But I did learn to be wary when the windsock starts dancing and can't make up its mind.

New Guy checkout with squadron "Top Gun"

F-100 (Itazuke Air Base, Japan)

As a brand new "certified" fighter pilot, I arrived for my first operational assignment at Itazuke Air Base, Japan in May of 1962.

I was about to be one of the "Flying Fiends" of the 36th Tactical Fighter Squadron and fly their F-100 Super Sabres. The new guy was affectionately called an "FNG" (funny new guy) until he had accumulated over 1000 hours flying time. We even had an FNG patch with a colored star attached when we reached 750 hours. Well, with only 300 total hours and about 140 hours in the F-100, I had a long way to go before I achieved "old head" status. But I didn't care. I was living my lifelong dream ... to be flying fighters with the big boys.

The new guy is not exactly accepted with open arms by the "old heads." He must earn that acceptance by demonstrating his flying prowess. That process began for me, in earnest, when the squadron "top gun" (the best pilot in the squadron ... according to his gunnery scores and the respect given him by his peers) arranged for me to fly with him. Captain Jacob was a stereotypical "top gun" ... young captain, athletic build, spoke with authority, confident, kind of looked like Alan Ladd, and just knew that he was the best fighter pilot in the world ... I liked him. But who was I to say, I was just a green first lieutenant who wanted to fly fighters. Even though I had been tops in my class at pilot training and had won most of the trophies at fighter training (including the "Top Gun" trophy), I was still just an untrustworthy FNG until the old heads said different. When I found out that I was going to fly with Capt. Jacob, I was thrilled ... a chance to learn from the master! I was really up for this flight.

Jake decided the best way to evaluate the new guy was to climb up and do some ACM (air combat maneuvering ... called dog fighting in the old days). But since I was such a beginner and he was the expert, he allowed me to set up in an easy position behind him and then at his command, I was to try and stay behind him as he demonstrated his skill in getting behind me. So, after we got to about 25,000 feet he had me position my aircraft in the "perch" position (about 1500 feet behind him and 500 feet above and to one side).

On the first maneuver, he called me to "roll in" on him and when I was established in the pursuit position (nose pointed at him, accelerating towards him like I was making a gun attack) he began his "display" of superior airmanship. Well, he pulled up and into me, and with a little rolling and pulling of my own I just settled into his 6 o'clock position about 600 to 800 feet back and just followed him through his dips and doodles just like it was in-trail acrobatic training. It was great fun ... I was finally flying behind someone who could really make the F-100 dance.

Flying Tales

Apparently, Captain Jacob wasn't satisfied, because when he saw that he wasn't gaining a positional advantage on me he called it off and had me reposition to the perch position for a second go.

This time he didn't allow me the extra time to roll in on him, but as soon as I was in the perch position, he started his turn up and into me again. But being in such a perfect beginning position, I would have really had to mess up to not get in his 6 o'clock and stay there again. This didn't seem to please him very much, so he called it off and we tried it a third time ... with much the same results, except his maneuvering seemed to take on more frantic movements and his airspeed variance more dramatic, with use of afterburner and speedbrakes. And his radio calls were more curt, as well.

I was too new and naïve to realize that this scenario was supposed to end with the new guy sliding out in front of the old head, who could then later say at the debriefing *"This is what it's all about, son."* But really, he had given me such a distinct positional advantage to begin with. He shouldn't have been upset that he couldn't get behind me.

When we did get back on the ground, he didn't say too much, except to say, *"Well, I guess I shouldn't have given you so much of an advantage."* But I could tell that I had won his respect and, through him, the respect of many of the other old heads. It was after that flight that I was given the call sign "**Stick**." It was a feather in my cap, but I knew it was not for me to boast. It's much better for others to do the talking.

No emergencies allowed

T-37 (Moore Air Base, Texas)

"**Primary**" ... a word that will always ring a bell in an Air Force pilot's heart. For Primary Pilot Training is where it all began ... opening a new world of adventure into the wild blue yonder. I attended Primary at Moore Air Base in the remote southern tip of Texas. It lasted six months and encompassed flying the T-34 for a short introductory period, and then the rest of the time in the T-37 jet trainer. My instructor was Bill Conroy, a man who had a profound influence in my life. In those days Primary was conducted by civilian instructors. Bill had thousands of hours and was very influential in getting me through the initial phases of flight training. He had three second lieutenant students to nurture through this demanding course ... Dick Schaefer, Lee Salmons, and myself. All three of us made it successfully through Primary, a tribute to an excellent instructor. When we flew with our instructor our call sign was Hotbox 14 (Bill's call sign). When we flew solo, our call signs were Hotbox 34, 44, and 54 (my call sign).

Certainly one of the big deals in pilot training is flying solo, and when I first soloed in a T-37 ... now Hotbox 54 ... jet pilot ... now there was a thrill! After I had acquired a measly 10 or 12 hours in the T-37, I was out on one of my first solo rides, doing some maneuvering, having a ball, when all of a sudden a malfunction occurred in the airplane. Malfunctions are emergencies. We train for those kind of things but never expect anything like that to happen. I noticed as I was maneuvering that my elevator trim was not working properly. And, in fact, it soon ran away to full nose up trim, which meant that I had to hold a lot of continuous forward stick pressure to keep the aircraft flying the way I wanted. A difficult and uncomfortable way of flying! I quickly went through all the checks from the checklist, made sure the circuit breaker hadn't popped, recycled the system ... sure enough it was broken. So I did the recommended thing and declared an emergency and asked for a straight-in approach to landing back at Moore Air Base. The landing was quite a challenge, but went fairly uneventful. Pushing forward on the control stick while I was trying to land was an interesting new experience! The flair for landing was a little touchy (releasing force rather than pulling back on the stick) ... an anxiety builder for a budding Air Force pilot.

Once I was on the ground I was greatly relieved as the trim forces had no effect there. Then I taxied in, pleased that I had successfully managed my first in-flight emergency. I noticed as I taxied to my parking spot, that Mr. Conroy was standing there with his hands on his hips, big staring eyes looking right at me ... obviously concerned about one of his students (he'd been notified by the radio transmissions coming from "Hotbox 54"). As soon as I opened the canopy and shut the engines down, he came rather quickly over to the side of the cockpit, looked at me and said, *"I never authorized you to have any emergencies."*

But as I described what had happened his big grin let me know that he was pleased with how I had handled the emergency. I couldn't wait to go up again.

I wonder what will happen when we hit that cloud?

QU-22B (Eglin Air Force Base, Florida)

Many years ago I was flying a little airplane called the QU-22. It was really a modified Beech Bonanza, a little single-engine airplane that the Air Force was buying, and I was the test pilot. I had a lieutenant test engineer as my assistant. But he didn't really want to fly. He didn't mind being a test engineer ... but not one on flying status. Recognizing the challenge before me, I had him fly with me all the time ... so he could learn about flying ... that it wasn't as terrifying as he might think. He reluctantly began to learn more and more about flying as I nursed him along, sitting in the right seat and taking data while I flew the airplane from the left seat. I worked at being a calming influence ... everybody should love flying!

On this particular flight we took off from Eglin Air Force Base and headed out over the water, climbing up to do some testing at altitude over the Gulf of Mexico. It was a nice pretty day but right in front of us, as we were climbing over the bay, was this great big round puffy white cloud. It looked like a giant cotton ball, about the size of a football field. It was right in front of us and I could see we were heading right toward the middle of it. I could easily have flown around it ... it was the only cloud in the sky ... all by itself. But I noticed as I looked at Vic Auterio, my engineer, that as we got closer and closer to that cloud he kept leaning apprehensively towards the instrument panel with his eyes fixed on that cloud.

A marvelous and mischievous idea crept into my head. I'm thinking ... *he's never flown into a cloud* ... he doesn't know what might happen when we go into the cloud. And I could see he was getting real tense, his body flexing, his face leaning forward as we got closer and closer to it ... just staring at that cloud. I could see Vic was expecting some great cataclysmic effect.

I just couldn't disappoint him, so I flew right for the center of the cloud and just at the moment we entered the cloud, with Vic's tension at its highest, I hollered out real loud ... BOOM !! Vic jumped and flexed all around and hollered and yelled at me *"You dirty rat !!"*

In a moment we were through the cloud with no impact at all, of course ... except for the muscle spasms in my stomach from laughing so hard. For Vic, it was another mythical terrifying flying moment put to rest. For me, I'll never forget his whole body spasm as we crashed into that little white cloud that went ... **BOOM** !!

Pull Up ...
So this is what it feels like to die!

F-100 (Nellis Air Force Base, Nevada)

Training to become a fighter pilot is filled with exciting and exhilarating moments. Some of them are more memorable than others. Fighter pilot training began for me with six months of flying the F-100 (a single seat, single engine supersonic jet fighter) at Luke Air Force Base, Arizona. Following that was three months at Nellis Air Force Base, Nevada, where we practiced different kinds of weapon deliveries than we had learned at Luke. Much of the training at Nellis focused on low-level navigation and simulated nuclear weapon deliveries, because that's what a lot of F-100 unit's missions were at the time.

One of the deliveries we learned was called a manual laydown, where we would fly level at 1500 feet above the target and release a high drag parachute retarded weapon. It was called a manual release because we used a grease pencil mark on the side of the canopy as an aiming point (very high technology!). The reason we used a grease pencil mark was because at that altitude, with the parachute retarded weapon you would be almost right over the target before you had to release and you couldn't see the target through the gunsight over the nose, so we had to roll up and see the target from the side. Flying at the right airspeed (on this particular delivery we flew at a very high speed for an F-100, about 550 knots) we rolled up into about a 90° bank and waited until the grease pencil mark crossed the target, and then pressed the pickle button to release the weapon. That would provide the right slant range to release a high drag or parachute retarded weapon to hit the target.

On this particular "memory" mission I was in a flight of four F-100s ... one instructor pilot (IP) and three students. The object was to take off in five-minute intervals, and each fly a low-level route of about 45 minutes up in the mountains and desert north of Nellis. The IP would orbit the target and wait for us, grading us on what time we got to the target ... whether we achieved our time-on-target (TOT) precisely. We each had a specific time to put our weapon on the target (I always tried to be within 10 seconds and was usually within two seconds of the desired TOT). We were dropping a little practice bomb, called a Mark 106, and it would leave a little white phosphorous smoke charge when it hit the ground. When that smoke went off the IP would know what time we arrived at the target. He would also grade our accuracy by estimating how far the smoke was from the actual target. In this particular case, the target was an old abandoned shack out in the desert mountains.

As I approached the target, which was in a small valley in a mountainous area, I noticed there were clouds that might cause a problem in the target area. At 1500 feet I would be just below a solid layer of clouds. Many of the surrounding mountaintops rose up into those clouds. "*No sweat,*" I thought. My low-level navigation had gone perfectly and I was right on time. I saw the target, rolled up to my left, pickled when the grease pencil mark passed over the target, and then rolled right and picked out a place that I could go to the right, because the instructor was just above me below the cloud layer and I didn't want to pull up into him. I saw over to the right, there was a kind of a saddleback, a dip in the mountains, with a few hundred feet of space below the clouds where I could maintain visual contact with the ground. So I thought if I just fly through that saddleback below the clouds I will get out away from this mountain range and over into the desert valley, a couple miles away, where there were no clouds to contend with. Then I would pull up, slow down, and come back into the target area and join up with the IP.

Well, fighter training is not without its perils and lessons learned. And in this tight turn into the small opening between clouds and mountains it became apparent that I was not yet familiar enough with a critical flying quality of the F-100. As speed is increased, the same stick force provides a higher 'g' ... a rather dramatic and foreboding increase at higher speeds. The F-100 didn't have a speed sensing device to change the force feedback. So when you were doing 550 knots and pulled the same force that gave you four 'g' at 400 knots (the normal release speed for other weapon deliveries in an F-100) now produced about eight 'g'. **And that's what happened.** I rolled into a tight right bank of about 80 to 90 degrees and figured if I just pulled about four 'g's it would put me right through the saddleback into the desert valley. It turned out I was not pulling about 4'g', but was pulling about eight 'g' ... the ominous result was that I started to gray out! ... that perilous condition where one's peripheral vision shrinks.

So I eyeballed, with what limited vision I had left (my vision field of view was shrinking dramatically) and mentally estimated how much time I needed to go through this mountain pass ... this now seemingly very tiny saddleback in the mountains. As I pulled through the saddleback the gray-out progressed ... my vision was closing in on me. Pretty soon, I am just looking through a little tunnel of vision. I knew, however, that I had to pull a little bit farther or I would hit the side of the mountain. Even though my eyes weren't functioning clearly, my mind was still calculating (turn rate, timing in the turn, etc. ... just like the engineer I thought I was!) just how much longer I had to pull. I couldn't see very well in front of me so I looked down to the side. That only validated what I already had surmised ... I couldn't see too well! And then I heard on the radio: *"Two ... **Pull up !!**" ... "Two ... **Pull up !!**"* That got my attention! And I quickly, and wisely, decided that I had turned far enough, and it was time to relax the 'g' ... **now !!** So I rolled out and released the 'g'.

My vision came back, and I could then understand why the emphatic *"Pull-up"* call by the IP ... **I was only about 100 feet above the ground, if that!** ... instead of pulling level, I had actually been descending! (so much for mental calculation precision!) I had been going parallel to the desert floor, which fortunately was sloping down, away from the mountains. If the desert floor had not been descending, hadn't been sloping, I would've hit the ground a long time before.

The weirdest part of this episode, though, was the strange thought I had as I went around the corner and began to slowly gray-out, losing consciousness (graying out just precedes a blackout where one loses consciousness ... kind of like going to sleep). I thought *"This must be what it is like to die ... kind of just fade out"* ... I don't know where that thought came from. **I never liked that thought.**

Of course, as soon as I relaxed the 'g' I immediately rolled wings level and pulled up and everything was okay, except that in the eight 'g' turn I had burst one of the hydraulic systems. But that's another story.

Who's flying that?

T-33 (Webb Air Force Base, Texas)

"**Basic**" Pilot Training ... the second six months of the yearlong Air Force pilot training program ... for me was accomplished in a T-33 single-engine jet trainer at Big Springs, Texas. The first task at hand was to check out in the venerable old T-33. When checking out in a new airplane the first flying skill which must be mastered is how to land the airplane. We worried through this phase by flying, with our instructor in the back seat, out to an auxiliary field about 20 miles away from the main base. This austere field consisted of a solitary runway ... and a mobile control tower, manned with another instructor to control the traffic and help grade the student.

It must have been exciting for the mobile control officer to watch the new students learn how to land a T-33. All of us students worked extra hard to avoid his most humiliating radio call for us to *"Go around ... Go around ... You're not safe."*

But sometimes even a student pilot can get it right. And it happened for me ... on one memorable day at auxiliary field number two. On that day I just happened to be what we called "in the groove." Everything was just perfect. I wired my airspeed throughout the pattern. The procedures just clicked. The base to final turn was smooth, steady and consistent. The line up to final approach was precise and I had a consistent approach angle to the runway ... there was none of the usual wing rocking trying to line up with the runway. And to top it off, my touchdowns were just "greased on." I flew several of these "wired" landings and they were all just perfect. The instructor in the back seat must have been satisfied, because he wasn't saying much ... usually instructors yelled at a student when he was off profile just a little bit.

Then I noticed some banter on the radio between my instructor and the mobile control officer. After my third or fourth greased landing, the mobile control officer made a comment I'll never forget ... He said. *"Who's flying that ... Eddie Rickenbacker?"* My instructor chuckled and made some comment back to the mobile control officer. I don't remember exactly what he said. I just knew that I had received a supreme compliment and relished it very much. I kept my mouth shut. I was reminded of an old proverb, which says "Let another praise you and not your own mouth, a stranger and not your own lips."

Oh no, I'm going to be cut in half by a Gatling gun

OV-10 (Chu Lai Air Base, Vietnam)

In combat there occasionally comes a moment when eternity looks you right in the face. One of those moments was etched into my memory when I was in Vietnam, flying an OV-10 Bronco observation aircraft.

It all began in the middle of a very dark night at one of our army installations ... on a small mountaintop way out in the boonies ... a firebase called "Mary Ann" ... about 50 miles away. "Mary Ann" got overrun by some Vietcong. Carrying bags of explosives, called satchel charges, these "sappers" came crawling through the concertina wire and minefields undetected. They got into the firebase and started throwing these explosives into all the perimeter defense positions, killing and wounding the guards, and then blew up each of the big howitzers. They got in so quickly that it took a while for our soldiers to respond.

I was sound asleep and I got the call to get out there in my OV-10 ASAP to control all the air activities out there ... that's what a FAC (forward air controller) does. Maintenance folks had already gotten the call and had the airplane ready when I got there a few minutes later. I was airborne in a flash.

When I got to the firebase there were already many helicopters coming in to pick up the wounded and many Cobra gunship helicopters trying to find and destroy the bad guys. Our main job was trying to find out where the bad guys were and where they were going and administer quick retribution. I'm talking to all the guys on the ground with one radio, the guys back at headquarters on another (they could give me some air support), and the helicopters that come in for rescue on another radio, and the helicopter gunships on yet another radio ... there is just one person who directs all those resources and that is the forward air controller. That was my job.

About the best thing the Air Force can bring into such a battle in that situation was a gunship ... at that time we had C-119 "Specter" gunships ... an aircraft which had a 20mm Gatling gun pointed out the left side which could spit out about 100 rounds per second. I called for one immediately upon knowing about the attack and the Specter gunship arrived there shortly after I did. I had them start firing where we thought the bad guys were dee-deeing (getting out of Dodge). They were probably all fleeing because they had already done all the damage they could do. There were nearly 125 Americans wounded and being evacuated by the time the Specter gunship got there. And all the howitzers had been destroyed.

Without knowing exactly where the bad guys were I had the gunship start hosing the most likely area with his Gatling gun. He settled into a circular orbit, and firing from the left side of the airplane, just put a steady stream of 20mm projectiles into that area. It was a pitch black night and it was easy to tell where he was and where he was firing because every few rounds is a tracer. So there is this nice stream of light going from his airplane to the ground where the rounds are impacting.

Once I had the Specter firing into that area I diverted my attention to directing all the rescue helicopters (called "Dust Offs") and the Cobra gunships trying to keep some order in all of the confusion. I'm also talking to the commander on the ground trying to get a good assessment of what is needed to help their situation. So, you can see, I was kind of involved in a lot of different hectic and urgent types of activities.

Now the title of this flying tale kind of tells you what's coming next. While I'm orbiting the firebase so I can look down and see everything, totally engrossed with the frenzy of activity that's going on, I occasionally glance up in my cockpit to make sure I'm flying safely. On one of those glances my heart pulsed violently and I'm totally shocked to see a brilliant beam of light right in front of me. I'm headed directly toward a stream of 20mm bullets coming out of Specter's Gatling gun at 100 rounds per second !! That line of tracers was directly in front of my windscreen and I only had moments to react to keep from flying right through that sword of annihilation. I knew that I was a second or two away from being sawed in half.

All I had time to do was to push the control stick into the far right corner of the cockpit. That rolled me inverted and pushed the nose down into pitch blackness, hoping I was between the mountains. But my immediate concern was to avoid that hose of iron light. After a second or two I knew I had missed the 20mm chain saw. But now I had to recover from this split-S into the darkness over the mountains.

After a few terrifying moments with no ground references at all ... only the instruments to guide me ... I got the nose pointed up and was finally at an altitude that I knew was safe. I could breathe again.

As is often the case, one doesn't have too much time to dwell on the terrifying moments when eternity looks you in the face. There were too many other things left to do. The mission was far from over ... someone was calling me on one of the radios ... forget the near disaster. But later, back at the home base, laying on my comfortable cot in my hooch, I realized that visual image was now a part of my permanent memory. Apparently God's prevenient grace was in action then, but it was years before I realized it. I thought it was "skill and cunning" that had saved me.

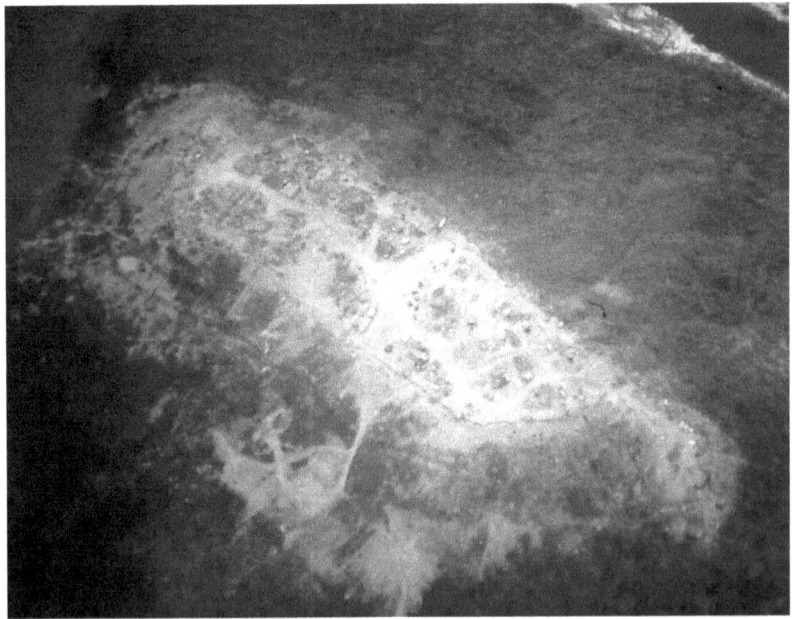

Firebase Mary Ann

First solo ... boom the hermit

F-100 (Luke Air Force Base, Arizona)

There I was ... at last ... about to become a bonafide fighter pilot, taking my first flight in a single seat airplane ... the awesome supersonic F-100 Super Sabre. I had been looking forward to this for years ... the sole occupant in a one-seat airplane! The profile for this flight was standard curriculum. Takeoff in afterburner (of course the F-100 really wouldn't takeoff without it) was followed by a climb to above 35,000 feet towards a specified area northwest of Luke over an unpopulated desert area.

Then came the joy of relighting the afterburner (it was always a rush to light that big bang) and rolling inverted and pulling into about a

30-degree dive. Speed thrills. Keeping that clean (no external stores) F-100 in afterburner, the airspeed in a dive increased rapidly. Going right through the Mach, soon I was going 1.2, then 1.3, then 1.4 times the speed of sound ... pretty fast for a wheat farmer from Kansas. Man, I was king of the hill.

But, alas, I noticed the ground was coming up pretty fast, so I had to come back to reality and pull out of the dive and reluctantly come out of afterburner (but I kept it in mil power (full throttle)). Everything was going so well. I thought I would just continue a gentle descent to a very low altitude. Wow, at 100 to 200 feet the ground goes by very fast at this speed. As I maneuvered along an old dried up riverbed in the desert I noticed an old mobile home just ahead ... probably a modern hermit's home. I wondered what he might think as I roared over his abode at such a low altitude.

As I went by, however, it dawned on me that I really hadn't slowed down much since I had pulled out of the dive. In fact, I was still probably dragging a supersonic shock wave through the desert. I hope I never have to explain that big sonic boom to the hermit!

Squadron Commander gives New Guy the once over

F-100 (Itazuke Air Base, Japan)

When I arrived at my first operational squadron (the 36th Tactical Fighter Squadron) the commanding officer was a Lieutenant Colonel by the name of Obenshain. I sure don't remember his first name, because the new guy NEVER got on a first name basis with him. Obie, as we called him behind his back, was known by all the fighter jocks at Itazuke as the "Original MGF" (mean grouchy fellow). He was some kind of mean. He was ugly, with a capital U. He had the foulest mouth I had ever heard. And, I'm telling you, he ruled with an iron hand.

Colonel Obie personally checked out each new guy. In fact, he usually checked them out before they even got there. I knew of one guy who never made it into the squadron because his flight from the states was delayed due to his immunizations being out of date. Another new guy was shipped right off to another unit when he arrived because he had indicated on his assignment preferences that he wanted out of the Air Force as soon as possible! So, when I was scheduled to go up on a two-ship flight with the Squadron Commander, I was just a little bit apprehensive (scared silly). It didn't take a steel trap mind to figure out this was an evaluation flight for the boss to see what kind of a "kid" he had inherited into his squadron.

The flight briefing didn't take long. I just remember saying "yes sir" a lot and making sure I had all necessary forms filled out (I had worked on them all night long and had my flight commander, and anyone else who could help, check them over for me ... local area map, check list, flight pubs, briefing card, flight plan, mission card, etc.). He didn't check any of that stuff.

But, I sure do remember one significant thing that happened just before we left the squadron to go fly ... one of the "old heads" took me aside and told me *"Now watch out. When you're lined up on the runway ready for takeoff, and he looks around to see if you're ready, you better release brakes."* That turned out to be very sage advice, but at the time it seemed kind of strange, cause normally, when you line up on the runway (two-ship formation takeoff) the lead looks around to see if you are ready (after he has given the run-up signal and you have checked your engine instruments) and then he looks forward and nods his head to release brakes and then another nod of the head to light the afterburner. After that, you just try to stay even with lead. When he begins to rotate (lift the nose) for takeoff you just rotate with him and takeoff together in formation. The next hand signal from lead is a thumbs up to raise the landing gear (an upward nod of the head is the moment of execution) followed (after sufficient airspeed is attained) with a palms down forward hand movement to signal flaps will be raised at the next head nod.

When we taxied onto the runway for takeoff, I lined up farther forward than normal. I wanted to have a little advantage, cause I also had heard he always took the fastest airplane. He turned around and looked at me and gave me the run-up signal. So I ran the engine up to full power, but didn't take but a quick glance at the engine instruments. I wanted to be ready. Lead is supposed to pull back a couple of percent from full power to give his wingman a slight advantage. I guessed that the "Original MGF" would probably ignore that gratuity. I was now as prepared as a new guy could be, and with the old head's advice still going through my mind, I awaited the boss's look back at me to see if I was ready to roll. He slowly looked over at me. I nodded my head that I was ready for his release brake signal.

As soon as he turned his head back, I didn't wait; I released brakes and lit my afterburner. The "old head" was right ... Colonel Obie never gave a release brake or light afterburner signal. He just started his takeoff as if he was the only plane on the runway. However, I had a bit of a head start on him, and was, in fact using my brakes to keep from going past him. He never noticed though, because he never once looked back to see how I was doing until we were half way down the runway. When he did look back, I thought his double take would hurt his neck. I don't think he really expected me to be within sight, cause he always left his wingmen behind (I learned later) ... and there I was ... right beside him ... the young lieutenant was hanging in!

Well then, he rotated and I rotated right with him. I didn't wait for his gear up signal, but immediately pulled my gear up so that wouldn't slow me down. And then I put my flaps up as soon as I thought it appropriate. I didn't wait for any of his signals, which by now I didn't expect. True to form, he never looked back at me ... just kept his head down, brought his gear and flaps up ... never gave me any signals. But that was his way. Then he turned to look at me and saw that I was right there with him.

Again his head just shook, like he just could not believe what he was seeing. You could tell that he was a little stunned ... someone must have told on him ... or the new guy was "not too shabby."

Well, the takeoff was only the beginning of Colonel Obie's once over. I might have passed that test, but more challenges loomed ahead. He took me up to about 30,000 feet, where the F-100 was not known for stellar performance, and signaled me for a "pitch-out and rejoin" maneuver. During this maneuver, which begins from close wingtip formation, lead abruptly pulls into a level 60 degree bank turn (2 'g's) and the wing man waits about five seconds and then follows the leader. The task then becomes one of quickly rejoining up on lead, who, after 180 degrees of turn begins another gentle (30-degree bank) turn. The standard procedure for such a maneuver is for lead to maintain a constant speed from which the joining wingman can assess closure rate and make appropriate adjustments.

I should have known this wasn't going to be a "standard" rejoin! In my exuberance to impress the boss, I went full power and picked up as much speed as possible so I could rejoin in the shortest possible time. It didn't take too long for me to figure out that this was going to be a record short time rejoin ... something was fishy ... then I noticed that he was at an unusually high angle of attack. Oh, oh ... he had gone to idle and was going about as slow as an F-100 would go at 30,000 feet. I did all I could to kill my excessive airspeed (idle, speed boards, as much 'g' as I could pull) and through pure "skill and cunning" I kept from committing the most grievous error of overshooting (going in front of lead). But even though I stopped even with him, I was still about 200 feet out, ready to close slowly back into wingtip formation.

However, Colonel Obie wasn't finished with me yet. He now had me just where he wanted me ... as I came up beside him, with my speed brakes down and my engine at idle, I could almost see him chuckling. He had anticipated my actions and already had his engine at full military power! Since it takes about 10 seconds to achieve such an advantage, I had my work cut out for me. By the time my engine was back up to full power, he must have had a 50-knot advantage on me.

I had no choice but to lower my nose and try to light the afterburner (not a sure thing in an F-100 at 30,000 feet and 240 knots). I was fortunate that time ... the afterburner lit and I soon had sufficient speed to complete the straight-ahead rejoin. But my cautiousness (what is he going to do now?) delayed the final closure to good wingtip formation. Needless to say, I was embarrassed. And determined to not let that happen again.

I soon got my chance. He immediately signaled me for another pitch out and rejoin maneuver. This time I thought *"I'm not going to take 5 seconds, I'm going to turn around as quick as I can and stay as close as I can."* I figured he wouldn't be looking back for me, but looking straight ahead like he usually did. Also, I decided not to go full power right away. I should have known!

This time, after he pitched out, unbeknownst to me, he went full power. I took about 2 seconds, pulled promptly towards him, and, right away, noticed that he was pulling away from me. But because I was on edge and rapidly becoming more wary of his tricks, and because I was much closer to begin with ... the judicious use of afterburner allowed me to make a more reasonable joinup. Not the fastest I had ever done, but at least it was acceptable. When he looked back at me and saw that I had actually joined up on him and wasn't lost back there somewhere, he was either disgusted or pleased (I could never tell the difference with Colonel Obenshain).

He never even looked at me again the rest of the flight. In fact, we never even debriefed. I thought, Oh my gosh, I am in big trouble. But as time went on, I still remained in the squadron. Eventually, I surmised that I must have pleased the Squadron Commander on the day he gave me the "once over" and he decided that maybe I could fly an airplane and was worthy to be in his squadron. In fact, that flight might have been a factor in my selection as the first lieutenant to be awarded the Eighth Tactical Fighter Wing pilot-of-the-quarter award.

Formation roll ... PULL-TWO!

F-100 (Osan Air Base, Korea).

Flying formation can sometimes be more exciting than you realize. One day, while on temporary duty to Osan Air Base, Korea, I (a lowly lieutenant) got to go flying with one of the senior captains in the squadron ... Timothy Z. Ogle ... affectionately called T.Z.O. He was a bachelor ... one of those bachelors that got caught up in buying a Rolls-Royce for a speculative sale in Japan ... but that's another story.

Tim and I were scheduled to fly two F-100 single seat fighters on a training mission (call sign "Tiger") to a nearby gunnery range where we would drop some practice bombs and do some other interesting flying. On this particular day Tim and I took off in formation, always a delight for me. I was on his wing (Tiger Two) ... he was leading (Tiger Lead). I just love to fly formation. After we took off we just started doing formation acrobatics as we headed out to the range. Tim was having fun and I was really enjoying it. I like to fly real close formation with my wing tucked under leads wing (overlapping) ... kind of like the Blue Angels (the Thunderbirds don't overlap wings). As we got close to the range he decided to do more formation acrobatics close to the range tower ... no doubt to impress the range officer and the other troops there with our flying acumen. Not a good idea!

A formation barrel roll is a beautiful thing to watch and a great rush for the wing man. It is begun with a slow pull up to gain a little altitude and then the roll is initiated. At the completion of the 360° roll the aircraft is pointed down and a slow pull back to level flight is initiated. The roll is done rather slowly, so the wingman can stay in position precisely. We had practiced many of these on the way to the range. Since the range wasn't ready for us to begin bombing practice when we arrived we did a few barrel rolls right by the range tower.

As we did the rolls we seemed to be getting lower each time ... I say seemed, because the wingman is only looking at his leader and can't look at the ground. On the last pass we started a slow roll to the right. I was on the right wing. As we came around finishing the roll, out of the periphery of my eyes, I could tell we were pretty close to the ground, but couldn't tell exactly. And as we start the recovery Tim starts pulling more and more 'g's, and he transmits on the radio *"**Pull - Two!**"*

That was an unusual call, filled with foreboding ... are we going to hit the ground? All I could think to do was to stack high on him (about 5 or 10 feet above his wing) so that if we hit the ground he would hit first !! Then I might have a slim chance. But we obviously made it (I'm here to tell about it).

When we came out of it, somebody keyed the mic and said *"**WHOAAAAA !!**"* I don't know if that was the range officer or Tim.

But it told me we came very close to the ground! I never knew how low we got that day. I don't think I wanted to know. Thank God I was able to pull smooth with him and not go bobbling underneath him.

We went on and did our normal bombing range work as if nothing had happened. But that last roll was the only thing I remember from that flight.

My first combat

F-105 (Korat Air Base, Thailand)

My fighter squadron deployed to Thailand during the summer of 1964. We were the first F-105s to operate there in response to the Gulf of Tonkin situation which, more or less, began the US military presence in Southeast Asia. As soon as we got there we started preparing for any combat that might ensue.

My first combat experience was soon to come. We had four F-105s on cockpit alert to go up to Laos to provide assistance, if necessary, in a covert military operation there. While we were waiting, sitting in the cockpits, we got the word that an Air America helicopter pilot had been shot down and they needed fighter escort up there ASAP. The four of us took off within minutes of the call to scramble. Captain Ted Shattuck was flight lead, Captain Rick Layman was two, I (First Lieutenant Larry "Stick" Van Pelt) was the element lead (#3), and the squadron commander (Lt Colonel Donavon L. McCance) was on my wing (#4). We were loaded with 38 rockets and, of course, a full complement of over 1000 rounds of 20mm high-explosive, incendiary (HEI) ammunition ... a rather modest weapon load for the mighty Thud (nickname for the F-105). The takeoff was rather hurried ... so much so, in fact, that Rick made the first-ever no-flap takeoff in an F-105 !! But that's another story.

We took off, and soon rendezvoused with an Air America C-123 twin engine cargo plane (Air America was the front for the covert CIA operations in Laos). The C-123 pilot knew where the downed pilot was located (in a heavily forested, low mountain area typical of most of Laos). He essentially performed the Forward Air Controller (FAC) role for our mission. We circled over him while he appraised the situation on the ground. He was a pretty excited individual, because things were pretty hectic down there. I can still hear him saying, ***"That's an American boy down there, and we've got to get him out*** !!"

The chopper had been attempting to infiltrate some friendly Laotian troops and was in a hover when he got blasted from behind. He went down fast and considered himself fortunate to have survived the crash, even though he suffered some major injuries. The enemy was real close (100 to 200 yards) and was being held off by the few remaining survivors. The C-123 pilot didn't have any way to mark where the chopper was exactly (usually a FAC puts a smoke rocket on the desired target) so he had to describe the location very precisely to us so we could fire our rockets on enemy positions, and thus provide time for the rescue helicopter to make a pickup. Finally, Ted was comfortable with the description of the target area and where the bad guys were located and rolled in to put a load of rockets on the enemy position. Ted's rockets were exactly where the C-123 pilot wanted them, and the rest of us could now see exactly where the target area was since the rocket explosions stirred up a lot of dust and smoke.

There I was, my first time in combat, about to fire angrily at the enemy, not knowing what the enemy was going to fire back at me. My mind raced to analyze the situation. It would only be one hot pass ... dive at the target, fire the gun for a few seconds to scare the enemy out of firing back and then fire all the rockets, and get out of there without being hit myself. A few things sprung up in my mind as I positioned my Thud for the attack. I suddenly remembered that my bomb-bay fuel tank was empty, but pressurized ... a normal situation. But I thought if I unpressurized it, it wouldn't be so vulnerable if it was hit (a fallacious thought, no doubt, but one that seemed logical at the time). Secondly, I figured I would be a harder target to hit if I went really fast! That meant recalculating release parameters for the rockets I was about to fire ... a dubious task since we had always and forever practiced firing rockets at a specific airspeed (450 knots). I knew precisely the aiming reticle (gun sight) position for firing rockets at 450 knots, but now, with my mind racing, I decided that 450 knots didn't seem very fast when you are being shot at.

So, with the steel-trap mind that every fighter pilot thinks he has, I quickly recalculated (guessed would be a better description) a gunsight depression for firing at 600 knots !! Now I could roll in (from about 5000 feet above the target, flying at a 30-degree or better dive angle) and light the afterburner ... instead of retarding the throttle! Now I felt invulnerable, going down the chute at 600 knots. And confident, not realizing that rockets had probably never been fired at that speed. It just seemed at the moment to be the "prudent" thing to do ... to just go as fast as I could before firing rockets in a combat environment.

It was just a good thing that the target area was large (usually the case when the target is enemy ground forces). Since you never see where your rockets hit (if you watch them all the way to impact, you will impact with them!), I was confident that my last second calculations had not affected my accuracy ... but, who knows? I didn't have time to wonder if other fighter pilots in the past had made such profound last-second calculations.

All of these mental gymnastics were almost for not, however, during those few seconds plunging towards the enemy. I was so concentrated on bringing my weapon system to bear on the enemy on my first combat mission that I didn't notice that the C-123 had circled directly between me and the target. I passed about 100 feet or so in front of him (probably the closest I ever came to a mid-air collision). It happened too fast for me to pay much attention ... I was just at the point of weapon release ... but he sure let out a squeal over the radio.

The pullout after firing on an enemy target for the first time was exhilarating. Especially after I had jinked my way back to a safe altitude and position. As fast as I was going, that didn't take long. I had just survived my first combat! Probably hadn't hit anything but trees, but the excitement of the C-123 pilot was contagious. He was able to watch the enemy hightail it out of the area (they didn't want any more to do with the mighty Thuds). With the enemy threat taken care of, the rescue of the downed chopper pilot was soon successfully completed! Now it was time to return to base and regale my squadron mates with my calm, cool approach to combat.

A sidenote: They evacuated the chopper pilot to a field hospital at our base and the four of us who provided the air support were able to spend time with him. That really made the mission special, and allowed me to forget about my questionable first combat mission mental gymnastics.

Dive bombing at night

F-100 (Eglin Air Force Base, Florida)

In 1967 the Air Force was developing the world's first laser spot seeker/tracker for use on a fighter aircraft and I was the test pilot. The device was enclosed in a small pod attached to an F-100 single seat jet fighter. The seeker was very sensitive and could "see" a laser spot on the ground from many miles away. And then it would slave (point) the gunsight so that the little pipper (spot in the center of the gunsight) would point directly where the seeker was looking.

We tested this quite often and found that the seeker (called Pave Penny ... it is now on most fighter airplanes) could do just what it was supposed to do. It was amazing. During flight test, the seeker would lock on to the laser spot on the ground, and I could fly directly to the area and when close enough I could visually spot the "target" ... directly behind the pipper.

Well, we thought it worked so well we would just take it one step further and have the seeker slaving, not only the visual gunsight, but the instrument landing system (ILS) as well, so the seeker pod could be used for dive bombing at night. There are two needles in the ILS indicator, a vertical and a horizontal needle. Centering the vertical needle kept the aircraft flying directly to the laser spot, and the horizontal needle was mechanized to be centered at the particular angle needed for the dive bombing ... we set it for 30°.

The idea was to test the device to see if we could actually do dive bombing at night on instruments. So we pick the darkest night (no moon), and then put the ground laser and target up in the darkest area of the range ... miles from any lights. I would just have to use the instruments to fly toward the laser spot on the ground. And it worked fine. I would fly straight and level at 5000 feet, centering the vertical ILS needle to fly directly towards the target. And when the horizontal needle was centered at the proper dive angle ... 30°, I would just push down, a negative 'g' maneuver, into a simulated dive bomb run. I would then hold those two needles centered until reaching a precise bomb release altitude.

Well ... that was the procedure. But one of the dilemmas we had on this early test was that every time I pushed the nose over in the F-100 the negative 'g' would cause the electrical system to glitch. Warning lights would come on, and the DC generator would go off-line. I would have to manually reset it by turning the DC generator switch off and back on. Not a big deal. As I pushed the nose down, the caution lights would show that the generator needed to be reset.

But everything else was working properly. So I would continue to pushover and establish the proper dive angle, and then I would reach over and reset the DC generator and everything would be fine.

Everything was going well. The system seemed to work perfectly except for this little nuisance alarm, which any "Golden Arm" test pilot could handle. **Until** ... I was about to discover that a little aircraft "glitch" could precipitate a test pilot "glitch." On the last of many test passes, as I pushed over, the DC generator did its thing as usual. Calmly waiting until I had pushed over and was precisely on the 30° dive angle, I reached over with my finger to reset it. Unfortunately, my usually trustworthy finger hit the switch next to it instead, and turned the **AC** generator off !! **Not a good thing !!**

Now, with both generators off, the cockpit went completely black, and more critically the AC generator powered my most important instrument for flying at night ... the attitude indicator, which tells me when I'm wings level and climbing or diving. I quickly reset the AC generator, but that didn't help me much, because the attitude indicator had tumbled and it had turned upside down. There I was plummeting down at a great rate in the pitch black night, not knowing which way was up or what was wings level ... with only about 10 seconds before I would hit the ground. I looked outside the cockpit for some sort of help, a ground reference, but all I see is darkness. I knew I was diving, but if I started a pull out and was not wings level I would just be pulling into the ground. I finally saw a couple of lights way over by a small town about 20 miles away. A couple of lights. But that was enough to help me and I managed to get wings level and made a pull up to ensure I wasn't descending anymore.

I remained silent as I gradually climbed back up to a safe altitude. I figured if I talked on the radio the engineers on the ground might hear my fast heartbeat and a high-pitched voice they were not used to. I finally calmed down and told the engineers that that would have to be our last pass, but I didn't tell them why. I'd had enough diving at the ground in the dark, and I didn't need any more test pilot "glitches" to interrupt a perfectly good test mission.

Hi, Carolyn

F-4 (Eglin Air Force Base, Florida)

Being stationed at Eglin Air Force Base as a test pilot came with some interesting "perks." One of those was flying single ship ... solo without escort ... allowing some mischievous deviations from standard protocol ... such as flying a special route that allows one to wave hello to one's wife.

Returning back to land at Eglin after a scintillating test mission provided just such a memorable opportunity. You see, our house was located right beside the high school football stadium in Ft Walton Beach, and so was very easy to locate from the air in a fast moving jet fighter. And since this location was only a mile or so beyond the normal traffic pattern entry, I could (rationally) deviate "slightly" to fly right over our house just before landing at Eglin.

Now I must tell you that most fighter pilots can readily tell you that they know which circumstances create the most noise from their airplane. And the F-4 was a champion at making a very unusual sound (noise). Just lighting afterburner on most fighters will provide a large BANG which can be heard for a great distance. The F-4s afterburner ignition, unfortunately for my purposes, was not a great noise maker because of its progressive and very smooth ignition.

After much experimentation (which coincidentally terrified my brother's cattle) I discovered that the F-4 noise was most terrifying when accelerating at full military power (not afterburner) from very slow speed to mid speed (incidentally, used when entering the traffic pattern !!). Now it took several seconds to accelerate thru this speed range, and during that time I found that the F-4 made the loudest, most awful roaring, screeching sound (perfect for announcing my arrival to my wife ... and the entire neighborhood).

This became most apparent when I put this knowledge to use right over our house, while "officially" entering the traffic pattern to land at Eglin (at, of course, the low altitude required for the traffic pattern entry!). Carolyn quickly learned to easily identify this noise (as could the rest of our neighborhood) and knew exactly when I was overhead.

I can still vividly remember flying a hard, fighter pilot turn right over our house (pulling a few 'g's just to amplify (and aggravate) the noise) and looking down to see my lovely wife step out of the house onto the porch to wave at her husband. What a thrill to see my wife, waving to me as I completed another daring test pilot flight.

Fortunately, our neighbors were friendly and didn't turn me in for disrupting the quiet, urban life style. They probably thought that was just the way the airplane flew. I didn't tell them any different.

It was just my way of saying *"Hi, Carolyn ... I love you."*

Clearing the face mask at 35,000 feet without losing consciousness

F-104 (Edwards Air Force Base, California)

"**Zoom**" flight! Even the name is exhilarating. And exhilarating was exactly what the zoom flights were at the Air Force Test Pilot School.

The objective of the zoom flight was to try to fly an F-104 (affectionately called the "Zipper"), a really fast little single seat fighter, to as high an altitude as possible. We did this by first getting the "Zipper" going as fast as we could (above Mach 2) and then pull up at a high angle and let her "zoom." We flew several of these flights trying to get higher and higher ... 70,000 feet ... then 80,000 feet ... maybe even 90,000 feet!

In order to get that high the engine had to be shut down because it wouldn't run very well up there. Without the engine running, there was no pressurization in the cockpit. And at those altitudes consciousness is impossible without some kind of protection. Consequently, we had to wear a full pressure suit (like the astronauts). In a full pressure suit your body is contained inside what I called a "man shaped barrel" where the pressure was maintained at survivable levels. If you were not inside that suit, they say your blood would boil. That sounds kind of ominous and weird, but losing consciousness ... now that's serious when you're flying a single seat fighter.

Suiting up in preparation for the zoom flight was a major ordeal ... putting on the complex suit with zippers in funny places, hooking it up to a portable air/oxygen source, checking all the connections, and then hobbling out to the Zipper ... which had already been pre-flighted, fortunately, by a classmate. The full pressure suit is very bulky, even when <u>un</u>pressurized, but once established in the cockpit and strapped in ... the takeoff and climb to 35,000 feet was routine.

Then the fun really got started. The pressure suit was inflated, and then the aircraft was depressurized. The cabin pressure was now the same as outside ... 35,000 feet. But the pressure in the suit was well below that. At 35,000 feet pressure one is safe for about a minute or so before you would lose useful consciousness. So at 35,000 feet, we would check the pressure suit to make sure all the functions were working properly ... holding its pressure and everything. That included checking the facemask seal.

The helmet (like you see on the astronauts) had a clear Plexiglass facemask, which you could pull up with just the push of a lever. That action, however, would completely depressurize the entire suit.

The zoom mission was incredibly interesting. Probably the most demanding, task-filled flight that I had ever flown. I loved it! What with all it took to get to this point in the flight, I sure did want the suit to work perfectly so I wouldn't have to go back and land and start the process all over. But on this flight my pressure suit began to have a slight malfunction. I was turning around at 35,000 feet to position for the high-speed run. I might have been breathing a little hard, who knows, but my facemask began fogging and I couldn't see through it. Being a quick thinking fighter pilot, I realized that one sure, but precarious way to get rid of the fog was to dump the pressure and let the dry air at 35,000 feet evaporate the fog on the facemask. So I just opened my visor ... the pressure in the mask, and consequently the suit, soared to 35,000 feet ... and voilà ... the facemask was clear. Of course, I closed the full facemask real quickly ... so I wouldn't succumb. Only took a couple seconds. I must say I was comforted when the suit re-pressurized ... I wanted to do the mission so much.

Unfortunately, the facemask fogged again, so I repeated the quick fix! This happened maybe three or four times before I had to focus on other critical tasks like precisely positioning the Zipper in the supersonic corridor, lighting the afterburner and accelerating to the maximum speed, and achieve all the parameters at the exact point over the ground where a pull up should be initiated ... this time to the maximum angle!

Just before the pull, with my F-104 going as fast as it could (without the engine inlet temperature being exceeded), my facemask began to fog again! One quick mask open and shut ... mask clear ... pressure okay ... go for it! ... pull back on the stick and begin the "zoom." The moment seemed worth the risk!?

The excitement of the moment is hard to explain ... once the aircraft is pointed up its going up ... up ... up! There is no stopping it! The engine really doesn't like that high altitude and the afterburner eventually has to be shut down and then the engine temperature has to be controlled by slowly retarding the throttle until eventually the engine itself must be shut down also ... 75,000 feet maximum . The Zipper then became an unpowered glider with my attention riveted on angle of attack to maintain control, slowly pushing the stick forward to maintain a gentle zero 'g' float over the top. The indicated airspeed gets down to about 90 knots, too slow for a Zipper to fly normally, but at zero 'g' ... pitch and yaw can still be gingerly controlled.

Even the best have encountered trouble here. Chuck Yeager had told us that his Zipper went out of control as he went over the top and it entered a flat spin that was not recoverable and he had to eject. I thought about that as I approached the top, hoping that my facemask stayed clear so I could see to keep the Zipper flying straight. Even a momentary clearing of the facemask was out of the question now (one student's glove disconnected during the zoom and he went unconscious in seconds and was lost). Well, the mask did stay clear (prevenient grace?!), and I even had enough time going over the top to take a quick glance outside ... I could see from Los Angeles to San Francisco and the sky was very dark ... and I had just set the record for attaining the highest zoom altitude for our class ... an even 90,000 feet!

Was the risk worth it? ... don't ask!

Last fighter flight from Itazuke

F-105 (Itazuke Air Base, Japan)

Itazuke Air Base, which many would call the last real fighter base, was writing its final chapter. The base was closing down. All of the fighters had been reassigned to Yokota Air Base. The Strip Club was closing down. No longer would anybody be singing the famous song *Itazuke tower* with the same fervor. So it was only appropriate that the last flight of fighters from Itazuke be a memorable one.

The last flight of fighters from Itazuke, four sleek silvery F-105 "Thuds," would be led by the stellar commander of the 36th Tactical

Fighter Squadron, Lt. Col. Donovan L. *"See me"* McCance. He had three sharp, seasoned fighter pilots under his wing ... #2 Captain Ed *"Muscles"* Fox ... #3 Captain Larry *"Stick"* Van Pelt ... and #4 Captain Dick *"The Man"* McKinney. This is their story.

We knew this was going to be a special flight when the flight briefing consisted of: *"We'll take off ... fly to Yokota ... and land. Any questions?"* We did have a little discussion of what our flight call sign should be. Since the 36th Tactical Fighter Squadron was known as the *Flying Fiends*, that was considered. But one of the captains thought that *Pukin' Pups* might even be better. In the end the boss's selection ... **Zuki flight**, was deemed most appropriate. Now all we had to do was wait for the flight to begin. We knew enough to keep a close eye on our boss and be ready to start engines when he did.

The cacophony of four simultaneous cartridge starts of the mighty J75 engines must have echoed ominously between the mountains surrounding Fukuoka, a sound never to be heard again ... like a bell tolling for all the F-51s, F-84s, F-86s, F-102s, F-100s, and F-105s that had once called Itazuke home. We knew to keep a tight formation as we taxied to take off ... to commemorate all the fighters who had lived here. Our formation takeoffs were perfect we were told. And then *Zuki Flight* was off for Yokota, or so the three of us captains thought.

We joined up into a tight fingertip formation over Hakata Bay in anticipation of soon going route formation for our trip northeast. However, our adventure was just beginning as *Zuki Flight* reversed course over Brady Beach and headed back towards Itazuke, accelerating and descending. Now, it didn't take a steel trap mind for us captains to figure out what was happening. We were going to make a high-speed pass, saying goodbye to the Strip Club (where the bell would never ring again) and Itazuke tower (where the song would never be sung the same again), and anybody else who might be melancholy minded.

We knew this flyby had to be good, so we tucked-in as close as we could. However, with all our concentration on maintaining tight formation, we couldn't really spare a quick look inside to check how fast we were going. But when the shockwave formed outside on all our canopies, that gave us a pretty good idea that we were close to 600 knots (maybe .96 Mach) and explained why the flight controls were so sensitive. Well, Zuki flight's wingmen worked hard and the pass went well. The folks on the ground must've been impressed ... we sure were !!

Now we began to have thoughts about what was coming next. Slow down we didn't ... we were well past Dazaifu to the south before we started to climb and turn back on course. "On course" took on new meaning, however, as we took a heading very similar to the same heading we would have had if we had gone north after takeoff. But we were so glad to begin climbing and move into route formation that getting on course right away was not a high priority. It gave us a chance to do some after takeoff checks ... like disconnecting our zero delay lanyards! ... and loosening the white knuckle grip we had on the stick. When the flight finally settled down, and we arrived at our cruise altitude, we noticed that we were heading east instead of northeast. But we all kind of decided to delay advising the boss that we were getting farther and farther off course.

He was our noble leader, and we would follow him anywhere ... unless he headed us out over the Pacific Ocean. We knew he had a lot on his mind, and being an excellent pilot we trusted that he would soon remedy the situation. Being good wingmen, however, we were all checking our TACANs closely ... watching the needle move farther and farther to the left (pointing to Hiroshima). When we went feet-wet over the Pacific Ocean, Dick finally broke the silence with his tactful radio call: *"Three. What does your TACAN say?"* Being a discrete element lead, I replied. *"My TACAN shows Hiroshima 40 degrees to our left."* These two subtle radio calls resulted in an abrupt formation turn towards Hiroshima TACAN. A collective sigh was apparent as each Captain clicked his mic button and signaled thumbs-up to each other. Rest easy we thought, the rest of the flight will be a piece of cake. Some cake! Fighter flights that begin ominously often have ominous endings. Our story was no exception. The flight was unremarkable after we recovered on course, until we were about 75 miles out from

Yokota and we unexpectedly began a rapid descent. We knew this had all the markings of a low-level entry into Yokota. Excitement was being injected into an already memory filled flight! It was obvious that we were going to approach Yokota from the West and at low altitude, popping up over a small mountain range ... just before arriving at the base. Boy, was Yokota in for a surprise! So were we!

This low-level approach tactic unfortunately blanked out the Yokota TACAN, so it was pilotage by landmarks the rest of the way. No sweat - that was our expertise. In order to impress those waiting for us, we were again called into close formation and speed was increased ... dramatically of course. No time to look around and help navigate for the boss. As we crossed the mountain range, we obtained radio contact with Yokota Tower where Captain Rod *"Cool Hand"* Beckett (one of our own F-105 jocks) was assisting the tower operators to ensure a professional arrival at Yokota of the last fighter flight from Itazuke. The contact was intermittent, and we didn't understand Rod's querulous comments. But, not to fear, the boss quickly found the runway ... put us into echelon formation ... called for a five second break ... and prepared to pitch out and land. We were all working hard to maintain an excellent formation and couldn't look around much, but we began hearing some strange radio calls, many of them in Japanese ... strange, since the international flying language being English. Well, lead broke smartly, then two, then three, and finally four.

We now had our first chance to look around, and it was not a welcome sight. There were four JASDAF F-86s in the pattern ... **in opposite direction**!! They had just pitched out too! There were now eight aircraft trying to land on the same runway at the same time in opposite directions. Most of our immediate attention was now taken up just trying to avoid each other ... Zuki Flight certainly didn't need a midair collision to enhance its image. F-86s and F-105s seemed to fill the sky. And, of course, everyone was talking on the radio ... with tension filled shrill voices.

The Japanese voices on the radio were difficult to understand, but when Rod "Cool Hand" Beckett's voice came over Guard channel, transmitting: *"**Zuki Flight on guard ... you're at Johnson Air Base**"* we knew exactly what had happened. Dick's calm voice also confirmed the now obvious: *"**Zuki's, this ain't Yokota** !!"* Zuki flights "arrival show" had just become infamous.

From then on Zuki Flight wasn't really a flight at all. We each kind of wove our way thru the traffic and found our own way to Yokota, about 10 miles south, and landed single-ship. Not the glorious arrival we had anticipated. Not the precise formation landing ... not the four ship formation taxi in ... not the canopies opening at the same time ... not simultaneous engine shutdowns ... no welcome committee (they somehow had lost their enthusiasm and disbanded). Just a routine ending to a nonroutine flight.

Perhaps it was as it should be. Sadly, the last fighters had departed Itazuke. The last fighter flight from Itazuke just had to mark the occasion with a performance that would be filled with memories ... the more ignominious the better. **It did just that!**

That evening all of the displaced fighter pilots from Itazuke met at the Yokota officers club stag bar and destroyed it!

All those hits in one pass ?!

F-105 (Nellis Air Force Base, Nevada)

Checking out in a new airplane does have its moments ... some embarrassing and best forgotten ... but occasionally a magic moment one doesn't want to forget. I began flying the mighty F-105, affectionately called the "Thud" (the biggest single engine, single seat fighter ever made) at Nellis Air Force Base, Nevada. Our whole fighter wing rotated, one squadron at a time, from Itazuke Air Base, Japan back to Nellis to check out in the F-105 ... a transition from the F-100 Super Sabre we had been flying.

It takes a while to transfer loyalties from one airplane to another, but in this case, the F-105 had a capability that was particularly endearing ... it was the first airplane I flew that had a Gatling gun. The F-100, which I had been flying for three years, had four 20 mm cannons. Impressive, but the firing rate was pretty slow, and we rarely fired more than two cannons at a time. Not even a close comparison to the awesome 20 mm Gatling gun which would fire 6000 rounds per minute ... and to top it off the cannon made this cool brrrrrrrrrrrrrrpppppp sound when you fired it, not a wimpy rat-tat-tat.

When we went to the gunnery range strafing was usually the last event and was, by far, my favorite event. Firing rockets and dive bombing were great; skip bombing was a hoot, but strafing was the ultimate thriller. When you strafe on a gunnery range you descend in a shallow, high speed dive directly towards the target, which was generally a white cloth about 20 x 20 feet square, suspended between two telephone poles. The minimum distance to fire at the target was 1500 feet slant range to avoid running into the ground. See why I call it a thriller? So at 1500 feet you had to be done firing and begin a sharp pull-up. This generally put you about 50 feet above the ground when you completed the pull up. So when you fired you were maybe 100 feet or so above the ground, moving fast ... in the F-105 we strafed at about 450 to 500 knots. Strafing was most challenging and exhilarating (besides throwing yourself at the ground at high speed) because of the flying finesse required to aim the airplane so precisely ... using the gunsight (or pipper) for proper alignment. The F-105 made it easy ... it was a great gun platform ... rock steady ... very stable.

It was my first time strafing at the Nellis gunnery range and we (there were three students and one instructor ... a flight of four) were only given one hot, firing pass at the target, because of an ammo shortage. So I made a dry pass to see what it was like to position the pipper on the target and then I came around again for a second pass, my only hot pass, and fired the gun. I figured that if I was only going to get to fire once, I was going to make it a good long pass (the cannon fires about 60 rounds in the first second and 100 rounds a second after that) ... to heck with the ammo shortage! I figured if I start firing at about 2500 feet from the target, as I'm moving about 700 or 800 fps, that I could get off a good long burst before firing beyond the 1500 foot slant range minimum. But this meant I had to place and hold the pipper right in the middle of that target for one or two seconds, an extremely long time at these speeds and closure rates.

Sounds easy enough, but the pipper is a very tiny spot on the gunsight, and the target looks very tiny at that slant range. Anyway, I came around and everything was looking good ... dive angle and airspeed were looking good ... pipper was on line and drifting up towards the target very nicely ... no major directional corrections needed ... I let the pipper move smoothly right up to the middle of the target just as I approached the proper slant range, held it there momentarily ... and squeezed the trigger down for a real long brrrrrrrrrrrrrrrpppp (that wonderful sound I never got tired of!) ... the pipper stayed right on target ... and then I pulled up.

You can actually see the bullets impact the target just before you start the pull (just don't fixate and stare or it will be the last thing in your life ever seen!). If you hit the target all you can see is dust <u>behind</u> the target. That's all I saw that day. It was the kind of strafing pass a fighter pilot dreams of. I was tempted to key the microphone and say "beautiful." But I resisted the temptation. The range officer said it for me though!

We completed our mission and returned to Nellis, not knowing our strafe scores. After we left the range they replaced the panels and counted the number of rounds in each target. When they counted the hits in my panel they found 114 holes! 114 rounds had gone through that 20 x 20 foot panel on my single, maybe 2-second, firing pass! No one had ever shot that high before !!

Later that day, when I was over at the officers club eating, some of the instructors came running in, and hollered *"Do you know what you shot??!! ... How did you do that? ... That was fantastic!"* Quite a compliment, coming from the old head instructor pilots to a first lieutenant with just a few hours flying the F-105. I tried to let them think that it was "skill and cunning" ... instead of just a lucky shot. Whatever ... it was a magic moment I haven't forgotten.

I've been hit ... uhh, disregard

F-105 (Takhli Air Base, Thailand)

During combat a fighter pilot must be prepared for many different types of missions, and more importantly, able to revise or change missions in-flight.

One of these scenarios that comes to mind involved Rick Layman and myself when we were stationed at Takhli Air Base, Thailand during the early days of the air war over North Vietnam. We were tasked to fly two F-105s on a rescue combat air patrol (RESCAP) mission in support of a strike mission being flown by one of our sister squadrons. Their target (on an island just off the coast of North Vietnam) was a radar station surrounded and protected by some antiaircraft guns. Our job (for Rick and I) was to be overhead that island when the strike attack was going on. In case any of those pilots got shot down we would be there ready to provide cover (CAP) ... for any rescue (RES) efforts that would be needed (hence RESCAP).

Rick and I circled the island in fighting wing formation (Rick, my wing man, flew behind me about 600 feet back and offset about 30°) and observed the attack on the radar site by the other eight F-105s. They hit the target squarely with napalm and rockets and whatever else they might have had ... finished their mission and departed. The need for us to be a RESCAP was no longer there. There we were ... with a full load of rockets and ammunition ... over enemy territory ... and our mission was over!

However! ... This time we came to the war with an unusual secondary mission ... the kind that makes fighter pilots drool ... **armed recce**! Armed recce meant we could go looking for targets of opportunity! ... at our discretion! ... at a low altitude! This was the first time such a mission had been authorized. With eager anticipation, we began looking for small targets like trucks and other military vehicles on the road (we were authorized to fire our rockets and 20 mm on such targets). For fighter pilots like Rick and I ... new into combat ... this seemed like a golden opportunity to go in there and find some lucrative target that intelligence had missed and win the war single-handedly!

I put Rick about 1000 feet behind me ... as I would jig to the right he would jig to the left ... a kind of mutual support. That way, we were always looking out in front of each other for any sort of ground targets worth destroying ... and any antiaircraft fire that might try to destroy us! We always kept our aircraft moving erratically ... up, down, left, right ... we called it jinking ... so that anybody firing at us would never have a straight target to shoot at ... to pull lead on. There we were, two overconfident, well-trained fighter pilots taking the fight to the heart of the enemy homeland. It was easy to think that I really had control over the situation. Enhancing that attitude was a comfortable cockpit ... cool ... quiet ... an environment I was very familiar with, having flown many hundreds of hours in it ... during peacetime, of course.

As the recce continued up one road and down another, I was intently focusing my attention looking for targets ... getting disappointed because I couldn't find any ... hoping to find that special target before my fuel got below Bingo (a code word for just enough fuel to get home). Totally engrossed, focused on the mission, when *all of a sudden* ... **KERBANG !!** Man, my whole body jumped ... I knew I had been hit. I instinctively pulled back on the stick and gained several hundred feet of altitude. My mind was reeling ... here I was right in the middle of North Vietnam and no RESCAP for us! I better let Rick know about my problem ... start calling for help.

But wait a second ... what's that stuff flying all around my cockpit? Why it's nothing but ice pellets! I hadn't been hit. My cockpit air-conditioner had just built up pressure and blown clogged up ice out of the cooling ducts. Wow ... I'm glad I didn't hit that microphone button and squeal like a stuck pig for all the world to hear. A loud belching air-conditioner was not an uncommon occurrence in the F-105 ... it'd happened before, but that was over friendly territory. This time I wasn't exactly prepared for a big loud **KERBANG !!**

The lesson learned was an insightful one. I remembered thinking just before it happened, how calm and cool I was ... not realizing that inside I was as tense as a cat about to get attacked by a dog. I jumped and spasmed and a plethora of thoughts went through my head ... *"Yeah, you're pretty calm and cool aren't cha?"* ... outside maybe ... but I was obviously covering up an inside all wound up ... my spring was wound tight and I didn't know it.

I collected my thoughts in as calm a way as I could, keyed the mic, and transmitted: *"Two, I guess it's time we head on back. I'm about to Bingo"* ... trying to keep Rick from ever knowing that I had just had a confrontation with my own fears.

Sir, I think I found the problem

F-104 (Edwards Air Force Base, California)

All of the students at the Air Force Test Pilot School were filled with apprehension when it came time for us to be evaluated by the Commandant ... a ritual Colonel "Buck" Buchanan took seriously. He always flew with every student at least once to check them out. And we surely wanted to impress our Commandant, because we knew he had the "yea" or "nay" whether his students could continue in the course.

When it came my turn to fly with him I was scheduled to fly as a safety chase in a two-seat, single engine, F-104 jet fighter ... while the primary airplane, a student in a single seat F-104, was going to fly a Zoom profile (accelerating to maximum speed at 35,000 feet, and then pulling into a steep climb to gain as much altitude as possible). My job, as safety chase, was to fly a close, observing position until the aircraft zoomed. At that point, chase would stay at 35,000 feet and wait for the Zoom airplane to come back down ... and then join up with the Zoom airplane and escort him to his landing ... making sure everything was okay.

On the morning of this particular flight Colonel Buck came into the preflight briefing ... came over to me, and with a very nasally tone said, *"I've got a bad cold today, and I don't feel very good. So I don't know if we will be able to climb up to altitude or not ... I don't know if I can clear my ears. We will just take off and see how my ears clear as we climb. If we can't go up with lead we'll just orbit while he goes to altitude to accelerate and zoom ... we will catch him when he comes back down."* He was obviously in some kind of misery. This complicated my task. One is always up for it when the commander flies with you. But now I had the additional task of keeping my boss comfortable. No sweat ... I was up to the task! At least I thought I was!

Well, we took off and began our climb out ... Edwards is about 2300 feet elevation ... and as we went through 5000 feet Colonel Buck said he was having trouble clearing his ears. Then, to my chagrin, I noticed that the pressurization in the cockpit was not working. As we went through 5000 feet the cabin pressure was 5000 feet. As we went through 8000 feet the pressure was 8000 feet. When we went through 10,000 it was 10,000. Colonel Buck said *"I don't think we should go up to altitude, if we can't pressurize the cockpit. Let's just orbit down here ... we will go as high as we can ... about 20,000 feet."*

I knew he was going to suffer without normal cabin pressurization, which usually was maintained below 8000 feet ... even with the aircraft at 35,000 feet. So we told the Zoom aircraft to go on to the turnaround point where he would start acceleration, and we would just wait over the town of Barstow. After we separated from lead we climbed up very slowly, as Colonel Buck worked at clearing his ears and sinuses. I'm thinking *"Oh no, I'm a student and I don't know how to run the air-conditioning system."* Something failed here that's probably my fault ... no pressurization as we climb ... and it's making my boss ache, causing his head difficulty ... great pain! We finally got to about 20,000 feet, and that's what the cabin pressure was! It was a good thing we were breathing 100% oxygen. We began orbiting, waiting for the Zoom aircraft. After much effort, Colonel Buck was finally getting his head clear ... the inner pressure relieved. He'd been in pain all this time. Finally his ears were clear (pressure in the inner ear the same as cabin pressure), and he says. *"I think we'll be okay."* When the Zoom airplane came back at 35,000 feet we'd be able to see him ... he'd be conning (making a very visible contrail as he zoomed). And we could go after him.

As we orbit there I'm looking around in the cockpit to see if there's something that I haven't done. The F-104 had an unusual cabin pressure system. It had a little door on the left side of the cockpit ... about 2 inches square. If you pushed a button on a little handle on the door you could open the door and depressurize the cockpit. You could also then close the door and re-pressurize the cockpit. The button that you push also had an electric switch which turned the air-conditioning system on and off. As I looked at that door, it appeared that maybe it wasn't all the way closed.

So in my best "<u>try to please the boss</u>" attitude, I said. *"Sir, I think I found the problem."* And without further comment (or thinking) I reached down and opened and closed the door real quick. Lo and Behold! ... that **was** the problem! ... I was proud of myself ... but only for an instant ... for **all of a sudden** the cabin pressure went to 8000 feet ... just like that! We pressurized in about two seconds!

I should have thought this out a little better though, before acting, because the next thing I heard on the interphone was the most painful, groaning, moan I had ever heard in my life ... *ooooooooooooooohhhhhhhhhhhhhhhh!!* I knew I had just pushed his eardrums into each other! I thought, *"Oh my gosh ... my flying career is over."* By solving the problem, I had almost put the boss into cardiac arrest!

What a brilliant comment ... *"Sir, I think I found the problem."* ... true engineering revelation! But spontaneously acting upon that revelation bordered on lunacy.

Fortuitous mission timing kept me from dwelling on the cockpit misery I had just precipitated ... at just that moment the Zoom aircraft magically appeared overhead ... focusing our attention on his zoom and recovery. During the ensuing time of concentrated safety-chase work, Colonel Buck was gradually able to clear his ears again. Without discussing the rapid and dramatic pressure change in the cockpit, we finished the flight.

The post-flight debrief never really occurred, as Colonel Buck went back to his office to recover. I did eventually graduate, but I don't recall Colonel Buck speaking to me much after that. I figured he would always remember me as the guy who pushed his eardrums down his throat ... but I'll always remember him for the sudden groan emitted just after I said those infamous words: *"Sir, I think I found the problem."*

Instructor vs. Rookie dive bombing challenge

OV-10 (Hurlburt Field, Florida)

It had been over six years since I had flown combat in Vietnam and it was time to go back. This time, instead of flying fighters, I was assigned to fly the OV-10 "Bronco" ... a twin engine, propellor driven observation airplane. The "Bronco" was used in the forward air controller (FAC) role and was very versatile ... in combat it normally carried four pods of rockets and four machine guns. But it could also carry small bombs ... which brings to mind an interesting event during my training in the OV-10.

I went through OV-10 training in the spring of 1971 at Hurlburt Field, Florida. During that training we had two missions to the gunnery range to learn dive bombing in the OV-10. We carried four little 25 pound practice bombs and a pod of rockets. Most of the OV-10 instructors had never flown any other type of aircraft since their pilot training days ... all were Captains. However, they considered their skills were exceptional at any OV-10 task ... and took great pride in their dive bombing acumen. And well they should ... they had gotten as good as you could get in dive bombing in an OV-10 with just OV-10 experience. I, on the other hand, was a Major with years of fighter experience, but I had never dive bombed in an OV-10. However, manual dive bombing was about all I had been doing for several years, first in a fighter outfit and later in a controlled flight testing environment. Manual dive bombing required that the pilot fly the airplane to the precise dive angle, release altitude, release airspeed, and desired aim point simultaneously ... achieving all four conditions at exactly the same instant ... bomb release (done manually by pressing the pickle button) ... an incredibly complex and difficult task.

The OV-10 instructor on my first training mission to the range (Captain *"Buzz"* Halprin) was eager to demonstrate his skill against a seasoned dive bomber like myself, and during the pre-mission briefing challenged me to a wager when we went to the range ... who would get the best bombs.

After a second or two of thought I said *"Sure, I'll do that."* I figured ... my goodness, I've got to be able to do well in an airplane that goes about one half of the speed that I have been used to ... down to about a third of the release altitude that I have been used to. Dive bombing in this little plane ought to be a piece of cake.

With a wager made, and the briefing completed, our four ship flight (one IP, three students ... Snapper Flight ... I was Snapper Two) proceeded and we headed to the range. The first event was dive bombing and the first pass is always dry ... no bomb release. This gave me a chance to explore the OV-10 dive bombing qualities before I released my first bomb.

My goodness, I was astounded ... you come down the chute in an OV-10 at about 250 knots ... I had been used to 450 or 500 knots. When you're going that slow you can come very close to the ground and get a very accurate aim point before you release your bomb and begin your pull up. I was satisfied ... ready for the competition to begin.

The IP, *"Buzz"* rolled in, released his bomb ... and the range officer scored his bomb ... bull's-eye! Oh, Snapper Lead was crowing *"Lead got a bull's-eye Two, watch out."* With the pressure on, I rolled in for my first delivery ... 10 foot! Not bad for a first bomb ever in an OV-10, but I didn't say anything. On the second bomb Snapper Lead got a 20 footer ... *"Buzz"* is pretty good I must say. I rolled in, corrected for my first bomb and ... bull's-eye! After two bombs I was ahead ... but only by 10 feet. We came around for the third pass ... the tension was building. Lead goes in and drops another 20 footer. Now a 20 foot manual dive bomb is a very, very good bomb score. Snapper Three and Snapper Four were getting 50, 75, or even 100 foot bombs.

Accepting the challenge, I rolled in behind Lead for my third pass and got another 10 footer ... now I'm 20 foot ahead with one bomb to go. Lead is now getting concerned ... he's having a great day and he is behind. He knows the pressure is on ... I could tell in his voice as he said *"Okay Two ... one more bomb."*

Buzz rolls in for his fourth and final bomb ... I'm looking for the bomb impact ... it looks very close ... wow! ... another 20 footer ... very impressive. Even an old-timer like me could get butterflies ... but I embraced the challenge, knowing that if I get a 50 footer or worse the young IP will win the wager ... and enormous bragging rights from beating a "real" fighter pilot.

I rolled in, got my dive angle, watched my airspeed, altitude, and aim point come together nicely and released my last bomb. As I pulled up and looked back ... I could see that my bomb smoke was right on the pyramid that marks the center of the target ... and I heard the range officer cry out *"bull's-eye."*

As I continued my pull I said, with much aplomb, ... *"Two is off hot ... with another bull's-eye, Lead."* Lead responded with a shallow *"Okay ... let's set up for rockets." Buzz* had just had his best day ever on the bombing range ... a 15 foot average ... and the rookie (albeit a veteran at dive bombing) had beaten him. An old saying came to mind ... something about age and cunning overcoming youth and talent.

FLAMEOUT!
Don't worry boss, I'll get you there

F-100 (Eglin Air Force Base, Florida)

On one memorable occasion I had the opportunity to take an F-100F (a two-seat version of the famous single engine jet fighter) on a weekend cross-country flight to southern California to attend my brother's wedding ... my own personal jet to go to a wedding! Official recurring flight training, of course.

This was available because on the same weekend the Wing Commander, Colonel West, needed to attend his daughter's wedding up in the San Francisco area. A great opportunity! Colonel West wasn't F-100 qualified (he wasn't even fighter qualified) but he could go along in the back seat of the F-100F. I would drop him off at Moffett Field, just south of San Francisco, and then take the airplane solo down to March Air Force Base, near Los Angeles, where I could catch a ride to my brother's wedding in Garden Grove, California. Beautiful plan! How could anything go wrong?

Preparations proceeded without delay ... the airplane was ready ... the weather was great (VMC ... visual meteorological conditions all the way). We put a travel pod on the wing of the F-100 so the colonel could carry all his gear (wedding presents, formal clothes, and even his fancy golf bag ... which fit in the pod quite nicely). The travel pod was a 220 gallon external fuel tank converted to an empty pod with a large side-mounted access door. We loaded our gear and off we went. We stopped at Cannon Air Force Base (New Mexico) to refuel and then headed on towards San Francisco. Colonel West was pretty quiet for a colonel and a Wing Commander ... he was probably thinking about the good times ahead. So was I.

It was a beautiful day, and as were crossing the Sierra Nevada mountains going into California, at 35,000 feet, the sun was setting right in front of us ... a beautiful sunset. We could see forever ... such a calm and serene environment ... soon to be dramatically altered ... when <u>all of a sudden</u> the engine just rolled back. By rolled back, I meant it was just like I had pulled the throttle back to idle ... FLAMEOUT !! And we were a long way from anyplace ... right over the high mountains of California. The quiet rear cockpit passenger quickly noticed the sudden loss of thrust, and, of course, said. *"What's going on?"* I told him *"We've lost our engine ... and I can't get it back."* That must have given him a surge of confidence in the captain in the front seat! Then I tried to reassure him by saying *"Don't worry boss, I'll get you there."*

I didn't know how ... but began pursuing options by declaring an emergency ... telling the air traffic controllers that I have an engine flame out, and sure do need a long runway close by to land on. They were quick to respond and pointed me toward Castle Air Force Base (about 80 miles southeast of San Francisco ... a SAC base for KC-135 aircraft). We were 50 miles from Castle when our dilemma began. I did some quick mental calculations and figured I could "just" make it in my 15 ton glider. We were at 35,000 feet, which I maintained until the airspeed slowly bled off to best glide speed, which (with our gross weight and configuration of external fuel tanks and a travel pod) was right at 230 knots. I figured, with best glide, I could arrive over Castle at 10,000 feet ... the best altitude to execute an overhead 360° flameout landing pattern. When you do a flameout landing you try to come directly over the field (at what we call **high key**) ... lined up with the runway (going the same direction that you're going to land) ... and at least 10,000 feet above the runway, and then fly a gentle 360° circling, descending pattern to the runway ... putting the gear and flaps down at the appropriate time.

As we approached Castle the sun was going down ... below the horizon. So this was going to be a **night** flameout landing! ... **not** recommended. But I didn't see any choice! Everything seemed to be going well ... I could still see the runway visually, even though it required runway lights. As we approached Castle, I'm continually mentally calculating whether we are going to be able to make it or not. That decision must be made before going below safe ejection altitude. I also had the option of extending our glide range by jettisoning the wing tanks and the travel pod! That cost me some concern, because I thought *"I can do almost anything, but if I jettison his golf clubs unnecessarily I am probably in really big trouble."* So I better make this a good approach and landing.

I could see that we would not be able to enter a **high-key** at or above 10,000 feet, so I opted for a 270° pattern as I arrived over the Castle runway at 8000 feet. The critical point in a flameout landing is **low-key** ... a position abreast of the runway with 180° turn remaining. It's where one can best visualize the proper glide path to the desired touchdown point on the runway ... and then make adjustments during the turn-to-final approach. Those adjustments also included when to lower the landing gear and flaps and whether I would need to jettison that precious travel pod. **Low-key** is a critical point, because once you set up your conditions there and begin the base turn-to-final, you are pretty well committed.

Fortunately, when I got to the desired **low-key** position everything looked good ... having a lot of experience flying simulated flameout landings at Edwards Air Force Base really helped. The Castle runway was a long concrete runway ... typical of what all SAC bases had ... for that I was most thankful. The 180° descending turn from low-key to final approach really had me focused, and as I rolled out on final I could tell the touchdown point was going to be just fine. That reassurance was certainly welcome, easing the tension that had gripped me for so long.

Such a comforting feeling to finally touchdown after gliding for well over 10 minutes. I even touched down at the rarely achieved optimum speed for an F-100 ... when the tailskid drags on the runway (the tailskid sticks down about a foot on the F-100 to protect the afterburner tail cone). This also provided some humorous relief to break the tension, for it was dark enough that when the tail-skid dragged on the runway the tower operators noticed the sparks and thought there was a fire (they had been monitoring our flight all along on the radio, and they seemed to be more nervous than we were ... not many flameout landings at Castle I guess). I reassured them that it was okay, and inwardly I chuckled, knowing that after a flameout landing in an F-100, I had touched down at the optimum airspeed ... a feat rarely performed in an F-100, even under normal conditions. A huge sigh of relief ensued ... we made it!!

As we coasted to a parking spot I just couldn't resist reminding the colonel that I had assured him that *"I'll get you there."* He was visibly pleased. However, *"there"* was his daughter's wedding, not Castle Air Force Base ... but he took care of that by commandeering an Air Force staff car to finish his trip. I, on the other hand, had to find a friendly KC-135 crew who took me to March Air Force Base that very night on one of their training flights. As I reflected on the days "activities" I was unable to assure myself that it was my skill and cunning that had prevailed. Deep down, I knew differently ... **"Someone"** up there must have been looking after me!

This is the worst formation flying I've ever seen!

OV-10 (Danang Air Base, Vietnam)

I was going back to Vietnam!

The first time I had been there I flew the mighty F-105 "Thud" ... bombing targets in North Vietnam. This time I would be flying the twin engine observation plane, the OV-10 "Bronco" as a Forward Air Controller (FAC) directing air power in support of our ground troops.

I was excited ... a chance to help our soldiers ... the real warriors battling the enemy face-to-face. But getting into action was not immediately forthcoming ... there was first a week or so of "orientation" ... boring lectures, with lots of idle time.

Flying Tales

Not being the patient type I volunteered to fly one mission in the back seat of the OV-10 as an observer while awaiting my assignment to a regular unit. No problem flying ... since the OV-10s were usually flown solo and the back seat was usually empty. So what if I, a major with a few thousand hours flying time, was put in the back seat behind a junior lieutenant barely out of flight school!

It turned out that the mission flown that day was not much help for our troops ... the weather was poor and we were over a solid under cast most of the time. So I didn't see much. I did see the huge Vietcong (VC) flag up by the demilitarized zone (DMZ). The North Vietnamese had a great big Vietcong flag hanging on the border between North and South Vietnam ... surrounded by lots of anti-aircraft if we were foolish enough to get too close.

The boring flight did take on a more ominous tone however as we returned to base. Our navigation aids failed and since we had to fly down through a solid under cast cloud layer we joined up on the wing of another OV-10 to come back down through the weather for landing. No sweat ... formation flying was always a favorite of mine ... any Air Force pilot can do it! Boy, was I in for a surprise!

I was sitting in the back just relaxing ... the formation was going well. The lieutenant was holding close formation position reasonably well. **Then** we entered the clouds and **the chaos began**. The clouds were bright white but they were very thick so we had to get much closer to keep the other OV-10 in sight. The closer we got, the more erratic the lieutenant became. We would surge down ... well below the other OV-10. And then we would surge up! ... up and down ... in and out. The lieutenant's breathing became loud and often. The control stick was moving all around. The oscillations became bigger and bigger. There soon occurred a surge up so far I could not see the other aircraft below us! ... The most dangerous position !!

My thoughts immediately escalated ... *"My gosh, we're going to have a midair collision up here because this guy can't fly formation in the clouds."*

It was then I decided to take control of the airplane. In that instance however we broke out of the clouds. And we were able to rapidly move away from the lieutenant's nemesis and flew formation at a distance. A huge sigh of relief (from both of us).

We made it back, but I wondered what a different story it would have been if I had just ended my Vietnam tour flying in the back seat with a young inexperienced lieutenant.

I didn't know an OV-10 could do that!

OV-10 (Chu Lai Air Base, Vietnam)

Never discount the opportunity to put awe on the face of your contemporary.

I had one of those occasions when I was stationed at Chu Lai Air Base in Vietnam in support of an Army unit. That unit had an aviation component with which we shared a runway. The runway was short, narrow and constructed of aluminum planking. The army was flying the Beaver aircraft, a single engine propeller airplane, which was quite capable of very short takeoff and landing (STOL) performance.

The Army pilots were always parading that capability in front of us ... making occasional fun of our obviously "less capable" OV-10 ... a twin engine observation airplane we used for forward air control (FAC) missions. They would generally always take off in front of us, beginning their takeoff roll at the second taxiway instead of using the entire runway, but when they landed they would land at the beginning of the runway and turn off the runway at the second taxiway (which was about 1000 feet down the runway) ... very impressive routine performance! We, on the other hand, would generally taxi to the end of the runway to begin our takeoffs ... with the entire runway ahead of us. There was a taxiway about 500 feet from the approach end of the runway but it was rarely used.

Now takeoffs in light aircraft are rarely impressive ... so neither the Army nor the Air Force (us) could cause any jaws to drop during takeoff. But landings are another matter ... the shorter the landing roll, the more impressive, and the Beaver's landing roll was very impressive ... we were envious. But I had a little secret that I thought might be able to reverse the image ... and one day I got a chance to demonstrate the Air Force superiority. Whereas we always landed the OV-10 using one half flaps or less, the OV-10 could do a really impressive full flap STOL approach. We did not allow that however because we had so many junior people flying with us. With full flaps down the OV-10 could fly as slow as 45 knots which is a very, very slow approach speed ... giving you a very steep approach. However, if you lost an engine in that configuration it would be pretty difficult to recover because much of the lift was provided by the massive airflow from the propellers over the wing. Consequently, if one engine quit the other engine must also be shut down to avoid a rapid roll ... not good when close to the ground at an airspeed that needed both engines running to sustain.

So we just didn't allow the young inexperienced pilots, lieutenants, to fly STOL landings in the OV-10. However, as an experienced "Golden Arm" test pilot I had practiced it on occasion ... and I can tell you, it was a hoot! It was just like coming down in a parachute in that airplane ... for if you had a 10 or 15 knot head wind you would only be doing about 30 knots over the ground. Nobody had ever seen that approach at Chu Lai because we normally came down at about 80 knots, a very gentle approach with no flaps or just a little bit of flaps not requiring high power settings. We would normally land long and turn off at the 2000 foot turn off point ... that's where the Army aviators were used to seeing us land and turn off the runway ... and they were prone to make occasional snippet remarks over the radio about our "airliner" landings.

Payback was soon to come! One day I arrived back at Chu Lai to land and there was also an Army Beaver approaching his landing. I was pretty close behind him but he said he needed to land right away and could he stay in front of me ... he said he would turn off real quick so that I could have all the runway (he emphasized the word **all**) to land on.

I thought ... *"Here's my chance ... I'll just do a STOL landing here and come in right behind him."* So I reduced speed, put down full flaps and added a lot of power (to provide for the massive airflow needed over the wings for a STOL approach) ... and began a very steep, slow approach behind him. I was still a few hundred feet above the ground and coming down like a parachute when he turns off the runway at the 1000 foot point and says, in a rather haughty tone, *"The runway is all yours, Air Force."*

It was his next move that I most welcomed though ... he turned around to watch me! <u>Perfect! ... a STOL landing in an OV-10 deserved an audience!</u> I touched down close to the end of the runway stopped in about 300 feet and then added power to taxi up to the first taxiway 500 feet from the approach end.

The Army pilot's awe was most apparent. He just couldn't believe what he saw. He keyed his mic and said *"I didn't know an OV-10 could do that!"*

I keyed my mic said *"It's just routine, Army chap !!"*

Why do my eyes hurt?

T-38 (Holloman Air Force Base, New Mexico)

At last ... a longed for view of the Pentagon ... in my rearview mirror ... as I drove away for the last time! I had just finished a four year tour there and was off to Edwards Air Force Base and a most desired flying assignment ... back to the cockpit ... hurray!

Since I had flown nothing but a desk for so long I talked my new bosses at Edwards to send me to a jet requalification flying course at Holloman

Air Force Base, New Mexico while enroute to Edwards. Holloman was home to a bunch of T-38 fighter-like supersonic jet trainers used to train beginning fighter pilots and also to requalify fighter pilots who had not been flying for a while. A perfect TDY for me ... just flying ... no additional duties ... I was eager for the opportunity. So I went to Holloman and stopped there for two or three weeks to get 20 hours or so to get back into the flying routine. It was mainly transition flying with some formation flying and some instrument flying ... it was sure good to be back at the controls.

One thing puzzled me though ... I hadn't been flying for a couple of years and I noticed as we got way up to altitude, where the sky is clear and the sun is bright, that I was squinting all the time. The standard dark visor on my helmet did not seem to relieve the eyestrain so I did something I had never done before ... I put my sunglasses on and then put my dark colored visor back down. To my chagrin ... I was still squinting! I asked myself *"What's going on? Why am I squinting up here? I never used to squint like this."* Other than that little concern the flying went marvelously and memories of the Pentagon soon faded from my spirit.

Now it was on to Edwards Air Force Base ... the most desired assignment for any test pilot. I soon began flying there and quickly noticed that I was still squinting up at high altitude, where the sky is clear and the sun is bright. But test pilots are resourceful. I pulled out of my coveted flight paraphernalia a never before used, gold plated, very, very dark visor. That should solve my problem, I surmised. I installed it on my helmet and when I got up to altitude I put that visor down ... and voila! That did the trick! No more squinting!

There was one little detail, however, that foiled my masterful plan. When I looked down in the cockpit the visor was so dark that I could not see my instruments! A real bummer, I thought. My fighter pilot eyes must be going out of commission. I guess I will have to exercise a pilot's last resort ... go see the flight surgeon!

As per usual, the dreaded flight surgeon's appraisal provided relief, and not grounding (why do us pilots always fear the worst?). He told me he had seen this symptom on many pilots as they returned to flying fighters after a long absence. It takes a while for the eyes to re-acclimate to the environment of flying at high altitude, where the sky is clear and the sun is bright. *"Just give it time"* he said. It was the kind of therapy I could handle.

My eyes finally did learn how to reverse dilate again and I eventually returned to a normal visor without even sunglasses. But those first few weeks of getting re-acclimated to flying in the upper atmosphere were kind of anxious moments for me. I thought something had happened to me physically. All that really had happened to me was I had spent too many dark days and nights in the Pentagon ... good riddance.

Safety chase ... you're too close

T-38 (Edwards Air Force Base, California)

Boy was I excited to be back at Edwards Air Force Base ... flying test missions ... flying in a test environment. Edwards is the home, the heritage, of flight test. Anything that has ever flown, particularly in the Air Force and many of the commercial airplanes and even Navy airplanes had made their early flights at Edwards Air Force Base. **All** test pilots want to be assigned there.

One of the jets I flew there was the T-38 which is used as a chase airplane ... primarily a safety chase ... to observe the primary test airplane. It is also used as a photo chase, carrying a photographer in the back seat to photograph particular events of the primary test airplane.

One of my first flights at Edwards in the chase role was flying safety/photo chase on an F-16 that was going to go out to the gunnery range next to the dry lake at Edwards and do some strafing ... to test a modification to the gun. I thought this is great ... I get to fly right next to him down low while he is strafing with the F-16's 20 mm Gatling gun. When you strafe you generally fly a gentle low angle ... flying close to the target which would be a 20 x 20 foot white panel suspended between two telephone poles. Strafing usually opens fire at a maximum range of about half a mile and terminates prior to about one quarter mile. At that point you had to stop firing so you can recover from the dive without hitting the ground.

Well ... I just love to fly formation and this was my chance to get right in there close with a low-flying airplane that is strafing. I initially positioned myself on his left-wing, the same side as the control tower and most of the range personnel. Ground cameras were located on both sides.

The F-16 flew a rectangular pattern ... turning from base to final (rolling in) at about 1000 feet above the ground and then flying directly towards the target. As he rolled in I flew just to his left, nearly line abreast, right beside him. I liked flying Thunderbird style formation ... really close so I could observe in great detail. Having flown a lot of photo chase at Eglin Air Force Base I knew exactly how to get in good position where the photographer could get just the perfect picture. So he comes down and fires his gun ... bbbbbbrrrrrrrrppppp ... that comforting noise a 20 mm Gatling gun makes. He pulls up and I pull with him and we just clear the ground by about 50 feet or so.

I'm thinking *"Boy ... this is a good mission ... this is going to be fun."* My reverie was interrupted, however, when the range officer in the control tower called on the radio though and said *"Two, we couldn't see lead that time because you were in between us and him. How about getting on the other side?"* So I switched over to the right wing and we came around for another firing pass. I'm right there next to him and just loving it ... flying really close formation ... I can see every bit of smoke that comes out of the gun ... and watch for the bullets.

The photographer in my backseat is ecstatic ... he's never flown that close to an aircraft strafing before (I didn't tell him I hadn't either!). The F-16 came around for another pass and I'm right there next to him ... bbbbbbrrrrrrrrppppp ... another long burst from the Gatling gun. As we pull up, missing the ground by a few feet (doing about 400 or 450 knots) we get another radio call from the range tower gruffly saying *"Chase ... our cameras can't even see lead ... because you're in the way ... you're too close ... **back off!**"*

Well, I was disappointed, because I like to be right down there close when the going gets really exciting. Embarrassed ... but pleased (it must have been pretty impressive formation flying to warrant a radio call like that) ... I pulled back and then began flying about 200 or 300 feet away from the F-16 ... flying a *"good"* safety/photo chase position.

But I sure did miss those low altitude close formation pull ups.

My first violation ...
I wouldn't have hit that airliner

A-7D (Edwards Air Force Base, California)

While stationed at Edwards Air Force Base I was fortunate to serve as the Operations Officer, Deputy Commandant, and even Commandant of the Air Force's Test Pilot School. While assigned there my two primary aircraft (as an instructor pilot) were the T-38 (a small, two-seat, fighter-like supersonic trainer used for all phases of training) and the A-7D (a single seat, single engine fighter) used for some special missions to teach systems test ... it was the only aircraft that had some good inertial navigation, terrain avoidance, terrain following, radar type systems you could teach budding test pilots how to evaluate. We also did departure training in the A-7 ... it did a wonderful departure from controlled flight ... kind of like a spin but instead of a spin it would tumble.

One would think that by now I had acquired a high level of flying proficiency, which I had, but experience and position do not guarantee infallibility! This became apparent one day when flying the A-7 from the East back to Edwards.

The A-7 had long-range capability and on occasion I would take the airplane cross-country. On this particular flight I was flying over the high desert, returning to Edwards, somewhere in Nevada and I was cleared to descend from 31,000 feet down to 25,000 feet ... what's called flight level 310 down to flight level 250. Before I started my descent (it was clear weather ... you could see 100 miles), I acknowledged to air Traffic Control that I was cleared to descend to 230. As I'm coming down I am thinking *"Did he say 230 or 250?"*

As I went through 250 and further on down "something" told me I better check. I called Center and said *"Los Angeles Center this is COBRA 02 ... was I cleared to descend to 230?"* They came back immediately ***"Cobra 02 climb up immediately to 250 ... you were cleared to 250."*** In response to Centers panicky radio call I soon observed right in front of me was a Boeing 727 commercial airliner at 230 going the same direction I was going ... about half a mile ahead of me. LA Center had good reason to be alarmed. I was on a collision course with an airliner if I had continued descent to 230.

I had obviously not been cleared to 230 ... I had been given instructions to descend to 250 and had misunderstood, and Center didn't catch my incorrect acknowledgment. When I had some doubts about what altitude I should be at and asked about it that's when I found out that I was wrong. So I immediately headed back to 250. I had only gotten down to about 240, but that was cause for concern.

The climb back up to 250 went normally and I didn't think anything more about it ... continued on my way back to Edwards and landed. However, about a couple days later the Wing Commander came walking into my office and put a paper down on my desk and says *"What's this all about?"* I looked at it and my jaw dropped ... I had been issued an FAA violation for descending below my authorized altitude. I looked up at him with a sheepish grin and said *"I wouldn't have hit anybody ... really!"*

But I knew it wasn't skill and experience that prevailed ... it was more like prevenient grace.

Double flameout – while taxiing?

T-38 (Eglin Air Force Base, Florida)

There I was – a full bird colonel on flying status! I had convinced my Wing Commander that I could do a good service to the unit if I was allowed to fly ... you know ... bring my experience and wisdom to the fore so the young, inexperienced test pilots could learn.

But the roles got reversed one day when I was taxiing out in my T-38 (a twin engine, fighter like aircraft) with a photographer in the backseat.

We pulled out of the parking spot on the ramp and started taxiing north on the long parallel taxiway. The primary test airplane (I was flying photo chase) was already in the "last chance" inspection area waiting for us to join him for takeoff.

As we were taxiing I was going pretty slow and was in a hurry (not good) so I pushed both throttles up rapidly to get a quick burst of thrust ... **WHOA! ... too much! ... speed building up too fast!** So I yanked the throttles back, rather quickly, and inadvertently lifted them right over the idle detent ... shutting the fuel off for both engines !! How could a seasoned test pilot do that? With both throttles in the idle cutoff position the engines don't run! They are supposed to shut down when you put the throttles over the idle detent. As a result of my incomprehensible action, both engines started unwinding unmercifully. **Double flameout! ... while taxiing!**

As long as there was some engine RPM I had some hydraulics to steer the airplane and the generator stayed on the line for a little while allowing me to make radio calls. So I immediately steered the airplane to the right to get it off the main taxiway and onto the parking ramp, out of the way of other taxiing aircraft ... **and** I keyed the mike and called maintenance control to send a starting cart out ... a call I later wished I had never made.

I had to think fast to recover from this self inflicted debacle. *Maybe an "air start" would work !?* Probably no one had ever tried to get an air start while taxiing ... novel idea ... and if it worked no one would ever have to know about my "incident." I immediately moved both throttles up into full afterburner range, which is the air start position which puts ignition into the engine and keeps the fuel flow going ... hoping for a restart while the engines were still windmilling. Then I carefully monitored the RPM and the EGT (exhaust gas temperature) because adding fuel and ignition at engine speeds below idle to get a restart risks over-temping the engine with that abundant fuel flow.

So I watched the temperature very carefully and it slowly began to creep up to the very maximum allowed and it stayed there and stayed there. I thought *"Oh no, if it gets above that I've got to shut it down and figure out how to get a maintenance unit out here to do a ground start to start me up again."* Then everyone will know! But the EGT stayed there, just below the maximum limit ... and gradually the RPM began to grow up, up, up ... finally, it got to idle again and there I was running again ... ready to continue the mission

Meanwhile, I had made this brief, strange radio call that I needed a starting unit at the parking ramp ... at a different place than I had started from ... somewhat unusual to say the least. Maintenance control called and asked me to clarify ... I calmly told them to "disregard" and, thinking the matter resolved without adverse publicity, returned to the taxiway to continue the mission without further "mishap."

Flying blunders are not easily concealed. Later on one of those young, inexperienced test pilots asked me what in the world that radio call and the turn off the taxiway was all about. Without thinking I said *"Well, both engines went to idle cutoff."* **The cat was out of the bag** ... I hadn't prepared a good story! I got the strangest look ... he said *"You're not supposed to go to idle cutoff on the taxiway ... You're not supposed to shut those engines down ... You're supposed to keep them running, man."*

I had to agree! Like Inspector Clouseau would say ... *"I know that."*

Carolyn's first roll

AG-5 Tiger (Eglin Aero Club, Florida)

I was retiring from a job with an engineering firm, and with the loss of income I knew I would have to stop flying, at least until I started drawing Social Security. My last flight then was in a Grumman Tiger AG-5 ... a little four passenger, low-wing, single-engine airplane. Last flights should be enjoyable so I took Carolyn with me so we could enjoy the experience together. I also had planned a "special experience" ... something Carolyn was sure to remember ... a little introduction to aerobatics!

The AG-5, like most light aircraft, is not known for its aerobatic ability ... but any aircraft will do a roll if you perform it properly. As a good test pilot, I checked the airplane out before and found it had good roll performance ... around 90 to 100° per second, which makes for about a four second barrel roll. Performing a roll in a light airplane requires pulling the nose up at a fairly good angle before you start the roll so you won't dish out too far at the bottom, or completion, of the roll ... and then exceed your limit speed at the bottom recovering to level flight. Most light airplanes, when you get the nose pointed down accelerate rather rapidly and you can easily exceed the limit speed. So on a roll the pilot has to be very careful to pull the nose up far enough before starting the roll so that airspeed control is maintained throughout ... and not exceeded by getting the nose too low at the end.

I was confident I could perform the roll in an AG-5 perfectly! It would so impress my lovely wife. So as we're flying along, enjoying our flight, I asked Carolyn *"How would you like to see a roll?"* She responded strangely ... kind of gave me an *"Oh ... what!"* I said ... *"Well, a roll ... here, I'll show you."*

Without waiting for further comment I eagerly began to prepare for the amazing event. *"Oh, oh, oh, oh ... I don't know"* she said. Disregarding her less than spirited response, and with a big grin of anticipation, I picked up a little speed (about 120 knots in the Tiger) and pulled the nose up to about 30 degrees above the horizon ... awesome attitude ... watched the airspeed bleed off to about 80 knots or so and then began the **BIG EVENT.** I put in full aileron to the right, and around we go! As we roll the nose drops slowly ... the horizon spins around us ... incredible experience ... beautiful slow barrel roll! ... dishing out about 10 or 20 degrees nose low ... came back to level flight ... never got over about 120 knots ... **perfect!**

Meanwhile I'm looking at Carolyn throughout the whole maneuver looking for that expression of inexpressible joy ... a delight to behold.

BUT ... there she was ... facing straight ahead with her **eyes closed !!** Oh, no ... Here I had gone to all this trouble to learn how to do a perfect roll so Carolyn could experience the overpowering thrill of going upside down in an airplane ... and **she doesn't see it!**

Oh ... the best laid plans of mice and men . . . .

You don't have to shout

T-33 (Webb Air Force Base, Texas)

Flight instructors are a different breed. They have to be! ... for each new student approaches the awesome realm of flight with a different set of apprehensions. The instructor pilot (IP) must reach deep into his tool chest of teaching techniques to meet the challenge. Some of the IPs don't have very deep tool chests.

My first flight instructor at Webb Air Force Base, where I flew the T-33 (T-Bird) was Captain O'Brien. I don't remember his call sign, but it should have been ***Shouter***, because that was exactly his primary teaching technique ... hollering at his students if they were making the slightest deviation ... to get their attention I guess. That technique didn't work well with me ... I didn't respond to shouting to do my best, to work hard. After about three or four flights Obie realized that and put that tool back in his teaching tool chest. He stopped shouting at me and just talked me through the maneuvers ... that worked much better.

However, old habits sometimes resurface at the most unusual times ... as happened on one flight after we landed in the T-Bird. I thought we had had a pretty good mission. He had not shouted at me the whole time ... all the air work had gone well ... or so I thought. We were taxing back to the parking ramp at Webb Air Force Base on a very long taxiway. We were about the only airplane on the taxiway ... it was just as quiet as could be. I was going over my after-landing checks ... listening to ground control on the radio ... really quiet. When all of a sudden **"WHAT THE 'EXPLETIVE' ARE YOU DOING?"** He **shouted** at me. I jumped, my whole body spasmed and I thought *"Oh, my gosh ... I must've just washed out of pilot training."* I had no clue what he was yelling about. Then he said *"Who told you you could taxi that fast?"* Well I wasn't taxiing very fast ... I was taxiing kind of a normal speed ... maybe going seven mph instead of five. But I sure slowed down after he yelled that.

It took us a long time to taxi that last mile to the parking ramp.

I can still vividly remember my body spasms when Obie hollered at me for taxiing too fast. I was somewhat taken aback by the severity of the charge. Yet, I was challenged and I think I even had the temerity to say *"You don't have to shout at me, you know."*

Obie never mentioned it again ... I guess he just had to get one more shout out of his system. Fortunately, I was soon transferred to another IP who had a much deeper tool chest. He taught so well I graduated number one in my class.

Sorry about that bobble four ...
Are you alright?

F-105 (Itazuke Air Base, Japan)

The F-105 was huge ... the largest single-engine aircraft ever built ... 15 tons empty ... 27 tons fully loaded! To make it maneuver like most any other fighter required some massive/powerful flight controls. The all moving horizontal tail, or slab as we called it, was particularly effective in creating rapid and large pitch attitude changes ... sometimes too rapid and large! Which brings me to this tale.

At the conclusion of many of our training missions, especially when there were four airplanes, if there was fuel and time remaining, we would join up and do some formation aerobatics. We would usually begin with some rolls and lazy eights while in close "fingertip" formation and then would progress into the more dramatic "trail formation" where we would get about one to two ship lengths between each other, between aircraft ... between your nose and the tail of aircraft in front of you ... flying a little below him so you could see the belly of his aircraft. Once we got in trail formation lead could maneuver just as violently as he wanted to ... doing loops, rolls, cloverleafs and high 'g' turns ... just any sort of maneuvering ... much more strenuous maneuvers than you could when flying fingertip formation.

The F-105 was a real challenge when flying in trail. Because of the powerful slab it was not too difficult to command more pitch change than desired, and then overcorrecting ... this resulted in what's known as a PIO, pilot induced oscillation. The slab was so powerful that when you pulled back and forth on the stick trying to maintain position pretty soon you could bobble the aircraft up and down ... not smooth at all. The F-105 had a stability augmentation system which would dampen out any roll or yaw oscillations ... it was also very powerful ... enough to generate large roll rates. If you ever got just one of your aircraft wings into the down wash or jet exhaust of the aircraft in front of you, you might experience some pretty violent roll excursions.

On one memorable day I was in a four ship flight just returning from a cross-country weekend. We still had some fuel to burn so Kurt, our flight lead, put us right into trail formation. I was three and Jim Fowler was number four (Jim was one of those who never came back from the war later on ... a really good friend ... at least until this flight). We were kind of tired, not getting the rest we should have during the weekend, so as we got into trail we weren't as ready as we should have been and we were all bobbling a bit. Whenever two would bobble a little bit I would bobble a little bit more. That made four's job even tougher.

We did some rolls and then we did some loops. When we were coming around out of one loop pulling a lot of 'g's, two bobbled pretty good and I bobbled even more. I went up into his jet wash and I really bobbled. I probably went two or three complete pitch oscillations. My airplane bounced up and down about 20 or 30 feet and I'm thinking as I finally settled out *"I wonder how four handled that?"* As we kind of settled down I said *"Four, are you all right?"* <u>The silence was deafening</u>. I didn't hear anything.

Pretty soon I heard *"Lead where are ya? ... This is four."* **Oh no!** We had lost four, probably due to my less than smooth flying. Lead settled into a gentle turn and wiggled his wings signaling for a join-up into fingertip formation so four could locate us and rejoin the formation ... which he finally did. By then we were low on fuel and landed at Itazuke, completing our cross-country mission.

Talking with Jim after the flight I discovered that when I did my big monumental bobble my jet wash went right through four's flight path and my massive jet exhaust went right in front of his nose ... **turned his airplane upside down ... threw him clear out of the formation!**

I don't think Jim really appreciated my precision formation flying after he got a ride like that. But more than that, he really didn't see the humor in it ... the humor that I couldn't conceal as I thought of his reaction to being thrown clear out of the formation ... wondering where his flight went ... and murmuring a few choice words at me.

What's that thump, thump, thump? WOW ... that was low!

F-100 (Itazuke Air Base, Japan)

Skip bombing was always a highlight of fighter training at the gunnery range ... because it was legal buzzing ... flying level at 50 feet above the ground and dropping a small 25 pound practice bomb on a small target ... exhilarating!

At the Ashia gunnery range near Itazuke the skip bomb target location provided some added excitement since this gunnery range was right on the beach and the skip bomb target was aligned so that you approached the target from over the water. Flying low over the water was the challenge ... to say the least! The typical weather at Itazuke complicated the challenge since it was usually very hazy ... limiting the visibility. Approaching anything over the water one must be very vigilant because it is very hard to judge your distance above the water.

Maintaining my altitude while approaching the skip bomb target at Ashia range was aided by flying parallel to a shoreline about one half mile offset from the desired run in course. As I approached the target over the water I could use the shoreline for altitude references. The main task was to try to be level at 50 feet above the target when releasing the bomb. The usual configuration we flew in the F-100 included two 375 gallon external fuel tanks. You can see those quite easily out of the side of the canopy as the tanks protruded forward from underneath the sweptback wings.

The presence of these fuel tanks played a significant part one day when the haze was very thick and from a letdown point from base to final on the skip bomb run in ... about a couple miles out ... it was very difficult to see the target at that distance. It was also difficult to clearly see the shoreline references to give me altitude cues. As I got within a mile or two I sure wanted to make sure I could see the target because I didn't have that many seconds left to get lined up with the target and established at the proper altitude. On this particular run it was very difficult to assess precise references ... and then I shifted my attention to look out the front windscreen trying to pick up the target.

I started hearing or feeling a ***thump, thump, thump, thump*** ... I couldn't imagine what that was. I don't know how many milliseconds went by before I became alerted to this ... but I sure felt this ***thump, thump, thump, thump*** and it wouldn't go away ... so I glanced around and when I looked out the side of the canopy and looked down at the external fuel tank I discovered that the bottom of the fuel tank couldn't have been more than three or four feet above the waves. **Wow ... that's low !!** Upon that revelation I sure did pull up fast! And not very smoothly! Gained a bunch of altitude !!

I must've been right in the ground effect action of those waves ... the interaction of the waves and the pressure under my airplane was giving me some feedback I guess. If there had not been any waves there might not have been any ***thump, thump, thump, thump.*** And without any ***thumps*** ... *well, I don't want to think about it.*

Maybe it was just some angels knocking on my canopy?! I sure lost a bit of my superb aplomb and coolness, and I don't remember whether I dropped the bomb or not ... I was mainly thankful that I had made the pass without making a splash.

You can fly close if you want, Fitz, but . . . . .

F-105 (Itazuke Air Base, Japan)

There I was, flying the mighty F-105 "Thud." After two years at Itazuke Air Base, Japan I was beginning to think I might one day be one of the "old heads." I wasn't an old head yet but I was getting close to 1000 hours flying time and I was a captain by now. I did have a little more confidence in my flying.

One night I was scheduled to fly a night training mission and one of the "real" old heads was going to be my wing man. Major Fitz Fitzgerald ... we just called him Fitz ... had been an instructor at Nellis when I checked out in the F-105. I had to respect him ... he taught me how to fly the F-105 and now he was my flight commander. But on this flight I was his flight lead! Was I ready for this role reversal? ... I was leading ... Fitz was going to be on my wing. Rank and age notwithstanding (Major Fitz seemed so much older ... he was probably in his 30s and I was still in my 20s!?), as flight lead I was in charge of the flight.

I gave the flight briefing and one of the things I emphasized was that when we came back to land we would fly the instrument circling approach, landing at Itazuke to the north (landing on runway 36). In that approach one came off the beacon at Brady Beach flying south towards the base ... and then flew until within one mile of the field and then turned to the right to set up on a downwind leg, maintaining one mile or less to the right of the runway and then turning a left base leg to land. The circling approach weather minimums were one mile visibility requiring us to stay a mile or less from the field. This was pretty close for an F-105 which maintained 220 ... 250 knots until established on final approach ... a very tight turn at those speeds.

So I briefed Fitz *"When I turn to take my spacing on downwind, you can go ahead and take spacing there and make your own landing. Or you can......"* Fitz interrupted me and said *"No, I'll stay on your wing and land on your wing."* I replied *"I turn base pretty tight ... are you sure you want to do that?"* I guess I was kind of boasting that I fly that pattern pretty tight ... tighter than most people ... flying right in buffet just above maneuvering stall speed ... he might be uncomfortable on the wing. He confidently said *"Oh, I can handle that ... you don't fly too tight for me!"* (He must have been thinking *"How can a young whippersnapper like you turn tighter than an old head like me?!"*). Well, I thought ... he's the old head ... no need for further comment.

The takeoff and night flight training maneuvers went well and as we set up for our circling approach and landing I wondered a bit how Fitz might respond. I wasn't about to relax my normally tight pattern. I maintained that one mile distance from the runway and it made for a pretty high-powered turn in a "Thud" ... a lot of drag ... on the backside of the power curve! ... particularly during the downwind-to-base-to-final turn where the airspeed is slowly decreased to final approach speed (185 knots in the F-105).

I put the gear and flaps down on downwind, started the power up and held the power at a pretty high setting so I could pull enough 'g' to get around the corner to make the landing. I looked over to my right (I was considerate enough to put Fitz on the outside of the turn) ... it was at night, but I could still see that Fitz was right there ... in close formation. He had said he could handle it ... so I just turned my attention to the runway on the left ... and made the turn. I could feel I was in buffet (maximum performance) all the way around. I wondered if Fitz had expected to be in buffet during the turn to final ... but when I glanced over ... there he was, right on my wing in excellent position as I rolled out on final. I was impressed! I transitioned to a nice smooth final approach so we could touch down together. Perfect! Always a pleasure to have a good wing man, especially an "old head" like Fitz.

When we got back down to debrief the flight Fitz comes running up to me and says *"**Boy, when you said tight, you meant tight!**"* I recognized that comment as a treasured compliment from a "real" old head. I just kind of nodded and hoped that someday he would regard me as one of the "old heads."

Carolyn's first flight

Cessna 140 (Manhattan, Kansas)

A new pilot's enthusiasm for flying must be shared ... I was sure of that. I had just gotten my pilot's license ... achieving a goal I had yearned for since a small boy ... and the first thing I wanted to do after I got my license was to take my lovely wife for a flight in an airplane ... to share my excitement for flight.

I could tell she was delighted that I was excited, but her eagerness to experience flight herself was not readily apparent. I assumed my enthusiasm was contagious, so as soon as I got my license we went out to the airport together and rented an airplane ... a Cessna 140... a small two-seater. Carolyn's countenance seemed to change as I helped her into the right seat ... a bit somber.

But I knew that would surely change as I got in the left seat and brought the quiet airplane to life ... thrilled to explain to her all the intricacies of being in control of a flying machine. There I am ... a newly licensed pilot and I get to fly my wife around to show her the K-State campus, the big earthen dam being built, the place where we live, and many other fascinating things ... freed from the bonds of traveling on the ground! Oh, I was so excited to be able to show somebody I love what it was like to fly! Especially, my first passenger ... ever!

As we were flying along, I was somewhat perplexed by Carolyn's response. She seemed to have a pretty good death grip on part of the instrument panel. And every time I would bank to the right, so she could look out the side window as I would point out the wonderful sites (I was expecting her to say *"Wow ... that's fascinating"*), but all I heard was a monotone *"yeah, yeah."* I could hear her speak but when I looked over at her she was not looking out the side window, but was just staring straight ahead ... her eyes as big as silver dollars.

I would bank to show her the dam and she would say *"yeah, yeah."* I would bank to show her our house and she'd say *"yeah, yeah."* But she never looked out the side ... she just had this frozen position with her hands gripping the instrument panel like it was her life saver. She would only look straight ahead. It was as if she thought that if she looked out the right she might fall out the door. Well, I figured, if I would just enjoy the flight she would too. I sure had a good time banking left, banking right, looking at all the marvelous sights on the ground, but I had a frozen mummy sitting next to me.

I obviously had a lot to learn about being considerate of my passengers. Carolyn sure was brave to weather my exuberance without once complaining. She did get that first flight, and because she loved and trusted me, she didn't stop flying with me. A few flights later on she learned that she could look out the right window and not fall out the door. But it took a while to learn that lesson. And it took me a while to learn that people have to learn that lesson.

Strafing record ... wow!

F-105 (Itazuke Air Base, Japan)

Competition amongst fighter pilots is notorious ... as each strives to be the "top gun" ... often characterized by the scores obtained while bombing, firing rockets, and strafing on the gunnery range.

Good manual dive bombing scores were difficult to achieve, at best. Good rocket scores were the result of luck (rockets don't often go right where they are aimed). But strafing ... that's where fighter pilots earn their reputation. Flying the F-105 and firing its Gatling gun made the competition interesting ... and very exciting. The "Thud" was a stable platform and the gun was incredibly accurate. Besides that, the gun made a beautiful bbbbbbbbrrrrrrrrrrrrrrppppppppp sound as it was fired. We knew we would all get good scores.

The F-105 could go through ammunition quite fast, burdening the logistics supply. In order to conserve ammo the Wing Commander restricted strafing training to two firing (hot) passes ... we could fly as many dry runs as we wanted to ... but that was no fun! Our strafing skill was now based on how many rounds we put through the target (a 20 x 20 foot vertical panel) in two passes, instead of a percentage of rounds fired (the normal way before the Gatling gun).

I soon learned that because the F-105 was so accurate I could get my score up by start firing farther out. I figured if I could get maybe a two second burst at the target then I could really put some rounds in and up my score. The first second takes about 60 rounds before the gun comes up to speed and then around 100 rounds per second after that, but to fire a two second burst really took some accurate firing. When there was good stable air (without any turbulence) and things were going well I found out that I could do just that.

I set the strafing record there one time when everything was just perfect. The air was marvelously stable that day and I found I could put the pipper (gunsight) right where I wanted it ... and then squeeze off a big long burst ... bbbbbbbbrrrrrrrrrrrrrrrppppppppppppp ... for about two seconds before ceasing fire at the 1500 foot cease-fire foul line.

On the first of my hot passes everything was just right ... a big burst and all of the dust was flying up right directly behind the target ... a good sign! I knew I had gotten a good score. I had really ripped that target. I came around and got another firing pass, almost as good as the first.

I just couldn't wait for them to count the hits in the target ... count the bullet holes. A lot of times the guys were getting over 100 hits in the target. When they called it in that night I discovered I had put 252 holes in the 20 x 20 foot strafing panel ... the most that had ever gone through the target in two passes. One feels pretty good when you have done well with that gun ... that is where that top gun moniker comes from. But glory is short lived in the fighter community. The competition is just too intense!

Flameout in an F-104 "Zipper"

F-104 (Edwards Air Force Base, California)

The F-104 (a single seat, single-engine fighter we affectionately called the *"Zipper"*) was the primary aircraft that I flew during the last six months as a student at the Air Force Test Pilot School. It was an airplane that everybody wanted to fly at that time. Called the *"Missile with a Man in It"* ... sleek ... small ... when I sat in that airplane I felt like I was a part of it. It was just an exhilarating experience to be in this sleek silvery fighter. It was the fastest airplane at the time. It had set both time to climb and speed records. Every fighter pilot dreamed of flying it.

And to top it off, it came with a set of nifty spurs which you wore on your boots. When you sat in the cockpit the spurs would attach to some cables that would retract your feet in case of ejection. That's what they were for, but I remember them most for the classy status symbol they epitomized. When the F-104 pilot click, click, clicked across the ramp with those spurs on he let everybody know ... *"I am an F-104 jet jockey ... the top cowboy around."* I still have my spurs. They hang on the den wall.

One of my training flights in the "Zipper" gave me quite a start ... a modest shock to someone supposedly prepared for any event. I was flying at high altitude in the supersonic corridor moving fast ... above Mach 2 ... two times the speed of sound.

I began examining throttle response at that speed (airflow changes into the engine at supersonic speed give a fuel control difficult problems to solve ... the F-104 engine/intake arrangement normally handled these variances quite well). On this one occasion I was pulling a few 'g's and as I pulled the throttle back to the idle ... **BINGO !!** ... the engine just quit on me ... **flameout!**

I was not overly concerned, because we practiced simulated flameout landings in the F-104 all the time. The runway at Edwards was three miles long and the famous dry lake bed had seven mile long runways. We would daily fly different profiles that simulated a space shuttle, X-15, lifting body, etc. ... any sort of space vehicle that landed without any thrust ... that was our training mission. And we got very proficient at it.

I was pretty close to Edwards when the engine quit and could see that I could set up for a simple emergency flameout landing on the lake bed ... no sweat! With the engine windmilling I still had hydraulics and electrical power ... radio contact could be maintained ... good !!

Everything was going well. There was an interphone in the F-104 and I could hear myself breathe (with that aural input I realized I was breathing faster than normal ... kind of told me I was more concerned than I thought). The engine rpm gradually decreased as I descended. An air start was not readily available until I got to a lower altitude where the airflow into the engine was strong enough to windmill the engine at the necessary RPM for an air start.

As the engine rpm decreased it finally got to the point where I got my "startle" experience ... all of the sudden the generators went off the line and it got stone quiet in the airplane! I had just experienced something I had never experienced before ... no interphone noise ... dead quiet in the airplane ... no warning lights ... total electrical failure. Now I could not transmit on the radio ... I was all alone! It was startling, to say the least!

But I continued with my flameout landing towards the lake bed at Edwards. As I got down below about 20, 000 feet, with only about 20 seconds left before I landed, the engine RPM began to increase and I tried an air start ... **VOILA!** ... there it comes ... a perfect start ... I soon had full thrust. I called the tower with my radio now working and told them I wanted to enter normal traffic ... continued my approach (now a *simulated* flameout landing) down to a touchdown on the lake bed ... did a go around and entered normal traffic and came around to land on the main runway.

Not really a big deal ... but I'll always remember how quiet it got in that cockpit when the engine really did quit on me and how startled I was when the unexpected silence occurred.

Oh no – I'm in a spin

F-100 (Itazuke Air Base, Japan)

The 8th Tactical Fighter Wing at Itazuke Air Base Japan upgraded from F-100 to F-105 fighters while I was assigned there. During this transition period each squadron would send their pilots to Nellis Air Force Base, Nevada for about three months to get checked out in the new airplane. My squadron, the 36th Tactical Fighter Squadron, was the last one to transition. I wasn't too happy about being the last, but because we were I got to do some interesting flying ... doing the work of some of the more senior pilots who were away ... like towing the dart aerial gunnery target.

Only a few pilots were qualified to tow the dart ... as a young lieutenant, it was quite a privilege for me to be selected. We called it a dart because it looked like a paper airplane. It was about 20 feet long ... made out of honeycomb material ... and towed behind the aircraft on a thin 1500 foot long cable. For takeoff it was attached to a rather ungainly rig under the outboard wing station of the F-100. After reaching the open area over the ocean I would release the dart and let it reel out 1500 feet behind me. Then I would clear the other F-100s to come in one at a time and shoot at it with their 20 mm cannons. I would first go into a maneuvering turn before clearing the shooter in-hot, because when you are in a turn there is no chance of them shooting you, especially with the target that far behind the tow aircraft. **And** we had special rules of engagement to ensure that would not happen

On the day before I was to leave for Nellis I was scheduled to fly my last flight in the F-100 (I loved that airplane) and I was to be the dart tow. What an ignominious ending in my beloved F-100 "HUN" ... I would have much preferred to be the 'shooter' on my last flight ... that's what fighters are for! But unforeseen circumstances have a way of turning the ordinary into extraordinary ... and this flight became particularly memorable.

On the very first pass one of the shooters shot the dart off ... one of their bullets probably hit the tow cable. So there I was with a full load of fuel ... my briefed dart tow mission terminated ... and it's my last flight in an F-100. I thought I'll just make the most of this opportunity and do some fun things. I'll just go to an area about 50 miles south of Itazuke and do some aerobatics ... just enjoy flying the F-100 for the last time. Improvising in flight, however, can often lead to undesirable results.

One of the things I liked to do when I was flying by myself, in the way of aerobatics, was what I called a Chinese Immelman. That's where I would build up as much speed as I could and then pull vertical (straight up). I would remain in the vertical ... look at the horizon over my shoulder ... and roll the aircraft so the wing tips would describe a line all around the horizon ... then I would stop the roll and pull so I would go over the top like doing a loop. As soon as I got vertical going down I would do another aileron roll and then pull out to horizontal again. Basically I came in level ... pulled to the vertical ... did a roll ... pulled over (make like a vertical hairpin turn) ... came down and did another roll and pulled out ... back to the horizontal. It looked just like a loop of rope being pushed together in the vertical.

On this flight, however, I had a very unusual configuration with a couple of external fuel tanks and that ugly dart tow rig on the outboard pylon creating all sorts of asymmetric drag. I had never done any aerobatics in that configuration and doing a Chinese Immelman in that configuration, I figured, would take a little extra judicious use of aileron and rudder to do the roll. I figured right ... and I was having fun ... great to have a fighter all to myself. With more zeal than wisdom, on my final Chinese Immelman I improvised and confidently did two aileron rolls on the way up ... not wise! As I completed the second roll I recognized I was going to be pretty slow going over the top. I pulled gently over the top ... but the "HUN" wasn't having any of my gentleness stuff ... she didn't like that slow speed ... especially with a dart tow rig far out on one wing ... and all of a sudden we departed controlled flight and entered into a spin ... a violent yawing, rolling motion.

Never having spun the F-100 and not being a spin expert at the time, I did, however, recognize that I had probably entered a spin and I'm thinking *"Oh my gosh ... I can't do the first step in the emergency response to a spin ... **jettison everything on the wing**! ... because I'm very close to a town"* about 20,000 feet up. I instinctively applied the other spin recovery procedures ... pushing full opposite rudder ... pushing the stick forward and ... putting ailerons with the spin (in the direction of spin) ... this supposedly provided proper controls for flying out of a spin (that's what the flight manual said ... so I had to believe it).

As I finished the first turn in that spin I'm thinking *"Oh my, I sure hope this recovery procedure works soon ... cause if it doesn't recover right away I'll just have to jettison all this stuff. Then, even if I do recover, I sure won't be going to Nellis tomorrow ... I'll be stuck here for a Flying Evaluation Board (FEB). And the results of that won't be good !!"* ... Strange thoughts one has when you're about to mess up!

Those thoughts quickly disappeared, however, when my trusty HUN soon recovered from the spin. I gave a big sigh, took a big bite of the humble pie I seemed to have acquired ... went back in and landed ... of course never telling anyone ... **until now!**

On the long commercial flight to Nellis the next day my mind wouldn't turn loose of the thought that my impetuous improvisation almost turned my last flight in an F-100 into my last flight in the Air Force.

Check ride – in a different aircraft!

Cessna 150 (Manhattan, Kansas)

I began my flying training via the Air Force's Flight Instruction Program (FIP) while a senior at Kansas State University. Air Force ROTC cadets were given pilot instruction in a light airplane and if we succeeded we would get our private pilot's license <u>and</u> be certified eligible for Air Force pilot training. I was anxious for that. I started my FIP out at the Manhattan municipal Airport southwest of Manhattan, Kansas. The program took us through 35 1/2 hours of instruction culminating in a <u>make or break</u> check ride.

When the day for my check ride arrived I was some kind of excited. Pass my check flight and I'm a licensed pilot ... a dream come true. I had spent the evening before going over all the maneuvers in my mind ... reviewing all the procedures and expected radio calls ... made sure I had all the paperwork ready. I knew I would have to demonstrate that I knew how to chart a course ... and answer lots of questions about flight rules, procedures, aerodynamics, etc. etc. etc. I was ready ... or so I thought.

However, when I arrived at the airport, I discovered a couple of surprises. My check pilot was an FAA flight instructor from Wichita ... that awed me ... I had only flown with local instructors. To me he was the most credentialed pilot in the world. We met in the flight readiness room. The first thing he asked me was *"Have you ever flown the Cessna 150?"* Well, I had only flown the 120 and 140, which are tail draggers. The newer version, the 150 had a tricycle gear and flaps and 20% more horsepower. It was really quite a nice airplane and this one was brand-new. The airport had just bought it. My check pilot wanted to know if I would like to take my check ride in the 150. I said, *"I have never flown it before."* He said *"That's okay, I haven't either!"* So I said, *"Why, sure"* ... I was willing to do that. What else could I say?

Now the task had a new scope ... I had to demonstrate that I knew how to fly ... in an airplane I had never been in before. With some foreboding, I saw it as a major challenge. As I preflighted the aircraft and prepared it for flight I found that the controls were all basically the same as what I was familiar with. There really wasn't much difference, except for taxing ... with no tail wheel and the rudder pedals connected to the nose wheel it was a whole lot easier to taxi with that tricycle gear. That was comforting! Takeoff was also easier ... didn't have to lift the tail before rotating for takeoff ... just get to flying speed, pull back on the wheel and takeoff. With the extra power all the maneuvers were easier too.

However, when it came time to land, I knew that was going to be a totally new experience, because I had never used flaps before. (The 120 did not have flaps and we weren't allowed to use the flaps on the 140 so all our training would be the same). After one no-flap touch-

and-go the check pilot said *"Let's do a flap landing."* I said *"I have never done that."* He told me he would talk me through it. The first thing I noticed after lowering the flaps was that it changed the pitch attitude for landing ... for the better! I'm thinking *"This is marvelous ... I am learning something entirely new as I get my check ride."* The check pilot seemed excited too. He had never flown in a 150 ... I'm sure he had many hours in the 172 or other planes that were much bigger and better.

Landing a tricycle gear airplane turned out much easier too ... no need to demonstrate the tricky "wheel" landing or the dreaded "three point" landing technique of the 120 and 140 tail draggers. I was thrilled. And I passed the check ride with flying colors (pun!?).

I was now a licensed pilot ... on my way to a flying career ... now confident that I could do more things than I ever thought possible. Little did I know how many more "things" were ahead.

Cessna 140

JD – Have you ever flown under a bridge?

F-100 (Itazuke Air Base, Japan)

All fighter pilots harbor an innate desire to fly **under** something. I don't know where that thought comes from. However, it usually remains idle in the hidden files of one's mind ... the files labeled "**reckless ideas ... do not access**." But that thought occasionally escapes from storage, usually whenever a large, high bridge is seen. But *reason and prudence* send it back to storage without acting upon it.

That thought did pop up, however, every time I flew past a large suspension bridge a few miles east of Hiroshima, Japan. As a young lieutenant, flying the F-100s out of Itazuke Air Base, Japan, flights to and from Yokota Air Base (near Tokyo) took me right over Hiroshima. Since we could fly visual flight rules (VFR) we were not constrained to a specific route or altitude. Occasionally we would circle briefly over Hiroshima, recognizing the terrain from the famous photographs taken many years ago.

On one of these flights I was in a two-seat F-100F with JD Phillips (my senior squadron mate and fellow fighter pilot) in the back seat. We were flying back from Yokota to Itazuke ... the weather was great (we would call it "severe-clear") and we were flying low-level (about 500 feet above the ground). Everything was going routinely **until** I saw this particular bridge miles ahead of me ... a high, long suspension bridge several hundred feet above the water and at least a half mile across. That bridge had always caused the "fly under it" thought to surface whenever I had seen it in the past. But this time *reason and prudence* were not being very effective ... the bridge seemed so high and the space below it so inviting. I tried to resist this growing temptation by thinking about my backseat copilot ... he might not approve. JD did out rank me ... but I was in the front seat that day and had command of the aircraft.

I had to think fast if I was going to take advantage of this tempting adventure. One doesn't get many chances to fly under something. So I asked JD an interesting question *"JD, have you ever flown under a bridge?"* Now JD wasn't born yesterday ... he knew immediately what I was thinking. His response, though, was rather vague and slow ... *"Well ... I don't know ... but I guess . . ."* I knew that same innate desire was working on him too. So, with fighter pilot bravado and confidence in my voice I said *"How 'bout we fly under **that** bridge?"* It took him a few seconds to say okay ... his assent was key ... because I knew that once he agreed we were both culpable in case something went wrong.

Now there was no resisting the temptation. I lowered the nose of our Super Sabre ... set a course directly below the center span ... and with calm fighter pilot assurance ... flew under the bridge ... Yahoo

... a couple hundred feet under it ... a couple hundred feet above the water. **Voilà**! ... I had just accomplished a rather obscure and reckless objective in my flying career.

As with many temptations in life though, the fly under was anti-climatic ... kind of ho-hum ... that bridge was too high! The thought of looking for a lower, more challenging bridge tried to surface but *reason and prudence* triumphed again and rather quickly put the whole idea away ... for good. I had just flown under something and didn't ever need to enhance the adventure.

Maybe an outside loop someday ... but that's another Flying Tale.

Come on, Stick, let's takeoff – we're doing 200 knots

F-105F (Yokota Air Base, Japan)

Fighter pilot egos can be very big ... and sharing a fighter with someone else can be humiliating. They're sure to notice your mess ups.

My fighter squadron in Japan was fortunate. We only had single-seat F-105Ds. But that freedom wasn't to last as the two-seat F-105F was being produced and we were destined to get our share.

Some of us were sent back to the states to pick them up and fly them back to Japan. On one of those missions four of us were sent back to Brookley Air Force Base in Mobile, Alabama to pick up two brand-new F's.

Bob Jones and I were teamed together and Cecil Powell and Carl Hamby paired up to get the other airplane. We weren't too excited as we first laid our eyes on this jet (fighter ?) with a <u>second seat</u>, even though they were brand new shiny airplanes with probably less than 10 hours on each. And to top it off, we would be flying them in a very 'non-fighter-like' configuration ... maximum gross weight! ... three huge external fuel tanks ... well over 50,000 pounds. The F-105F was the heaviest single engine airplane ever built.

The front cockpit of the F was essentially identical to the D, as were most of the procedures. Key differences in flying it were significant though ... which became readily apparent on our first takeoff. It was the first time we had ever flown the F model. Fighter pilots traditionally paid little attention to center of gravity (c.g.). We should have, because the F's c.g. was different than what we were used to ... somewhat farther forward. The F was also 2000 or 3000 pounds heavier than the D. These differences led to a very interesting, unanticipated, first takeoff experience.

A coin flip determined that I was going to fly the front seat on the first leg (to California) and make that memorable first takeoff. Bob Jones hunkered down in the back seat (Bob later rose to the rank of Major General in the Air Force Reserve). Prior to our recent conversion to F-105s Bob had a history of flying F-104s and I had been flying F-100s. Neither one of us had been flying F-105s very long ... just a few months. But we were confident. That confidence was soon to be shaken.

As we taxied onto the runway for takeoff we were well aware that the runway was only 9000 feet long with a bunch of trees and houses at the end and our projected takeoff roll was a little over 6000 feet (during takeoff all F-105s stayed on the ground a long time!).

A bit of trivia that stuck in my mind that day was the fact that tires on the F-105 were stamped <u>217 knots maximum speed</u>. The nose wheel lift-off speed for the F was 185 knots ... pretty fast before you ever had flying speed.

As we rolled down the runway the aircraft accelerated correctly ... we got the right check speeds. Bob is back there being a good backseater ... not saying anything. As we rolled and rolled and rolled ... we're getting towards 160 ... 170 knots ... we hit rotation speed and I started pulling back on the stick and that stick weighs a lot ... it's got a lot of force in it ... it wasn't anything like the D. I just kept pulling and pulling ... the nose was not coming off ... **nothing was happening !!** (that forward center of gravity and extra gross weight was talking to me).

We're going faster and faster and pretty soon Bob talks to me also, shouting *"COME ON, STICK, LET'S GET AIRBORNE ... WE'RE GOING 200 KNOTS!"* By that time I was really pulling on the pole ... and we're really racing to the end of the runway and the trees there were getting taller and taller. Finally, with both hands now pulling on the control and less than 10 seconds of runway left, the nose finally began to rise ... we finally rotated and soon thereafter that big F began to fly ... probably got airborne right at the 217 knots tire limit speed and probably used an extra thousand feet of runway.

Flight was never more welcome. But we only had a few seconds to clear those 'giant' trees. To compound the issue, we didn't climb as fast as I would have liked. But as we approached the trees I could tell we would miss them by a few feet ... I sure didn't want to gather any leaves with the landing gear. I was finally able to exhale as we cleared the trees and began our climb out. I quickly dispersed the impending derision that was sure to come from that "second seat" by telling Bob *"That takeoff was a piece of cake, Bob ... can't wait to see how you handle it."*

Years later I went back there and found those trees weren't nearly as big as I remembered them.

Sawing down telephone poles with a Gatling gun

F-105 (Itazuke Air Base, Japan)

One of the great thrills of flying the F-105 was firing its 20 mm Gatling gun (M61). What a tremendous gun that was. And it made a very special, loud, awesome bbbbbrrrrrrrrrrppppp sound when it was fired ... not a wimpy ratty-tat-tat sound. The "Thud" carried over 1000 rounds and fired 100 rounds per second. Probably about 60 to 70 rounds that first second as the gun came up to speed, and 100 rounds per second thereafter. The projectile used in training was just a solid piece of iron ... about 3 inches long and less than 1 inch in diameter, but even without an explosive warhead, it could do some awesome damage.

On the gunnery range, where we honed our strafing skills, we shot at a 20 x 20 foot cloth panel suspended between two telephone poles. We discovered that the F-105/M61 canon combination was so accurate that we could now open fire at ranges out to 3000 feet and still concentrate the burst in a very small area.

The idea occurred to me that with such a stable gun platform I should aim at a smaller target than that 20 x 20 foot panel. Why not just aim at the base of one of the telephone poles holding the panel up? Does the aiming accuracy improve shooting accuracy? ... I was about to find out. (Many years later that idea was promulgated in the movie "The Patriot" when Mel Gibson told his boys to "*Aim small ... Shoot small.*"

I could hardly wait to try out my new theory and on the very next mission to the gunnery range I got my chance. The air was particularly smooth that day and on the first strafing pass (which was always dry ... no firing) I was elated to find that I could hold the pipper precisely at the lower left corner of the strafing panel without great difficulty for the short time required ... the "Thud" was up to the task! ... Was I?

I must have been hyperventilating with anticipation when I turned final on my first hot pass ... acknowledging to the range tower "*India Two ... turning final* **hot** *... strafe.*" I wanted to say "*Watch my smoke*" but I wasn't that confident ... yet. I rolled in ... flew a gentle descent directly towards the strafing panel ... accelerating to 500 knots ... watched the pipper drift slowly up to the target panel, coaxing it towards the lower left corner ... approached firing range and squeezed the trigger ... bbbbrrrrrrrrrrrrrpppppppp ... watched the impacts directly where I had aimed ... and pulled up briskly to avoid the ground. Once in a climb I banked left and looked back at the target. Beautiful sight!

All that dust from the bullet impacts was coming from right where I had aimed. But then something unexpected happened. The telephone pole I had aimed at wiggled a couple of times and then fell backwards ... I had just sawed down a telephone pole with a Gatling gun !!

The range personnel were not too pleased about that discovery ... just one firing pass in the mighty Thud had created a labor intensive, time-consuming telephone pole replacement ... and that also had the effect of closing the strafing range for use. Pretty selfish use of strafing, I was told later. Boasting about such strafing prowess was not welcomed by my fellow fighter pilots either ... with the range closed nobody could strafe ... missing out on the best event on the range.

The light had just come on though and they could not resist the temptation ... many telephone poles fell the next few days before commanders gave the order to cease and desist. Shortly thereafter, however, we entered the war in Southeast Asia ... and soon discovered the F-105/Gatling gun could saw enemy wooden boats in half.

Taking control from the IP

T-37 (Moore Air Base, Texas)

I began my Air Force pilot training at Moore Air Base in the southern tip of Texas, near the town of Mission, Texas. There I first flew the T-34 (a single engine propeller airplane) for about 30 hours and then transitioned into the T-37 (a new jet trainer). Now I was flying jets ... big-time stuff.

This initial Air Force flying training introduced the prospective pilot to all the fascinating fundamentals of flight. Each day seemed to be filled with new and exciting experiences. The key to success in this venture rested squarely on the qualities of the flight instructor. At that time the Air Force contracted with a civilian concern to conduct the flight training. Without exception, these civilian instructors were very well-qualified.

My instructor was a bachelor named Bill Conroy from New York. I don't remember how many thousands of hours he had but he sure knew how to teach. I really liked Bill and still communicate with him. He seemed to have a knack for making sure I got the right kind of training. He was a great instructor. He knew when I was learning and when I was not ... and he could quickly redirect my efforts to learn the right way ... teaching me the things I needed to know ... not merely doing what he said.

There were several instances in my training that emphasized that point. An excellent example occurred during one flight when we were between maneuvers just cruising straight and level at 5000 feet altitude. We were talking about something ... kind of looking at each other (side-by-side seating in the T-37), or at the instrument panel ... when a sudden movement caught my eye. I looked up and there was a light airplane coming right at us. I didn't have time to say anything ... I just yanked on the stick (I think Bill might even have been flying the airplane at the time). When I saw that airplane I just reacted. I gave that stick a hard pull backwards ... instantly pulling a couple of 'g's, quickly gaining a couple of hundred feet ... watching the other aircraft zip a few feet under us. Bill hollered at me *"What are you doing, you . . . . ."* as his head bobbed down and nearly hit his knees. I looked at him kind of sheepishly and said *"We just about had a midair! ... I didn't have time to talk."* We were only about half a second away from a collision and if I hadn't pulled on the stick we might have been . . . .!!

Bill was smart enough, had enough wisdom to realize what I had just done and he calmed down very quickly even though I had caused him some uncomfortable concern. When he found out I had responded instinctively to seeing an imminent collision he was wise enough to compliment me for my action. His instructional mode surfaced and he emphasized that no matter what the situation is ... if you see something you have to respond to ... take action and then talk about it. It was a valuable lesson that set the pace for me in many respects for all my flying to come.

Bill's reassurance was a real confidence builder for me. Besides, I think maybe he was glad that I had saved his life.

First solo cross-country

Cessna 140 (Manhattan, Kansas)

When I was training to be a pilot, one of the flights I had to make was a long solo cross-country. Navigating across the country all by myself was a real confidence builder.

For this adventure I flew from Manhattan, Kansas down to Stillwater, Oklahoma ... just under a couple of hundred miles ... a little over two hours flying time. Of course flying in Kansas provides a very distinct advantage ... all the roads on the ground run North-South and

East-West so it is pretty tough to fly the wrong direction. Identifying the towns and the airfields and so forth becomes the challenge ... but as long as I was doing good navigation ... flying correct headings and identifying the landmarks using the aerial charts ... arrival at the destination was assured.

When I landed at Stillwater I had to go in and get my logbook signed by someone there to show that I really had gone there. I then refueled and headed back. With premature utter confidence in my navigating skills, on my way back to Manhattan I began to improvise. (My later training as a test pilot emphasized the foolishness of deviating from a plan carefully constructed before taking off).

In any event, the idea (temptation??) occurred to me to climb this little airplane as high as it would go! The idea seemed reasonable to me. However, up to this point in my flying career I had received no training in the effects of oxygen depletion at altitude ... hypoxia. I had done most of my flight training at or below 5000 feet. As my climb went above that I marveled at how things on the ground became smaller and smaller. Higher and higher I went ... but eventually (fortunately?) the Cessna 140 stopped climbing much when I got to 14,500 feet.

Now I may have known that the FAA regulations require use of oxygen above 12,000 feet but the little Cessna 140 did not provide that. I was aware that the air was probably a little thin up there. So I had a brilliant (??) thought ... that if I just held my breath and pushed real hard I could get more oxygen out of every breath that I took ... and I won't move around very much ... I'll be real still so that I won't be demanding much oxygen. Boy, wasn't that clever, huh? Here I could have been hypoxic at any moment, not knowing the effects of it ... which I discovered later in the Air Force (during altitude chamber training) could be very disabling. Here I was venturing into an arena that I was ignorant of.

They say "ignorance is bliss" ... and I must say I was blissful, or carefree, not realizing that that was one of my symptoms of early hypoxia. So in this case "ignorance was risky."

An interesting diversion soon occurred that brought me back to reality as I attained this "don't move" attitude. As I flew by Wichita I looked out and there was a B-47 jet bomber climbing out right through my altitude, right in front of me. With a carefree, oxygen deprived mind, I just thought *"Wow, I'm right up here with the big boys."* I'm sure he didn't expect to find such a little airplane up there and would have been really impressed to know it was a solo student pilot. If he had not turned to avoid me he could have turned me into aerial debris. If he had hit me he probably wouldn't even have noticed. But I was awed that I was up there with the big boys ... or was it the lack of oxygen that made me think like that.

I did have enough sense left to begin descending and get back down where I belonged.

In retrospect it seems I had been exposed to a lesson that I wasn't going to learn until I looked back on it many years later. I guess the Lord was watching out for me that day ... and kept that little airplane from climbing higher.

I'll never do that ... oops!

F-100 (Nellis Air Force Base, Nevada)

Training to become a fighter pilot is heady stuff, and one's ego can be overinflated quite easily. However, ego **de**flating, humbling, experiences usually occurred often enough to keep my nose out of the clouds, so to speak. Like in most of life's humbling experiences, it was usually the mouth that got me into trouble.

Flying Tales

I will never forget a time when I was nearly finished with my fighter training ... flying F-100s at Nellis Air Force Base, Nevada ... and my big braggadocios mouth opened to declare how invincible I was to making a mistake. This occurred during the preflight briefing for a low-level navigation flight culminating in a bomb dropped in a remote part of the desert in central Nevada.

On this day four of us students would fly the same route, dropping our small 25 pound practice bombs on the same target. The instructor would be in a two-seat F-100F with one of the students and would lead the formation and fly the route first. The other three students (I was number four) would take a couple of minutes spacing and then navigate on our own to the target, all following a prescribed low level course of about 45 minutes duration. The instructor would orbit the target and observe us as we came in.

The bomb delivery on this mission was to be a low angle toss ... that's where you pass over an easily identified Initial Point (IP) that was a known distance and bearing from the target. As you crossed directly over the IP a timer was started ... the setting based on distance from the IP to the target, winds, ground speed, bomb ballistics and so forth. When the timer expired a light would come on indicating when to start a four 'g' pull to a 45 degree climb. After a predetermined time in this climb a second light would come on and the bomb would be released. This type of delivery, in a 45 degree climb, tossed the bomb a considerable distance, allowing the aircraft to turn away, reverse course and get as far away from the target as possible before the nuclear explosion ... escaping damage from the blast (nuclear deliveries were weird!).

During the preflight briefing we were cautioned that these timers are initiated by one of the instrumentation buttons and not the pickle, or release, button on the stick ... *Great Scott, another button!* So when you came over the IP you hit that 'other' button and the timer would start. The instructor told us to be sure when you cross the IP **not** to hit the pickle button ... only hit the *'other'* button. The IP emphasized his point by repeating *"Be sure you do **not** pickle at the IP ... wait and hit the pickle button when the second light comes on."*

Being a confident, intelligent (smart alec?) guy, I loudly proclaimed ***"I'll never do that."*** A suave, albeit budding, fighter pilot like me thought it was ridiculous that I would hit the pickle button over the IP instead of waiting to hit the pickle button when I wanted the bomb to come off ... it seemed rather elementary to me.

After the briefing we all suited up, went to our respective aircraft, and began the mission. As I began the low level navigation portion everything was going fine ... there I was flying low level in a single seat airplane ... having a ball ... zipping along the desert floor at high speed. I arrived at all the checkpoints right on time. It was just something I really enjoyed doing and I knew I was doing it well.

As I approached the IP in this valley ... it was readily identifiable ... I knew all I had to do was drop a perfect bomb, and add another feather to my cap. I had my timer set and boy I was ready to go. I flew right over the IP, right on time ... and <u>mashed the pickle button like you would not believe !!</u> A few seconds later the instructor calls on the radio for all to hear *"Four ... you just dropped your bomb on the IP."*

All I could think to say was ***"Oops"*** as I absent-mindedly continued up in a useless 45 degree climb. I had just done the impossible ... making a gross mistake in front of my fellow pilots who couldn't wait to get back to Nellis and announce it to the whole class!

That ego deflation was painful ... but it accomplished an important milestone. From that point on I don't think I ever said *"I'll never do that"* ... because I now knew I was capable of doing just what I said I would never do ... something about Murphy, I think.

Never say never.

Bloody cold

F-100C (Luke Air Force Base, Arizona)

Training to become a fighter pilot had begun. Flying F-100 single-seat fighters at Luke Air Force Base, Arizona was probably the most enjoyable adventure of my young life. It was the culmination of years and years of dreams since childhood ... getting to fly a high-performance airplane by myself ... it was just exhilarating.

One of the things that can be a 'fly' in the ointment when you're flying (excuse the pun) is to come down with an illness. No pilot wants to be DNIF (duty not involving flying), particularly when doing something new and exciting everyday. That 'fly' bit me about halfway through the course at Luke (six months of flying F-100C aircraft) when I came down with a cold. The crucial criteria for pilots with a cold is being able to clear your ears ... because when you go up and down in altitude if your ears do not clear some serious problems within the ears can result. When I got this cold, I thought *"Well, I'll just continue to fly and not tell anybody"* ... as long as I can clear my ears by using the valsalva maneuver (hold my nose and blow) to get air back up into my middle ear to equalize the pressure. So I just kept flying every day and when my ears wouldn't clear normally I would level off and valsalva. After all, it was just a "minor" cold.

At that particular time in our training we were involved in learning a nuclear weapon delivery profile called "over the shoulder." This involved doing an immelman (the first half of a loop) right off the deck flying at about 500 knots, releasing the bomb somewhere just past the vertical ascent part of the immelman and then rolling out at the top of the maneuver and proceeding away in the opposite direction (another weird nuclear delivery technique). As you might surmise, this maneuver involved quite a bit of altitude change (about 8000 feet).

We practiced (repeated) the delivery several times ... which eventually led to my downfall. The ears will usually easily get rid of excess pressure when climbing ... forcing the air down the eustachian tube. However, the "over the shoulder" profile required descending down from the 8000 feet altitude to low level each time when approaching the target. During that descent is when I had to work at clearing my ears. They would clear but as the cold worsened I had to really blow hard. I also had to blow my nose a lot to clear out the voluminous drip. As time went on it was getting more and more difficult to clear my ears. I was really having to struggle. And then every time I would blow my nose I started to get blood out of my nose. My handkerchiefs were beginning to show a lot of bloody evidence that I had a rather severe problem. I had to throw them away after each flight because they were so embarrassingly bloody.

After about two or three days of this it finally got to the point where I could not clear my ears. I had to admit that it was past time to go in and see the dreaded flight surgeon. I guess I finally succumbed to the idea that I had to stop flying ... a sad day. My mindset seemed to be *"Oh no I'm going to miss out on a couple of weeks of flying with my buddies doing exciting things, while I'm sitting on the ground ... DNIF."* I was discouraged.

My trip to the flight surgeon tells the rest of the story. He looked up my nose and in my ears and said *"Yeah, you really have a clogged up system."*

The way they normally cleared plugged ears was to use diluted neosynephrine nose drops. But in my case I was so plugged up he could not relieve the pressure so easily. So he laid me on my back and filled my nose up with neosynephrine and then used a big syringe (kind of like a big syringe used to put water in a battery!). He put that neosynephrine in my nose ... let it sit there for several minutes while I was on my back. Then he got almost on top of me and he put the tube of that syringe in my nose and squeezed that bulb really hard to force the nose drops up into my middle ear ... **without success!** I do think my nose doubled in size though. Years later I wondered if waterboarding would have been more pleasant.

He even humiliated me more by calling in other flight surgeons to commiserate and enjoy the torture. He had never seen a eustachian tube plugged or swollen that badly. He joked *"You must really have wanted to fly."* To which I muttered a humble *"Yeah."* Eventually he used some higher strength neosynephrine ... let it soak in for a long time and finally, with much vigor and flair, forced the medication up into my middle ear. The pain relief was immediate. After a big chewing out (scolding) and some prescription medicine he sent me home ... DNIF !!

I did eventually return to flying. But I don't think my ears ever fully recovered from the damage I inflicted on them because of my inordinate desire to keep flying and not be DNIF ... the feared unknown of one who wants to keep flying.

In hindsight, a play on Forrest Gump's words might have been *"foolish is as foolish does."*

Dreamland

F-105 (Nellis Air Force Base, Nevada)

The following information appeared in a recently declassified history of area 51: *A flight of three F-105 Thunderchiefs, led by British exchange pilot Anthony "Bugs" Bendell, was on a practice nuclear weapon delivery sortie about 80 miles north of Nellis AFB when one aircraft experienced an oil pressure malfunction. One F-105 returned to Nellis while Bendell led the stricken craft to the airfield at Groom Lake.*

I was the 'stricken craft.' This is my story ... my trip to "Dreamland."

One of the mysteries when we were at Nellis Air Force Base, Nevada learning to fly the F-105 in 1963, was a secret airfield north and west of Nellis. It had no name and was located on a dry lake bed called Groom Lake. We were told that if we see anything strange near there to just pretend we had not seen anything ... and above all ... never talk about it. We also had to stay far away ... marking our maps with a 20 mile radius circle around it ... **stay out**! It would be bad news for us to try to find out what was there. (The airfield at Groom Lake later became known as "Dreamland" by the pilots, and "Area 51" by the media).

However, they did tell us that if we were ever flying near that area and had a very **serious**, repeat ... **serious** airplane problem we could use that airfield as an emergency landing site. Naturally all of us were hoping that if we ever had something serious, some real emergency, it would happen up there ... but we knew it would never happen. Then again !?!? . . . .

On 8 October I was on a training mission about 30 miles north of Groom Lake with two other single-seat F-105 fighters. Flight lead, the instructor, was Flight Lieutenant "Bugs" Bendell, a Royal Air Force pilot on exchange with the US Air Force. All of a sudden I did have a serious emergency ... low oil pressure. Jet engines do not like to fly with low oil pressure. In fact I don't know of any engine that likes to run with low oil pressure. I knew I had a serious problem ... not knowing how long the engine would continue to run.

So I said *"Lead, I've got an engine oil light and the oil pressure is low. I think I better land ASAP."* We decided to declare an emergency and land the aircraft at Groom Lake. Bugs got on my wing so I didn't have to manipulate the throttle maintaining formation ... keeping the engine at a comfortable rpm ... and I headed directly towards Groom Lake. As we approached Groom Lake we finally made radio contact with the control tower and told them I had an in-flight emergency ... and I needed to land. They asked several questions but finally agreed that I could land there.

The landing was rather uneventful until I slowed down and the Control Tower told me to stop on the runway ... not to get off. I also noticed that I had a nice Air Force blue staff car right next to me ... escorting me, and a USAF police vehicle on the other side. They finally directed me off the runway onto a taxiway and indicated that I should shut it down.

I shut it down and was soon surrounded by guards with guns drawn. The next thing I knew there was a ladder raised up to the cockpit and up the ladder came a **full colonel !!**. What a wonderful reception! I'm just a first lieutenant ... I had never been greeted by a full colonel before. He did not look happy! The first words out of his mouth were *"Who is that guy up there?"* ... pointing to "Bugs" who was now orbiting the field and obviously taking in everything that was on the airfield. I told the colonel that it was Flight Lieutenant "Bugs" Bendell, a Royal Air Force pilot. The colonel just about fell off the ladder ... and said *"Oh no ... not a foreign national."* A foreign national had just seen the "operation" !!

The "operation," I discovered as I was being towed to the parking ramp, was about a dozen of the super secret A-12 aircraft ... predecessors of the famous black bird (SR-71) ... all parked neatly on the ramp. I was just awed by the new airplane ... astounded that America could be building something that awesome and keeping it a secret. And here there was a foreign national circling overhead who could also see it all.

Bugs, of course, was forced to land so they could interrogate him as well. The interrogation really centered on our description of what we had seen. I later discovered that my description of the A-12 was remarkably accurate and they made sure it would be a long time before I ever described it to anyone else. We both went through an extensive debriefing and made to sign a ten year pledge never to discuss what we had just encountered.

Maybe it was just a 'dream' ... after all, it was called "Dreamland."

Get those Reveille Raiders

F-105 (Korat Air Base, Thailand)

Morale was getting low. As the first squadron to take the mighty F-105 Thuds to combat in the war in Southeast Asia, we were initially very excited. But soon we found ourselves **NOT** flying any combat, just sitting and waiting ... not even able to acknowledge that we were in Thailand (part of the agreement between the two governments to allow us to use their air bases.) We lived in wooden un-air-conditioned hooches ... sleeping on army cots ... watching the geckos climb up and down the walls ... eating C-rations ... and grumbling! We came to "fly and fight" not "sit and gripe."

Then, to make matters worse, we started getting an early morning get up call (reveille) from a bunch of Thai Air Force F-86s buzzing us and then beating up the field with lots of low altitude, high-speed, noisy passes. Fighter pilots hate having someone else do that to them. This went on for several days, driving our morale even lower. Each day we would plead with our boss to let us go out and meet these guys and show them what fighter pilots really are ... or let us fly over and beat up their base. *"Nope"* he said *"We're over here to be serious."* Boy, that sure cheered us up!

As our grumbling became more apparent, our commander, Lt. Colonel Donovan L. McCance, called Captain Ted Shattuck (my fighter mentor and flight commander) and Lieutenant Van Pelt into his office ... had us stand at attention ... we didn't know what we were in for ... for not being enthusiastic enough or something. He looked intently into our eyes and finally said *"We are going to get those reveille raiders tomorrow morning. I want you two to meet them in the air and show them some real fighter flying !!"* Wow, did that get our hearts beating fast !!

The word spread rapidly and planning began in earnest. Everybody wanted to help. The GCA unit (used for instrument landings) was the only radar we had and they offered to point their radars toward the direction the 86s came in from. Maintenance was eager to help so they downloaded all the external fuel tanks and pylons etc. off two F-105s so we would have clean 105s. Everybody in the squadron would be eagerly watching.

We knew F-86s could turn a much shorter turn radius than the F-105 so our tactic was to bounce them from above and behind at a <u>very high speed</u>. We could not go supersonic (might damage some things on the ground) ... but very near supersonic ... giving us over 300 knots speed advantage. We would go past them fast enough that they could not follow us ... then we would zoom up ... way high ... turnaround rather smartly and come in behind them again for another pass. That was our plan.

It was tough sleeping that night ... the whole base was abuzz about the coming tangle of two big F-105s against the gaggle of little F-86s. This was going to be a huge, needed morale booster ... **if** we could pull it off right. Many of the squadron pilots joined us for the pre-flight briefing very early in the morning, with GCA controllers and maintenance folks contributing their expertise as well. We briefed that Ted and I would do a close tight formation take off to start things off. In clean airplanes we ought to take off rather smartly and climb rather steeply in close formation. No one there could remember ever seeing a formation take off in clean (minimum weight) F-105s ... should be impressive. Then we would orbit and hope that those reveille raiders were on their way and hope that we could pick them up ... see them before they saw us.

It was a clear sky that day over Korat Air Base ... we started orbiting ... around 10,000 feet. I took spacing, went into fighting wing position which was about 600 feet behind Ted and about 300 feet off to the side. As the minutes ticked by I kept wondering ... *"I sure hope they come ... a lot of people on the ground are expecting us to put on a show for them."* **Lo** and **behold**, right about on schedule, GCA found them about 10 miles out ... gave us a heads up on the radio ... we looked down and ... sure enough ... there they came and they had already split up their formation ... there were three of them.

Lead and two were heading right for our flight line at low altitude and three was pulling off beside them. Ted said he'd take number three and I should take lead and two. Ted peeled off and set up for a pursuit path on his "bandit" while I did the same on one and two. One and two were flying a fairly close formation probably about two to four wingspans apart ... they let down to make a simulated napalm run right over our ramp where all the guys were standing and where all the airplanes were parked ... letting down to about 100 feet. They were going level right down the ramp so I rolled in behind them and made my pass so that I could pass underneath them just as they went right past the guys on the ground. The timing was perfect. I lit the afterburner and was approaching supersonic (a clean Thud really could accelerate in a dive!) so I opened the speed brakes, remaining subsonic ... barely ... indicating about 650+ knots. I was about .98 Mach when I went under them. They were nearly level with the control tower and I went underneath them !! ... and then pulled up smartly to about a 60 degree climb.

As Ted and I flew under those low-flying F-86s, going at least twice their speed, we were eager to observe their response. One of them announced our "arrival" by screaming into his radio "**Bogey ... Bogey ... Bogey**" in one of the most terrifying voices I had ever heard! Ted and I both rocketed up and looked back to witness a flight of F-86s in complete disarray ... now with lots of panicked Thai voices on the radio. They were not too fighter savvy though ... they didn't come after us as any good fighter pilot would do. They just kind of pulled up and went back to the field to continue their pre-planned simulated attack.

Perfect ... as they headed back down to "attack" our base we came right down behind them again ... approaching them just like we were shooting them down. As they made a pass down the field we would pass right behind them and then zip under them and then zoom up. This was perfect for the ground observers. We did this for about five or six passes. My reaction in this exciting flight was almost predictable as I was as close to hyperventilating as I had ever been ... breathing hard and fast because this was so much fun.

After the F-86s fled with their tails between their legs Ted asked me to join up with him. As I joined up in a very tight close wing position, overlapping wings, he signaled me with his rolling index finger indicating that we were going to do a formation "victory" roll right over the field. I'm thinking *"This is going to be a perfect capstone to a perfect mission."*

I put my canopy about five feet from his wingtip and we came over the ramp at a couple hundred feet at about 400 knots. He pulled up into a slight climb and we did a beautiful wing roll. Ted was smooth and I didn't quiver a bit ... just the perfect roll. The best wing roll I had ever done. We then came around, pitched out and landed. When we taxied in all the troops on the ground were jumping up and down yelling. They were just so excited ... the morale improvement was obvious. Some of the old heads came over later and said that was the best airshow they had ever seen. **Mission Accomplished !!**

We parked, shutdown, got down and shook hands all around ... went back into operations to sign in ... and the boss came out of his office ... said very sternly *"I want to see you two guys in my office."* We looked at each other and said *"Oh my gosh, what did we do wrong?"* We walked into his office ... saluted ... reported as ordered ... standing at attention. He didn't say anything ... he gave us his famous West Point grad glare ... didn't tell us to sit down or relax or anything. After an interminable long time he finally steeled his eyes at us and bellowed *"Who told you you could do that wing roll?"* Our hearts just sunk. Here we thought we had done the best flight of our lives and now we were going to get grounded for doing an impromptu wing roll. He looked at us for about five or 10 seconds, until we had wilted. And then a big smile burst out on his face and he stuck out his hand and said *"Good job guys ... that was really great!"* I'll always remember that hand shake from the boss. Well, that made my day. A good word definitely makes the heart glad.

The entry in the 36th Tactical Fighter Squadron operations log book that day said it all: *"The Thai F-86's came again today and we ate them for breakfast."*

Thai F-86

Get-home'itis

F-105 (Nellis Air Force Base, Nevada)

Transitioning from F-100 aircraft to F-105s took me temporarily (for three months) from Itazuke Air Base, Japan to Nellis Air Force Base, Nevada. The transition included extensive ground and flight training in all of the many systems in this new multi-mission capable jet fighter.

At the conclusion of that training I had the bonus opportunity to pick up a brand-new F-105 and ferry it back to Japan ... flying from Mobile, Alabama to Itazuke. Quite a trip ... I was really looking forward to it ... so much so that I succumbed to a rather ominous case of what is known as get-home'itis." When encountering this flying disease one is sorely tempted to make foolish (stupid?) decisions.

Flying Tales

This tale reveals the embarrassing details.

The final training mission I had at Nellis provided the first opportunity to do aerial refueling in the F-105. The importance of this training lay in the fact that I had to complete that training before I could ever go on a ferry flight. I was about the last one in my contingent to get scheduled for that refueling training and I didn't have but about a week before I was to leave and go to Mobile. The pressure was mounting ... I really wanted to get this mission done so I could do the ferry flight.

The day finally arrived and we took off ... one instructor and three students ... a four ship flight. Climbing to altitude and rendezvousing with the tanker was the initial event of the mission. On the way up my opportunity to make a poor decision surfaced ... the **AC GEN** caution light came on! *"Oh no ... I'll have to abort and return to Nellis!"* But wait a second ... I remembered that recycling the AC generator switch sometimes will bring the generator back on ... I turned the switch off and then back on and that brought the generator back to life. I sighed with relief and figured *"I'm okay."* However, the light soon came on again! Now, in an effort to "save the mission" (get that refueling square filled so I can do the ferry mission) ... I did a second recycle (not recommended) ... and then a third ... with the same results.

Eventually it became apparent that I was going to have to shut down that AC generator to keep it from turning and damaging itself more. The AC generator powered most of the navigation systems, the autopilot, the pitch and yaw dampers, and many other essential avionics systems. Fortunately the radios were powered by the DC generator.

I now knew that the AC generator was not going to stay on very long so I thought, I'll just save it till the end of the flight ... try to get by without it. After all ... it was still my secret! ... (the privilege (?) or penalty (?) of a single seat fighter). I knew if I told lead that I had an AC generator malfunction I would have to go back and land right away and we had only been in the air about 20 minutes. I'm thinking *"All I have to do is complete a simple air refueling."*

But *"simple"* was no longer an option as I knew that without the AC generator I would not have use of the yaw and pitch dampers. However, the foolish decision was made anyway. I was confident that I could refuel without any dampers on ... even though a few days before one of the students got into a pitch oscillation <u>(with all dampers working fine</u>) while on the tanker ... ripping the refueling hose right off the tanker wrapping it around his own horizontal tail!

As we got close to the tanker, slowing down considerably to match the tanker's slower airspeed, I noticed the aircraft was a little squirrely without any stability augmentation. Not to worry ... I can handle it! When it came my turn to hook up on the tanker I'm thinking *"Well, here goes ... be cool ... fly smooth."* (I sure did want to refuel as I knew if I refueled that would probably fill that square and I could go on to make that ferry flight ... "get-home'itis"). I got the refueling probe out ... the tanker was very steady ... was not bouncing around ... I approached slowly ... flew the smoothest formation I could ... and **hooked up!** I took on enough fuel to satisfy the training requirement and slowly backed away without ever having a pitch damper or any AC power and then I thought *"Larry, you really pulled off something."*

What I pulled off was a really stupid stunt. Forest Gump's mama tells us that *"Stupid is as stupid does."* I was secure in the fact that nobody but me knew that I had my AC generator shutdown ... at least not yet! I convinced myself that I was now sitting pretty ... all I needed to do was just fly a loose route formation for the rest of the flight ... should not be any problem.

I could now have easily advised lead that I had a problem. But without much thought, I now decided(?) I could also finish the rest of the flight, which included a little round robin navigation flight down to Davis-Monthan Air Force Base, Arizona. Nobody could tell by looking at me that I had an AC generator problem. So I kept my little secret of all the warning lights illuminated in my cockpit.

After that little side trip all I had to do was get back to Nellis, land, and then I could write up this airplane after I got on the ground ... as if the AC generator had failed just before I landed ... pretty dishonest wasn't it?

Our approach for landing at Nellis was a "jet penetration" begun at 20,000 feet just about right on top of Las Vegas ... doing a teardrop turn with a rapid, extended descent back into the TACAN down to 2000 feet and then an 11 mile straight in approach to the runway at Nellis. They say that ignorance is recoverable, but stupid is forever. Well, ignorance played a part in revealing my stupidity.

As we started down the penetration my deception caught up with me. I discovered that I could not get the AC generator back on the line! No sweat ... I thought ... **until** all of a sudden a little warning light came on and I couldn't keep the secret anymore ... this little light said **LOW FUEL**. Turns out that some of the fuel pumps don't operate without AC power (ignorance?) And fuel wasn't being transferred to the feed tank ... exacerbated by the steep descent. It was kind of critical now because I couldn't complete this approach and then fly around for an overhead pattern. I was going to have to land right away. I thought about it for a couple of seconds and finally I said *"Four has got low fuel ... my low fuel light is on."*

That really got the IP's attention ... suddenly he finds out I have a problem ... when it is critical. The IP did a smart thing ... told two and three to join up and go land by themselves. He then joined up on my wing and called Nellis Tower ... told them I had an emergency ... emergency fuel ... and needed to land straight in. He made the calls ... got on my wing said *"Okay ... put it on the ground"* and I just headed right for the Nellis runway.

I landed and rolled down the runway ... safe and secure ... but as I turned off the runway I remembered one of the little details about the F-105 that further uncovered my deception. Once you touch down on the ground without AC power the cooling to the radios turns off and the radios shut down automatically after about 30 seconds. So as I'm turning off the runway I called tower and told them I'm going to lose my radio in about 10 seconds ... send somebody out here to tow me in ... and then my radio quit and I had to stop.

Now ... everybody knows !! ... I had more than just low fuel ... I had an AC generator problem that I never told anybody about! After I got towed in, I went over to maintenance debriefing and began to write up the airplane. As I'm writing it up the instructor comes in ... **mad as hops**! *"What in the world is going on here?"* I sheepishly said, *"I lost the AC generator"* ... He took me by the ear (figuratively) and hauled me off to see the squadron commander ... who immediately pink slips me ... gives me a failing grade for that ride because of <u>poor judgment</u>.

I got chastised by all the IPs for making a stupid decision ... having an emergency and not telling anybody about it. Which really was a stupid thing to do. But deep inside of me I was still prideful ... thinking that at least I got refueling qualified and get to go and get that airplane at Mobile. Who cares about a failing ride (even though it was my one and only in my entire flying career)?

In the long run that kind of decision making ends a lot of flying careers and it was a stupid thing to do. Did I have "get-home'itis" or what? I later often wondered ... how could I have made such a collection of really dumb decisions? My desire to make that ferry flight clouded my judgment? ... "get-home'itis" ... it really was my motivator. The flight could have turned out disastrous ... I was lucky.

Chuck Yeager might have said it best in his autobiography ... *"And luck. The most precious commodity a pilot carries."*

Watch out for the Chipmunks

F-105 (Korat Air Base, Thailand)

My fighter pilot mentor was a fine man, name of Ted Shattuck. He was my flight lead when we were flying F-100s and later in F-105s ... and he was a really good friend. I always looked up to Ted as one who took care of me and helped teach me how to be a fighter pilot. I trusted him explicitly.

Then one day my trust was put to the test. We were at Korat Air Base in Thailand ... our squadron had deployed to Korat right after the Gulf of Tonkin incident ... the first F-105s into Southeast Asia. When we got to Korat we wanted to be a part of the war ... to be doing combat ... but all we did the first few weeks was just training flights where we would fly low level around Thailand simulating armed reconnaissance.

One day Ted and I were in a two ship formation ... that's normally the way we went out on training flights ... in two aircraft. I just got off Ted's wing ... in a "fighting wing" position (a few hundred feet behind and offset) so I could keep an eye on him and still look around and check for threats that might be causing lead a problem. The wingman's job was always to clear for lead ... make sure there was no threats bothering him while he attacks the target.

Simulating combat conditions we flew pretty low ... maybe 100 feet to 200 feet depending on the terrain, whether it was mountainous or flat plains. Ted was simulating road recce ... moving left and then right down a road ... steep banks ... jinking down the road looking for 'enemy' vehicles. I stayed behind him and kind of just moved back and forth behind him ... keeping him clear. We were staying mighty low. That was the best way to protect yourself against the defenses we thought.

We had been flying at low level for about 30 minutes and I wasn't paying precise attention to our exact location ... I was just trusting Ted's navigation ... keeping him in sight and protecting him. I began to see familiar terrain and thought we must be getting back close to Korat. I noticed that Ted got straight and level so I pulled in closer to him and as I looked down I saw Camp Friendship, a US Army outfit right next to our base in Korat go zipping right under us . We were so low (about 100 feet or so), probably making a really loud noise ... I wanted to holler *"Hey Ted, we just buzzed Camp Friendship."*

But I didn't have time ... as I looked up I could see we were headed right for the control tower at Korat !! We were about tower height and to complicate matters significantly, there were a whole bunch of Chipmunks (Thai Air Force training aircraft) in the traffic pattern making practice landings. Being a diligent wingman I called out to Ted, "**Chipmunks at 10, 11, 12 and one o'clock !!**" How are we going to avoid all those airplanes? Fortunately, they were all above us.

And then, an additional concern aroused my attention ... we were going to fly almost directly over our maintenance and operations headquarters buildings (hooches). I thought *"Oh my gosh, we're going* to buzz our headquarters (the bosses office) just as we go through all of these Chipmunks." In response to my radio call Ted whipped into about an 80 degree bank turn to the right, pulled about four 'g's ... so we wouldn't hit the tower ... and we went whistling across the ramp with our bellies turned to our operations and maintenance folks ... barely missing the Chipmunks. Ted kept it low and at our speed we crossed the field in just a few seconds.

But now another concern raised its head ... on the other side of the runway was Camp USARTHAI ... the **US AR**my in **THAI**land ... their major headquarters ... our turn put us right over the top of them. We were going a good lick ... probably 500 knots by then ... went by so fast that I thought *"Boy, I hope nobody saw us ... I know they had to have heard us."*

With those pulse elevating events behind us I now had time to think ... *"Did Ted just lead me through a hornets nest, or what?"* The rest of that flight I was besought with trepidation ... *"If the boss saw us, or if the Army or the Thai pilots or Korat tower personnel complained to our boss, we ain't never gonna fly again ... we're gonna to be grounded for sure."*

We came back later after we got our fuel down ... landed, taxied in and began looking around to see if anybody was pointing fingers at us ... nobody was! When we walked back into the personal equipment hooch to drop off our parachutes, helmets and other personal equipment no one there said anything either. We then went next door where the boss's office was ... to sign in at the ops counter and face the music. The boss came out of his office ... looked around ... but didn't say anything! Had we completely escaped notice? Finally we asked some of the other pilots if anybody saw us and one, with eyes big as saucers, said *"I saw you all come through ... but I wasn't going to say anything."* (What are friends for??) *"You came by so fast and so low it was over before anybody could look out and see."*

Hooray !! ... we escaped without any retribution ... we made it !! I could still trust my good friend and mentor to not lead me astray !! However he certainly provided me a memorable visual image ... whenever I think of the day that Ted and I buzzed Camp Friendship, Korat tower, Camp USARTHAI, and flew under all those Thai aircraft. I sometimes shudder at the memory ... but mostly thankful we didn't hit any of those Chipmunks.

How low can you go?

F-100 (Osan Air Base, Korea)

Fighter pilots talk about a lot of strange things, particularly when they are on alert with nothing to do but sit around in the alert shack (no matter how nice the facility was ... it was always referred to as a "shack"). When I was stationed in Japan we spent one week per month sitting nuclear war alert in Korea. Fighter pilots always talk with their hands when describing flying feats of adventure.

On one of those occasions someone postulated (boldly, of course) that there was a psychological minimum altitude that pilots won't go below when they are flying, demonstrating his profundity by 'flying' his hand low to the floor. As in most cases of fighter pilot jabberings, we just laughed it off and went on to other pontifications.

However, being the scientific type that I am, I thought, *"That's kind of interesting ... I wonder if that's true."* I couldn't get the idea out of my mind. A few days later, as I prepared to go fly ... once a week during that week long alert status we got to be on "flyable alert" where two airplanes (without weapons loaded), out of the twenty or so on alert, were flown on training sorties ... I was still wondering if there was a minimum altitude that I would not exceed. On that day the other airplane aborted so I was out there all by myself flying around the South Korean countryside.

The "marvelous?" idea occurred to me that since I was alone I could investigate whether there is such a thing as a psychological minimum altitude. The mere thought now sounds very risky ... but fighter pilots will do those kinds of things. Proceeding with this dubious plan I found a nice big old rice paddy area and, of course, checked it over to make sure there were not any telephone poles or wires to obstruct the test. I rationalized the experiment with the argument that if we went to war we would try to fly as low as we could and I thought *"If I have a psychological minimum that won't take me very low during wartime I better find out now."* However solid that reasoning might sound ... it was really just pure adventure I was seeking ... and I knew it.

With my attention finely focused, I let down slowly ... went lower and lower ... checking it out. I noticed the lower I got the more I concentrated on what I was doing ... eyes intensely scanning the terrain in front of me. I got lower and lower and finally I reached the point where total concentration was outside the canopy. There was absolutely no opportunity to glance inside and check engine instruments or the other things that a pilot must do. Being a somewhat reasonable person I thought *"That's not a very useful altitude"* but I proceeded anyway to go still lower! ... to see how low I really could go. I finally got to the point where I couldn't (wouldn't?) go any lower and it didn't take a steel trap mind to figure out this was not very comfortable and I pulled back up ... test complete!

I discovered that I really did have a minimum psychological altitude ... in an F-100 going about 400 mph ... and that minimum was about **20 feet !!** I could confirm that with just one data point.

I would probably never need to go to that altitude again ... 50 feet was much more comfortable !!

You're cleared to buzz

F-105 (Itazuke Air Base, Japan)

Buzzing ... or flying at an extremely low altitude with one purpose in mind ... to impress people on the ground ... is, of course, strictly forbidden. There is no room in aviation for buzzing. As one gets older in a leadership position one realizes the no-buzzing prohibition must be strictly enforced because it is so dangerous. However, that mischievous, annoying temptation is often found whispering in the back of the mind waiting for the chance to override prudence and good judgment.

On one occasion in my flying career that prohibition was overruled. It happened quite unexpectedly. I was in a flight of four F-105s on a training mission to a gunnery range near Itazuke Air Base Japan ...

Ashia gunnery range. This gunnery range was located right on the shoreline of the ocean and a Japanese fishing boat had come up to the shore trying to gather some of our spent ammunition ... scrap bombs. We could not do our practice strafing and bombing and rockets with that boat so close to our targets.

The range officer, who was one of us regular fighter pilots (each of us had to go out and pull range duty every once in a while as part of our duties), was exasperated. The interfering boat ... a 30 or 40 foot sail boat with a good sized mast on it ... was keeping us from using the range ... and stealing our scrap metal to boot. Under the range officer's controlling authority ... with a desire to "impress" the intruder ... he asked us to scare him off.

I'll never forget his exact words ... they were official words coming from the range officer ... his exact words were "***You're cleared to buzz.***" Boy, when I heard that I thought *"This is fantastic ... we've got clearance ... yeah, orders ... to go down there and do what has always been strictly verboten."* ... fighter pilots fantasize about such an "opportunity."

Consequently we eagerly responded to the "orders" ... taking spacing so we could "buzz" that boat at 5 or 10 second intervals. When we buzzed this boat (remember I said buzzing was an extremely low altitude) ... in order to make a "real impression" ... we flew at an altitude below his mast. He was surely impressed ... obviously terrified by the horrendous noise and air disturbance. As his boat rocked back and forth he got his auxiliary engine going and got out of there as fast as he could ... giving each of us the "opportunity" to impress him only a couple of times !!

Another milestone in my flying career was passed ... I had heard the words that every pilot secretly yearns to hear: "***You're cleared to buzz.***"

Goodbye Army tent city ... Goodbye Air Force wings!

F-105 (Osan Air Base, Korea)

The U. S. Army troops stationed in Korea were always requesting to see more of the Air Force's presence. However, when we flew in Korea we didn't go up near the DMZ (demilitarized zone) where the Army maintained most of their presence. I guess the powers that be thought us reckless fighter pilots would cross over the DMZ and start World War III. On rare occasions, however, the Army's ardent requests prevailed and we were tasked to fly up there ... to reassure them that they were not alone ... the Air Force really was in Korea with them.

On one of those rarities I was leading a flight of two F-105s ... my good friend Rocky Bowles was my wingman (Rocky later never came back from the war in Southeast Asia). We went up by the DMZ and rendezvoused with an Army engineering company that was constructing a surface to air missile site ... a Hawk site. They were located on a hill that rose up 300 or 400 feet above the surrounding rice paddy area. At the site they had four or five big massive tents ... a regular tent city. These tents were all right next to each other, like loaves of bread ... side by side. They were probably 50 feet long and 20 feet wide ... pretty good sized tents. One of them would be the mess hall, one of them would be an office area, and the others housed individual sleeping areas. Close by the tent city a knoll rose up another couple of hundred feet on top of which the actual building/constructing of their missile site was taking place. There was an Army forward air controller up there, accompanied by the site commander, that we established radio contact with. They were very excited and wanted their troops to see the jet fighters make simulated weapon delivery passes at the tent city.

We gave them a couple simulated rocket passes ... diving at 30 degrees ... bottoming out at about 500 feet. They liked that ... but then asked could we get any lower. I said *"We can give you some strafing passes."* On the strafing passes we came in at about a 10 degree angle going down to about 300 feet or so right over the tents. They liked that more ... but then they upped the ante by saying *"Could you make a simulated napalm run over the tent city?"* I looked down there, and since our normal napalm delivery was at 50 foot altitude, said *"That may create some real turbulence over those tents ... I don't know if we want to do that."* Not to be deterred, the response was *"We really want you to do that. The camp commander is here and he wants to see you come down really low ... those high passes were nice, but..."* Responding to a somewhat official request to buzz, I agreed and told my wingman, *"Two, set up for napalm ... let's keep it at about 100 feet"* and began my first low altitude, level pass over their tents with Rocky about 10 seconds behind me.

As I approached the tents I saw I was going to be closer to 50 feet above all those tents. ***"No sweat ... they asked for it."*** But then as I got closer to the tents something unexpected appeared in my vision. Just beyond the tents there was a mound about 50 to 100 feet higher than the tents ... directly in front of me. I would have to pull up rather smartly to avoid it ... in fact I had to snatch the stick back very briskly. When you do that in an F-105 the aircraft rotates quickly into a much higher angle of attack creating massive wingtip vortices. At low altitude these vortices are like miniature tornadoes that reach right to the ground. I had seen the effect before ... over the water these vortices created huge whitecaps. **<u>Too late</u> !!**

As soon as I got to an altitude where I could look back my mouth flew open ... all I could see where the tents were was <u>rolling and boiling dirt and debris !!</u> Rocky behind me said he couldn't see anything and he was going high and dry. I looked down and I thought "*Oh No ... I just destroyed the place*" ... I better start apologizing because I won't have my wings when I get back to base. They'll be waiting for me ... for going in there too low and destroying those facilities. As the dust cleared I could see that **all four tents had been flattened.**

I keyed the mike to begin my apology ... but before I could say anything my Army friend said "***Oh, that was great !! That was great !! Do that again. Do that again.***" I said "***WHAT*** *... you want me to do that **AGAIN**?*"

It didn't take a steel trap mind to quickly figure out that the Army liked that stuff ... they liked getting dirt in the face. To further convince me, the camp commander himself got on the radio and said *"Please do that again. We never see the Air Force as awesome as that."* With a new found respect for the Army, and a chuckle in my voice I transmitted *"Okay ... Two, let's go around and give them a show."*

We made one more pass directly over tent city, both of us this time, and we came over really low. But by now all the tents were laying on the ground and I didn't have to pull up briskly, knowing about that rise just beyond the tents, so all we had to do was fly over low, level, fast, and loud. Oh, happy day! We got to blow their socks off ... and they loved it !! The Air Force presence in Korea had been readily acknowledged ... and appreciated.

As I later reflected on the mission, the flight had impressed me in two ways: <u>one</u> ... you could really do some damage with the wingtip vortices on the F-105; and two ... the Army just loves to get messed up and have a lot of noise and low altitude flying. I'm sure those Army grunts took all day to get their tents back up and clean out their food and their beds and everything else, but I also knew they were ecstatic. They now had tales to tell their grandchildren for years and years ... embellishing on the power and audacity of U.S. Air Force fighter pilots.

When we got back to the base ... no one had said a thing ... my Air Force wings were still secure.

Oh no!
I'll have to fly through the fireball!

F-105 (Korat Air Base, Thailand)

My first combat mission was anticipated, as one might expect, with guarded excitement. I had trained long and hard for that moment. Was I ready? As that initial combat mission drew closer my pulse quickened and my excitement level escalated. The excitement generated by the first mission, I discovered, often leads to mistakes. I only had to wait for the takeoff to witness the first mistake. This "Tale" goes no further.

We were sitting cockpit alert in F-105s at Korat Air Base in Thailand on this particular day in August of 1964 ... which meant four of us were sitting in our cockpits with the aircraft fully ready to start engines ... all pre-flight checks complete ... just press the start button and go! None of us had ever seen combat before ... we were on edge. We were in cockpit alert status because the war in Southeast Asia was heating up and on that day there were problems in Laos where some covert operations were ongoing. Ted Shattuck and Rick Layman were lead and two. I was number three on this flight. Number four (my wingman) was our noble squadron commander Lt. Colonel Donovan L. McCance.

Suddenly we got a launch order ... there was a downed Air America (CIA) pilot in northern Laos who needed to be rescued. We were ordered to get up there to help as quickly as we could. We all hit the start buttons as the contacts/frequencies/coordinates/etc. were given to us ... and within a few seconds we were taxiing ... with a full load of rockets and 20 mm ammunition. We stopped momentarily in the "last chance" area where the ordnance safety pins were pulled and maintenance folks checked for any obvious problems. They gave us the okay and sent us all on with big salutes. The mighty Thud was entering the war !!

All four aircraft taxied quickly onto the runway at the same time. Ted gave us the run-up signal ... we checked each other over quickly (too quickly, it turned out) and lead and two immediately released brakes, lit afterburners, and started their formation takeoff roll. I looked over at my wingman who signaled that he was ready to go and then I gave a nod of my head to signal brake release ... followed by another head nod to signal lighting the afterburners together. We were on our way ... just a few seconds behind lead and two.

Things really got exciting then. As we gained speed I was keeping an eye on lead and two as they took off in front of us. I saw lead take off but two was nowhere to be seen !! That got my attention !! Then I saw this huge cloud of dust and debris at the end of the runway where two should have been. **Oh no !!** ... The thought immediately hit me, *"Two's going to be a huge ball of fire at any moment and I'm going to have to take my wingman right through it"* ... a strange thought to be having at the time, considering my good friend Rick Layman might be crashing at the end of the runway.

All I could do at the speed we were going was to keep going because we could not abort ... we might end up in the same ball of fire he was going to create. All I could see in front of me was this big cloud of dust and debris. I started our lift off and soon the colonel and I were airborne. As soon as I could, I signaled to raise the gear and flaps, hoping that we could get them up before we got to where Rick's airplane would hit the ground and create a huge, billowing mountain of flame.

I was paying as close attention to our flight path as I could, but I couldn't keep my eyes off the cloud of dust and debris we were rapidly approaching. Then I observed an amazing sight ... an F-105 struggling across the ground ... **still flying** !! Way out there well beyond the end of the runway just above a big cloud of dirt was Rick flying his Thud, hugging the ground at a very high angle of attack. Very gradually he began to gain altitude. *"Hang on Rick ... you're gonna make it!"* He continued his struggle and began to climb out normally and we soon all joined in formation. To say I was delighted would be a gross understatement.

I sure wanted to know what in the world had happened ... but as we joined up and headed for our first combat mission there were other pressing things on our minds. I would have to wait until we landed to find out the real story. **What a way to start my first ever combat mission!**

After we got back I found that Rick had probably made the first no-flap takeoff in an F-105 !! I also discovered that I had kind of helped precipitate that whole situation. When we took the runway for takeoff I was behind Rick and when we checked each other over I could have/ should have been able to see that his flaps were up ... and warned him. But I missed that because we were in a hurry ... all the excitement of our first combat mission ... enhanced by the fact that I had the squadron commander on my wing (facts, but no excuse).

In Rick's excitement he had inadvertently put the flaps back up as he taxied onto the runway. During his takeoff roll, when he tried to rotate with Ted his airplane would just not rotate at all. He didn't know his flaps were up. All he could think to do was to keep the nose on the ground, accelerate to a much higher speed, and wait until he got to the end of the runway and hope that it would fly then.

Fortunately it did ... but not very well at the high angle required to fly with no flaps ... but it flew !! It stayed low to the ground for a long, long time and his wingtip vortices really stirred up the dirt, amplified with his afterburner also creating great huge dust clouds. His next step might have been to jettison his external fuel tanks. But he wasn't thinking about that. He was just hanging on ... hoping that it would fly ... and it did. The rest of that first combat mission must've seemed dull for Rick.

The image of it all is still very vivid in my memory ... and the image recalled always triggers the thought that I was going to have to fly my squadron commander through a big fireball. There were also other "memorable" events to follow in that first combat mission ... but they were told in a previous *Flying Tale:* "*My first combat*," page 39).

Clark tower ... I'll just stop here.
I can't see the taxiway!

F-105 (Clark Air Force Base, Phillipines)

During my first combat tour ... at Korat Air Base in Thailand ... two of us were selected to take a couple of F-105s back to Yokota Air Base, Japan so the airplanes could be exchanged for fresh airplanes from the Yokota fleet.

On this particular flight Bob Beckel and I took off from Korat and headed for Clark Air Force Base in the Philippines. We would make a refueling stop there and then fly on to Kadena Air Base, Okinawa for another refueling stop (necessary when flying that long distance without air refueling support) ... and then on to Yokota.

Flying Tales

The flight from Korat to Clark was rather routine. There's a lot of blue sky and a lot of blue water between the two. As we neared our destination, though, we encountered some rather thick weather so I continued the flight flying in close formation on Bob's wing.

We began an enroute descent with radar vectors to a GCA (ground controlled approach) into Clark. However, if the weather cleared up our plan was to discontinue the instrument approach and go in and land from a normal VFR (visual flight rules) pattern.

As we approached Clark we were descending through rather thick clouds. Bob called the Clark weather forecaster on the weather frequency and said *"What's the weather there at Clark?"* With an authoritative tone, they informed us there was a 3000 foot ceiling with 3 miles visibility and rain showers in the vicinity. That sounded great to us ... we could get below the ceiling and then fly a VFR (visual) pattern at 1500 feet.

So we went back to radar control frequency and continued our descent. However, we remained in the weather all the way down to 2000 feet as we were being vectored to a downwind leg for our GCA. Since we were only 4 or 5 miles away from Clark while on the downwind leg Bob called weather again and again asked *"What's the weather there?"* They again informed us that they had a 3000 foot ceiling with 3 miles visibility.

A little miffed, Bob told them *"We're at 2000 feet and we're in the clouds."* They were not affected by our astute weather report and stood by their observation, reiterating their claim that Clark was VFR. Reassured by their certainty, we went back to our GCA frequency ... continued on the downwind leg and then flew a base leg which was about 10 miles from the runway ... descending to 1000 feet ... and found ourselves <u>still in the clouds</u> ... in solid weather ... and it was raining pretty hard ?! But never fear ... with the good weather reported over the field we knew when we got close it was going to be VFR and we wouldn't have any problems ... we were sure to break out into the clear.

We turned final on GCA ... and began our descent to land about 7 miles from the runway. We were <u>still in the weather</u> ... in fact the weather was pretty heavy. So heavy, in fact, that I had to get really close to lead and ask him to turn his lights on to help me maintain visual contact. I had to stay about 10 feet or less away from him, overlapping wings. This was incredibly dark weather, and it was the middle of the day ... about three o'clock in the afternoon !!

It was just raining cats and dogs! We got closer and closer to the runway ... getting lower and lower. We got to 500 feet and nothing ... we hadn't broken out. We got to 400 feet ... no breaking out. 300 feet ... nothing! Thank God GCA was giving us a good approach. As we approached our minimum altitude (200 feet) ... with nothing visible ... I decided I would ride a little higher ... stacking a little bit above Bob so if he hit the ground I'd at least have three or four feet to take care of reaction time ... such are the thoughts of a wingman!

We finally got down to 200 feet and Bob couldn't see the runway. He stayed at 200 feet for a few seconds and said *"I can't see the runway. I'm going around."* It was raining so hard that we could not see forward through the windscreen.

But just then, out of the left quarter panel of my windscreen ... which I was looking out towards Bob ... as he started his go around ... I caught sight of the centerline of the runway. I didn't want to go back up in that stuff as long as I had sight of the runway, so I said *"I've got sight of the runway ... I'm landing."*

Lead went around and I transitioned to my own landing ... I could <u>not</u> see the runway in front of me but out of the quarter panel I could keep the white runway centerline just to the left of me. I made my flare and landing ... popped the drag chute ... and came to a stop by keeping the centerline in view out of my left quarter panel. Finally I got to the 8000 foot point on the runway where a separate line veered off to the right leading to a taxiway. I followed that line until I crossed the border line of the runway ... I could see that border ... but then the line stopped and I couldn't discern the taxiway anymore. So I came to a stop ... it was raining so hard I couldn't even see the edges of the taxiway !! I sure didn't want to taxi off the taxiway and sink into the mud. I changed to Clark Tower frequency and transmitted *"Clark Tower ... I'll just stop here ... I can't see the taxiway."*

Meanwhile I'm wound up pretty tight, thinking those weather guys need a wake-up call ... they need to/ought to step outside. I called them while I was sitting there in the taxiway and coyly said *"What's the weather here at Clark?"* They replied *"1500 foot ceiling and 3 miles visibility."* With jaws so tight I could hardly talk I told them *"Well, I'm out here on the taxiway and I can't even see the taxiway to taxi in. I'm going to have a word with you when we get in."* Without waiting for their response (I wasn't in the mood for an argument) I went back to GCA frequency and monitored Bob's progress as he made his second approach.

There was obviously a heavy thunderstorm over the field but Bob made it in on the second approach ... pretty low on fuel. The storm finally moved off a little bit so I could see the taxiway and I started taxing in (very slowly) so as not to block the taxiway for Bob. After we parked and deplaned, Bob and I both shared a big sigh ... and then we immediately headed for the weather office where we had a little animated discussion with the weathermen. We **'suggested'** that maybe they ought to look out the window once in a while when there is a heavy rainstorm in the area.

That was undoubtedly the lowest weather condition I ever landed in ... when I couldn't see the runway in front of me but I could see a little out of the side ... about 50 feet or less ... and where the visibility was so poor I dare not taxi.

Butt Snapper fired ... what's next?

F-105 (Yokota Air Base, Japan)

I was flying in an F-105F (the two-seat version of the F-105) on a training mission out of Yokota Air Base, Japan with Marty Case in the back seat. Marty Case was a fellow fighter pilot, friend, and a general good guy ... from a sister squadron. I don't remember what the mission was but I sure do remember the landing.

I was in the front seat so I made the landing. I touched down smoothly (of course !) on the main gear, then kept the nose up and popped (deployed) the drag chute. I then held the nose up to provide some aerodynamic drag to help slow the beast down ... the normal routine in an F-105. That routine made for a graceful landing, requiring only that I keep pulling farther and farther back on the stick to hold that touch down attitude as the airspeed (ground speed?) bled off to about 80 knots.

During this landing, however, something totally startling and unexpected occurred ... a **loud explosion** in the front cockpit just as we were beginning to slow down. If the noise wasn't enough to get my attention, the rather instant discovery that my body was way up against the instrument panel sure did !! I found my head on top of the instrument panel and the stick . . . ?? ... I was instinctively still holding the nose up ... to do that with my body pushed forward I had to hold the stick all the way back into my crotch. I gradually (?) let the nose down and hollered to Marty *"Something has fired up here ... you've got it"* ... passing control of the aircraft to him.

I could smell the cordite ... the explosive gas that is produced when something in the ejection seat fires. I quickly realized that my seat belt had fired and it was separated from me. But of most concern to me ... the Butt Snapper had obviously fired ... pushing me out of my seat. The Butt Snapper was a piece of canvas strap that went under me from the front of the seat under my thighs to the back of my seat under the neck ... called the Butt Snapper because when one ejects from an airplane the seat gets shot out of the airplane and then a few moments later another cartridge fires opening the seat belt ... then the Butt Snapper fires ... rolling up the strap and forcing the occupant out of the seat so the parachute could then function. My mind was racing ... since the Butt Snapper fired and I was now way up against the instrument panel with my head under the canopy bow I was vitally concerned about ... *"What else is going to fire?"*

I told Marty *"Stop this thing now ... I'm getting out of here."* He brought the airplane to a stop on the runway while I was opening the canopy, preparing for my escape ... hoping that nothing else fired! I got the canopy open and took off my parachute to make my exit easier. As we came to a stop I quickly climbed up over the windscreen and soon found myself on the nose of the airplane with another new revelation to deal with ... how does one get off the nose of a big F-105 ?? ... which must have been 10 feet above the ground. Full of adrenaline, I overcame that problem by simply sliding/jumping and landing on my feet and rump ... not your classic parachute landing fall (PLF).

I must say, I was one happy camper when I got on the ground. If that seat would have fired it would have just cut me in pieces. With my head under the canopy bow, I was not in any position to be ejected ... I was not in the seat anymore.

Another opportunity to be thankful for divine intervention?

If that engine so much as coughs . . . .

QU-22B (Eglin Air Force Base, Florida)

One of the first things that must be done with a new airplane is to calibrate the pitot-static system so that the aircraft speed and altitude can be precisely known throughout the entire test program. This is so important that the first test technique learned at the US Air Force Test Pilot School was the tower flyby where the airplane is flown at a very low altitude past a tower. An engineer in the tower could visually measure the precise altitude when the aircraft flew by ... while the indicated altitude was recorded in the cockpit. At Edwards Air Force Base this technique was relatively safe because we approached the tower from over a dry lake bed. <u>Not so</u> when I did this test for real at Eglin Air Force Base in Florida.

While stationed at Eglin as a test pilot I was given the responsibility of planning and flying the entire USAF flight test program (known then as a category two (CAT II) test program) for a light airplane called a QU-22B ... a highly modified Beech Bonanza. Finding a place to do a tower flyby at Eglin, a highly forested area, posed a challenge. I selected an old World War II training runway ... Field 6 (location of the U.S. Army Ranger camp). The abandoned runway there provided a nice cleared area and there was a photo theodolite located on the field. The photo theodolite could track my airplane and measure its altitude precisely while the indicated parameters were being photographed inside the airplane on a photo panel. A picture of the photo panel was taken when I pressed the button on the control column ... that button also sent a radio signal to the photo theodolite so both measurements were made at exactly the same time.

All I had to do (?) was fly precisely down the runway centerline at the precise airspeed desired and perfectly level !! In order to aid in achieving precision these tests needed to be run in the very early morning when the air was calm.

My supervisor, Ray Hinely, a brave man, decided to ride along with me on these tests. I say brave, because we had to fly these passes at 50 feet altitude ... exacerbated by the fact that we approached the field flying over trees that were 30 to 40 feet tall. The test began by flying at the fastest speed possible ... Vmax ... where if there was some emergency there was enough energy to climb and get up away from the trees. Since I had to maintain a very precise and stable airspeed and altitude when I passed by the photo theodolite my concentration was very intense ... so I let Ray worry about us being only 10 or 20 feet above the trees.

After each pass I would fly a rectangle pattern and set up for the next pass. Each pass was flown at slower speeds until the final point was flown at 1.1 Vstall ... or only about 5 knots above stall speed. It was those final passes that caused the most concern. I told Ray ***"If this engine so much as coughs ... we're in the trees."***

Well, the engine did not cough and the mission went as planned ... very successful ... everything was routine (?). We got all the data necessary to continue with the rest of the flight test program ... now knowing exactly how accurate our airspeed and altitude indications were. However, after we landed, having flown a nice smooth mission on a nice cool morning, we did notice our flight suits were soaked ... with nervous sweat.

Why did that fuel tank go over my wing?

F-105 (Yokota Air Base, Japan)

As a youngster I was fascinated by a regular article in "FLYING" magazine entitled *"I learned about flying from...."* I wondered if I would ever have stories like that. When I began flying I soon learned those "learning experiences" happen all the time.

One such "learning experience" occurred when I was flying an F-105 on a solo mission out of Yokota Air Base, Japan. I had rendezvoused with some Army guys on the ground who were testing out various signaling devices to see how far away they could be seen by a pilot. They tried various types of flares, mirrors, etc. The most prominent one turned out to be the signaling mirror. I could see the signaling mirror glint quite easily from many miles away, even through the heavy haze ... so prevalent in the Yokota (Tokyo) area. ... One learning experience achieved!

But then a more ominous learning experience suddenly presented itself ... a huge **BANG** ... **a big explosive noise** ?!! I was in about a four 'g' turn to the left when it happened and I also felt a sudden jerk in that direction. I immediately looked out to the left and discovered that my external wing tank was not there anymore. The wing tank had exploded or imploded ... structurally failed or whatever ... but was no longer with me !! ... **EXCEPT** ... as I studied the damage site ... it was obvious that I still had about half of the tank, but it was wrapped around the leading edge of the left wing like a thumb and forefinger grip. There was about three to four feet of remaining wing tank on top of the wing and about the same amount below ... bent in a nice big U shape.

Very puzzling indeed ... why didn't the tank, when it came apart, just disappear completely below the airplane?? ... especially when I was pulling four 'g's. So much for knowing airflow over/under a wing! The lower air pressure above the wing must've sucked the leading edge of the tank up ... placing it in front of the leading edge of the wing. Since the tank had no structural integrity remaining ... in the high-speed airflow (I was flying at about 400 mph) ... the front half of the tank just got impaled around the leading edge of the wing.

The big F-105 Thud still flew quite well with this big piece of junk on the wing, so there was no immediate concern since I was over mountainous, unpopulated area. I did begin to wonder how long the tank pieces would remain wrapped around the wing leading edge, so I remained over unpopulated mountainous terrain and did some controllability checks ... down to landing speed. I didn't want the remaining pieces to fall off on a populated area. I wasn't about to move the leading edge flaps, figuring I could make a no-flap landing.

The tank (pieces) didn't move, so I set up for a straight in approach back at Yokota ... after notifying the Command Post that I had a piece of wing tank stuck on my wing, over and under the leading edge. That sure elicited some interesting questions from them !! I was a bit apprehensive flying over the populated housing and business areas close to Yokota, but the tank pieces remained stuck to the wing and a potentially hazardous situation ended routinely ... except for the bunch of curious colonels waiting for me as I taxied off the runway.

Bottom line ... I learned I wasn't an expert about the airflow around a wing and how the low pressure above the wing can cause some strange things to occur.

Okay Two – Where are you?

F-105 (Korat Air Base, Thailand)

One of the most challenging AND delightful training tasks in flying fighters is called air combat maneuvering (ACM) ... better known in the media as "dogfighting" ... where you try to get behind the other airplane who is trying to get behind you. The training usually began with an equal advantage with both aircraft flying towards each other. The task is to outmaneuver your opponent ... to obtain an advantage where you could be right behind the other airplane ... and attain magnificent 'bragging' rights.

A golden opportunity for a mass "improvised" ACM adventure occurred one day, flying out of Korat, Thailand, when we were still just doing training missions. We had six F-105s (three two-ship flights) launching at the same time and we agreed (to put some extra 'sport' in our mission) that after about 30 minutes of individual flight low-level navigation we would meet at a certain geographical location at a certain time. We'd arrive as three two-ship flights from different directions ... we wouldn't tell everybody where we'd be coming from ... we'd just try to find each other ... and then we would just have at it ... with six airplanes all going for each other (sometimes referred to as a "fur ball").

I had Rocky Bowles with me as my wingman and we flew a low-level and then arrived at the rendezvous point at a high altitude (above 30,000 feet) and a high speed (above .9 Mach) so we would have a lot of energy to start the fight with. I signaled for Rocky to get in a fighting wing position ... about 500 feet behind me and we began looking for the other four F-105s. Unfortunately there were a bunch of clouds in the area ... big high puffy cumulus clouds. Consequently we were not having much luck finding our "enemy."

Calls to each other on the radio, like *"Where are you, Curly flight?"* didn't help much either. It began to look like our adventurous plan was slipping away. Finally, after about 10 minutes of orbiting and getting low on fuel, we caught a glimpse of the other "Thuds" and the fight was on ... but the clouds interfered. I would catch sight of somebody ... go for him ... and then the clouds would get in the way. Then I would see somebody else and go for him ... and the clouds would get in the way and we would soon lose sight of each other. No one could find anybody else long enough to engage ... and when we did see each other we would be making passes head to head and then disappear behind or in the clouds. It was just chaos (does Keystone Cops come to mind?).

I was getting desperate. Suddenly I was startled to see a Thud a mile or so behind me. At last I had someone in sight that I could go after! But he had a positional advantage ... he was <u>behind</u> me! Not to be deterred (never give up!), I began to work on him ... trying to get him in <u>front</u> of me. Gradually after much maneuvering I began to reverse the advantage in my favor and finally, after just about running out of gas using the afterburner most of the time, I got behind him into a gun firing position. Victory at last !!

But now we were all low on gas ... everybody is hollering BINGO (that's when you have just enough fuel to get home). So we called off the maneuvering and I began a gentle orbit so my wingman could join up on me and we could return to base. I radioed *"Okay Moe Two, join up"* .,. and I looked behind me to monitor his join up. But I couldn't find him. Two is hollering *"Where are you, Moe Lead?"* I'm looking all over behind me, but Rocky is nowhere in sight. So I said *"Moe Two, rock your wings."* **Low and behold** ... the airplane in front of me, the one I had just shot down, was rocking his wings !! What a mortifying discovery ... the only guy I had gotten in the whole mess was my wingman !! Some bragging rights !!

Of course when we got back to the base, each fighter pilot claimed that they had shot everyone else down and nobody had gotten behind them. It was a classic fighter pilot story ... everybody getting everybody else and nobody getting shot down themselves, when in reality nobody had shot down anybody !! ... **Except me** ... I knew one thing ... I had shot down my wingman ... and I wasn't talking about it.

Now you know why I changed our call signs to *Larry, Moe, and Curly.*

700 mph at 50 feet ... cockpit fog!

F-4 (Eglin Air Force Base, Florida)

In the munitions flight test business the lowest we usually tested to was 50 feet above the ground, making sure the new experimental munition would function at the lowest practical altitude. **And** we usually did that at the maximum speed that would ever be seen in a combat environment. After a few of these kind of tests, speeding in a car really lost its luster. One of those test missions really stands out in my memory.

The test that day was to deliver a new cluster bomb unit (CBU) under the maximum conditions on a range east of Eglin Air Force Base. The delivery was made from an F-4 which I was flying solo (we often flew the two-seat F-4 solo on the hazardous munition tests). I was to dispense the CBU in level flight 50 feet above the ground at just over 700 mph. That was a bit fast for the brutish F-4 ... requiring a descending acceleration using full afterburners.

In order to set the scene for this "tale" I must tell you about a design deficiency inherent in the early F-4s. The air-conditioning system, like in most jet fighters, used air drawn off the compressor section of the engines. When that air was cooled a lot of moisture was extracted. But the F-4 did not have a water separator, so a lot of that moisture ended up in the cockpit. This was most notable at low altitude in a high humidity area ... like Florida (or Southeast Asia!). That moisture usually showed up in the form of fog in the cockpit ... not desirable. In order to eliminate the fog one had to turn up the cockpit heat (using a small knob just behind the throttle on the left console) ... making the cockpit very uncomfortable. Crews returning from an F-4 low-altitude sortie in Vietnam came back with very wet, sweaty flight suits.

On this particular test mission I flew a racetrack pattern, flying a downwind leg at a few thousand feet altitude and at a comfortable 400 mph where I didn't have to worry about cockpit heat ... so I flew with the air conditioner at a cool temperature. I made several dry passes without accelerating to the highest speed so I could establish a proper run-in heading and altitude, making sure the range control people were satisfied before making the final hot pass. Consequently, I had not really stressed the air-conditioning system before making my final delivery.

Everything looked good as I began my hot pass. As I turned from base leg to final I selected full afterburners and began a rapid acceleration while descending. Approaching 100 feet or so and still descending and turning slightly, the F-4 air-conditioner reached out and grabbed me by the throat ... or should I say eyes? **All of a sudden** the fog in the cockpit came in like a blanket ... and **the ground disappeared !!** I immediately turned my attention to the instrument panel so I could regain a climbing attitude ... but it had disappeared too !! The fog was so thick **I could not see the instrument panel ... two feet in front of me !!**

How was I to avoid the ground ? ... as I was descending rapidly toward the trees. Without telling it, my left hand had already reached for the cabin temperature (heat) knob and turned it full hot ... but turning the heat up would take a few seconds to clear the fog ... seconds I did not have. Without any references to my actual attitude, but knowing I was perilously close to the ground, I pressed my nose (oxygen mask) up against the canopy looking straight out to my left ... I could barely make out treetops whizzing by. That small visual input was enough, however, to direct my right hand (on the stick) to make the correct control movements and arrest my descent and begin a climb. **... Whew !!**

The cockpit soon heated up and the fog disappeared and those few hazardous seconds (memory moments !?) were soon passed (I'll always remember them, but I don't recall anything of the hundreds of seconds that preceded and followed them). I did have the presence of mind to key the mike and transmit, rather emphatically, *"This pass will be dry."* Somehow I had lost my concentration ... was not anywhere near my desired release conditions ... and I wasn't in the mood!

I did successfully drop the CBUs on the next pass ... but it sure was hot in the cockpit !!

Worst airplane I ever flew

Twin Pioneer
(Farnborough Royal Air Base, England)

Probably the best part of attending the Air Force Test Pilot School was the opportunity to fly many different airplanes ... planes I had never flown before. The most unique opportunities occurred on a memorable field trip visiting various European flight test facilities. Our first stop was at the Empire Test Pilot School located at Farnborough Royal Air Base in England. While there, each of us got to fly two different aircraft. I got to fly the Hawker Hunter (an English equivalent of our

F-86 jet fighter) ... <u>a real pleasure</u>. AND the infamous Twin Pioneer ... the worst airplane I ever flew ... <u>a real challenge</u>.

The Twin Pioneer was a twin-engine, propeller driven, cargo/passenger airplane about the size of our C-47 (Gooney Bird). To begin with it was frightfully ugly ... a tail dragger with tall ungainly fixed main gear that made it sit on the ground at such a steep angle that it looked like it might fall over backwards. It also had three huge vertical tails, which never look right on an airplane. I later found out that it needed more than three.

I knew I was in for a thrill when they announced my assignment to the Twin Pioneer and all of the English Test Pilot School instructors (IPs) and students hooted and hollered and wished me well. My apprehension grew as I heard the instructor pilots discuss how it was impossible to make a <u>good</u> landing in the Twin Pioneer (not just difficult, but impossible!).

The next morning as I approached the ugly airplane I noticed my instructor pilot was not too thrilled with his assignment either, having discovered that I had never flown a twin-engine propeller driven cargo airplane before ... ever! He helped me into the left seat and then strapped himself into the copilot seat. Starting and taxiing were challenging, and the takeoff was awful too ... trying to keep that beast going down the center of the runway, lifting the tail off, and then getting airborne. But the thrill (?) was just beginning.

As soon as that bird got in the air, it didn't take a steel-trap mind to figure out that it didn't like to fly straight ... the nose wandered around like a marshmallow on the end of a long stick (<u>Dutch roll</u>) and I had to constantly work the rudder pedals to maintain the desired heading. I began to think of those three vertical tails and wondered why they stopped with three. Then I noticed that when I banked to the right the nose initially moved to the left ... and vice versa (<u>adverse yaw</u>) ... more rudder work (coordination) required. This ugly ego-deflator also displayed <u>negative dihedral affect</u> (when I pushed the right rudder the airplane would initially bank left ... and vice versa). Besides directional stability problems, this user-**un**friendly airplane also displayed some less than desirable longitudinal dynamics ... forcing me to constantly work the wheel (what is a wheel? ... I had always flown with a stick) to keep the nose level. I also learned about synchronizing the props ... but that's a different story. All of these enlightening (?) discoveries were made as we flew towards an auxiliary landing field where I would be faced with putting the airplane to the real test ... LANDING.

The Twin Pioneer's reputation as a horrible lander prompted the IP to suggest that he demonstrate the first one. I noticed he got all tensed up and focused his entire being on the task at hand. I could see that he was giving the rudders, the throttles, and the wheel a pretty good workout as we approached for our first landing. Landing the Twin Pioneer, with its awful directional stability characteristics, was complicated by the fact that it was a STOL (short takeoff and landing) aircraft ... it had huge flaps that allowed the airplane to fly final approach at a very steep angle and slow airspeed, necessitating a very large pitch change during the flare to touchdown ... particularly challenging in a tail dragger. If this flare was misjudged and all three wheels did not touch the ground at the same time a huge bouncing porpoise was assured.

Well ... wouldn't you know it ... my IP made this marvelous, perfect three point touchdown ... no bounce, no problem ... maintained perfect directional control. I was impressed. *"Landing this Twin Pioneer must not be as bad as everybody made out"* I thought. However, I did notice that as soon as he got the airplane airborne again he immediately gave me control and moved his seat all the way back, crossed his arms over his chest, and <u>never</u> touched the controls again. He had obviously just made the best landing he had ever made in this impossible airplane and did not want to break the spell ... wanted to finish on a good note.

With a perfect landing demonstrated before my eyes it was now my turn to demonstrate my youthful prowess ... which went pretty well **<u>until</u>** I started the flare. I then realized this was not going to have a happy ending. The main gear hit and then the tail went down and we lifted off ... then we came down ... main gear ... tail wheel ... bounce, bounce ... like riding a bucking bronco. Fortunately, nothing broke and we got airborne again ... for <u>another</u> attempt! ... with much the <u>same result</u>.

A third attempt proved just as futile.

This airplane could be landed, but I soon figured out that if there were ever passengers on board they had better be healthy and buckled in securely. As my landing efforts progressed (?) I could sense that the IP was inwardly chuckling ... he knew I was experiencing **the** typical Twin Pioneer landing effort ... but he didn't want to spoil the **incredibly humbling experience I was having.**

When we landed back at Farnborough, we were met by several Brits with knowing grins on their faces, which I sensed were meant to be encouraging. I was now in good standing ... the newest member of a select group ... those who had tried to land the Twin Pioneer and been humbled by the task.

Much as I would never have chosen to do it, flying the Twin Pioneer was a great experience for a budding test pilot. I now knew what adverse flying quality characteristics looked and felt like. It turns out, I discovered, that the Empire Test Pilot School kept the Twin Pioneer for just that purpose ... an excellent demonstrator of what not to have.

Shake, Rattle, and Roll

F-105 (Eglin Air Force Base, Florida)

One of my jobs at Eglin Air Force Base, as a fighter test pilot, involved "certification" of numerous conventional munitions on a variety of fighter aircraft.

Before a munition could be carried on a fighter in an operational unit we had to demonstrate that it was safe ... at all air speeds (ensuring that no adverse flying qualities would be encountered with the never-before-used configuration) ... and at maximum 'g' loading (ensuring that nothing would break). We usually accomplished this by flying two back-to-back missions without downloading the munition, flying at all speeds from landing speed to maximum speed and from a positive six 'g's to a negative two 'g's (+6,-2).

This rather routine test flight was affectionately called a "Shake, Rattle, and Roll" mission, a name that didn't exactly endear itself to me. As a new test pilot I thought test flights should have more exotic, imposing names ... like maybe "Technical Assessment of Hazardous Flight Conditions" or "Golden Arm Envelope Expansion" (test pilots were called Golden Arms). But the catchy "Shake, Rattle, and Roll" moniker stuck ... even though we developed a detailed test flight procedure for the mission ... ensuring that each of the pertinent flying qualities were evaluated in a buildup of speed increments ... following a detailed flight test card schedule. The 'g' loading test points were flown by establishing a precise airspeed at a precise altitude and then flying a level constant 'g' turn.

One airplane, however, presented a particular problem ... the F-105 did not have a negative 'g' meter indication ... and attaining a precise minus two 'g's was problematic. When I arrived at Eglin the standard procedure for obtaining the negative two 'g' test point was to dive to achieve a high airspeed ... pull up to a nose high attitude ... and as the airspeed decreased (approached the desired (aim) airspeed) ... push on the stick until it "felt" right (uncomfortable)! This roller coaster ride had no real precision as the airspeed was never constant and the negative two 'g's was attained with what I called a wild guess (technically known as onageristic determination) !!

Having just graduated from the test pilot school I was not too impressed by this non-precision approach. My thoughts were: *"Why not establish the aim airspeed and aim altitude and then simply roll into a 120 degree bank angle and then fly a level turn ... **inverted**?"* ... (by pushing, not pulling on the stick). My engineering expertise assured me that a level 60 degree bank constant-speed turn provided exactly two positive 'g's ... so a level 120 degree bank turn would provide exactly two negative 'g's. (Use your hand to envision this maneuver !!)

Most of my fellow test pilots scoffed, but I soon had a chance to put the scheme to the test. I found that rolling to 120 degrees of bank was just as easy as rolling to 60 degrees of bank ... and I soon learned that, with practice, I could maintain a level inverted turn. **VOILA** ... a perfect negative two 'g's at the precise airspeed and altitude desired !! The safety chase pilots said it looked a little weird, but they soon learned how to keep me in sight.

I soon became enamored with this negative 'g' turning maneuver ... actually enjoyed it ... and it eventually became my trademark maneuver. Later, when I checked out in the brand new A-7D aircraft in Dallas, Texas the company test pilots there took note of my upside down turn and kind of nodded approval ... but I think they thought I was a little weird too.

Get off the brakes ... Get off the brakes

C-131 (Andrews Air Force Base, Maryland)

While stationed at the Pentagon I initially maintained flying currency by checking out in the Convair C-131, a twin-engine, propeller driven passenger airplane ... a novel experience because it was the first transport airplane I had ever flown. I now had to learn what the real meaning of "crew coordination" meant, which I often described as a "three act play" ... necessary in a multi-crew cockpit. I was always getting my role confused ... like reaching for the gear handle instead of just saying *"Gear up"* and letting the copilot do it. Or forgetting my lines ... like not saying the "correct" words when commanding a particular flap setting.

But flying a multi-crew airplane did provide some memorable moments not attainable in the single seat airplanes I had been used to.

One of those moments occurred during a training flight to an airfield in West Virginia ... with an instructor pilot (IP), whom I regarded whimsically as a "Nervous Nellie," seated to my right in the copilot seat. I had just completed a few normal landings when the IP asked me to do some single engine landings ... simulating one engine inoperative. The main difference in this type of landing was that reversing the propeller thrust on the one good engine to slow the airplane down after touchdown was **not** recommended, so the main method of slowing the airplane down was simply using only the brakes. I could tell this type of landing was the IP's most challenging maneuver because his voice began to elevate and he couldn't stop talking about how judiciously the brakes must be applied. His anxiety level was most telling as I prepared for the landing.

My first single-engine landing attempt was perturbated considerably when the Control Tower asked us to change to a different runway ... perpendicular to the one we had been using. This change forced me to turn the downwind leg I was on (for the prior runway) into an immediate base leg. This meant I had less time to set up for landing. **And,** to top it off, the runway change put us on to a much shorter runway, a real challenge for a single-engine landing.

This change in plans **really** got the IP talking ... making sure I was fully aware that with the short runway, and no reverse thrust, I would have to be extra careful on the brakes so as not to blow out a tire, and yet stop on the available runway.

I was able to make a pretty decent final approach and touched down on speed ... pretty close to the desired touchdown point. It was a good touchdown and I immediately pulled the good throttle to idle and began my slowdown to a full stop landing ... with the IP reminding me to *"Be careful with the brakes."* I began my application of the brakes, being as 'judicious' as I could ... as the IP raised his voice, saying *"Easy on the brakes."* We started slowing down rather briskly and the IP immediately yelled again *"Easy on the brakes!"* Then shortly thereafter another high-pitched *"GET OFF THE BRAKES."* I immediately eased the pressure I had on the brake pedals.

It was strange ... I could feel the braking action but I could hardly feel the brake pedals. I soon noticed that the braking action was still fairly aggressive. As he hollered again *"GET OFF THE BRAKES!"* I looked down at the brake pedals and noticed that <u>I wasn't pushing on them at all</u> !! When he hollered *"GET OFF THE BRAKES!"* again, I looked over at him and said ***"My feet are off the pedals!"*** He looked at me with a strange sheepish look, finally realizing that he had been doing the braking all along. When he took his nervous feet off the brake pedals the aggressive brake action ceased, allowing me to bring the aircraft to a stop with plenty of room to spare.

He didn't talk much after that. Now you know why I thought of him as a "Nervous Nellie."

Oh, the joy filled memorable moments of flying a multi-crew airplane.

Super Sabre vs. Spad

F-100 (Eglin Air Force Base, Florida)

In the fighter aircraft munitions test business the most exciting times often occurred after we had finished the test ... dropped the munition ... and had enough fuel remaining to engage in our favorite "training" event ... **simulated air combat**. Usually this would be with our wingman who had been flying photo chase or safety chase. But even when there was no chase aircraft to "tangle" with we would often just go looking for someone else to "bounce." One of those memorable times (one I have tried to forget) occurred when I was flying an F-100 Super Sabre.

I had dropped all my munitions on a test site a few miles east of Eglin Air Force Base. I didn't have much fuel left but I still went looking for an "enemy" aircraft to shoot down. I was flying at a medium altitude when I looked down over the beach near Destin and spotted an Air Force A-1E propeller driven fighter (a 1940s era aircraft used by our rescue forces in Vietnam, and affectionately called a SPAD ... after a famous World War I airplane). Attacking such a slow, helpless little old propeller driven fighter with my modern supersonic SuperSabre fighter was really not up to my standards, but since there was no one else around I thought *"Why not?"*

The little antique A-1 was doing some interesting and unusual maneuvering ... flying a race track pattern at a fairly low altitude. I figured he was out of neighboring Hurlburt Air Force Base (a few miles west of Eglin) and was just learning how to fly the A-1. Oh well ... one simulated firing pass at this training pilot would give us both some valuable experience. Since he was going so slow and I also had an altitude advantage to begin with, I would not have to use my afterburner ... saving the small amount of fuel that I had remaining. I dove in behind him ... a couple of hundred miles per hour faster than him ... and closed to within gun range. But just as I got to within gun range he broke (turned) sharply ... reversing course abruptly in a turn so tight that, at my higher-speed, I could not possibly follow. Well !! ... That was not nice !!

I pulled up briskly so I could reverse course and dive in behind him for a second attempt. He was cooperating nicely (ignorantly, I assumed) ... just going straight and level and when I got into gun range <u>again</u> he suddenly reversed course <u>again</u>, and I missed ... <u>again</u> !! He had incredible lucky timing I thought. How could a novice know precisely when to break? I began to wonder what he was doing ... but I thought I'd give it one more try ... but the result was the same !! He broke just as I got at the correct gun firing range. This was definitely no fun. Enough of that !!

Looking around for something else more challenging(?) I discovered a T-33 (a jet trainer) orbiting a few thousand feet above. Ahh ... a more formidable opponent !! Abandoning the futile A-1 shoot down attempt, I began a climb to engage the T-33. But alas, I was so low on fuel I could not use the afterburner to get up to his altitude quickly, constrained to fly at a lower power setting in a gentle circling climb. The T- Bird just orbited tantalizingly above me ... like he was waiting for me. Focused on this "enemy" I gradually approached his altitude and was about to pounce on him when something told me to look back. *OH NO!* ... right behind me, and in perfect firing position, was the A-1 SPAD !! *How humiliating! How mortifying!*

When I left him to go after the T-33 I had dismissed him as an unworthy opponent and had not paid him any more attention ... leaving him to his strange training racetrack patterns. But he obviously had other thoughts and pursued his attacker (me) with vigor. Oh, the remorse of having underestimated an opponent !! Out of fuel and out of ideas I immediately departed the area with my tail between my legs and headed for nearby Eglin Air Force Base to land ... hoping to keep my embarrassment a secret ... to no avail it turned out.

Later that afternoon at the officers club, I was regaling my fellow fighter pilots with my "tale" of attacking some strangers ... leaving out some of the critical details, of course ... when all of a sudden in barged three or four guys in flying suits from Hurlburt. They yelled loudly *"Where is the F-100 pilot that attacked us today?"* Having already fabricated a rather misleading account of the encounter to my friends, I could not deny that I was the one. With great smiles of triumph, these gallant warriors from Hurlburt proceeded to present me, in front of all my fighter pilot friends, the **"YOU'VE BEEN HAD BY A SPAD" award!** How embarrassing to be figuratively shot down in flames ... right in front of my peers!

The embarrassment was climaxed when I was informed that the T-33 and the A-1 that I tried to attack were a **team** ... both flying out of Hurlburt. Their training objective was to teach the A-1 pilot how to defeat a MIG (Vietnamese jet fighter) attack. Their normal training was for the T-33 to simulate a MIG attack on the A-1, teaching the A-1 pilot the proper timing for when to make a break. But this team had a much better training opportunity when a real MIG (me) entered (stumbled into) the foray! A golden opportunity for them ... they were delighted. A humiliating experience for me ... I wanted to hide.

I did my best to accept the **"YOU'VE BEEN HAD BY A SPAD"** award graciously. My only recourse was to treat them all to a steak dinner that night.

A-1

Uncontrolled Flight

A-7D (Edwards Air Force Base, California)

One of the major objectives at the Air Force Test Pilot School is to expose budding test pilots to extremes of flight ... training them to recognize and analyze unusual (weird!) flight maneuvers that may occur with the misapplication of aileron, rudder, or elevator. We often refer to these extremes with the technical euphemism "departure from controlled flight" ... or simply *departures*.

To experience departures in the training environment we intentionally abused the airplane ... forcing the aircraft to do things it did not want to do. We introduced this training by first giving the students instruction while spinning in gliders, then advancing to spins in the A-37 (small, two-seat, twinjet attack airplane), and finally completing the training in the A-7D (a single-seat, single-engine attack airplane). The A-7D was a perfect airplane for departure training ... it was easy to depart, and more importantly it was easy to recover from the departure.

I taught this portion of the curriculum, chasing the student in another A-7D to observe and critique ... flying a loose formation a few hundred feet away from the student. I would talk the student into the initial conditions, observe his performance, and be ready to help him, if needed, in his recovery. The most important part of the learning actually occurred after the flight ... in the debriefing session ... where I would ask them to describe the extremes they had encountered. Departures were usually characterized by a violent yawing, rolling, pitching motion ... with rolling and yawing usually in the opposite directions (an incredibly confusing motion). It was always interesting to ask them which way they departed, for when the aircraft yawed right it would push the student violently to the left often confusing him into thinking he had just departed **to** the left.

The test pilot must learn to accurately describe departures (including air speed and altitude changes as well as the rapidly changing attitudes ... and most of all, the appropriate recovery procedures). That information must be translated into a written report, most of which would usually be included in the flight manual for the benefit of all future pilots of that aircraft.

Nearly all of the students at the Test Pilot School were new to the A-7D ... had never flown it before ... making it a perfect learning experience. The departures were initiated above 25,000 feet altitude ... by flying to a near stall condition ... from both straight and level and turning conditions ... and then abruptly applying full aft stick, full aileron, full rudder, or a combination thereof.

The typical departure might include a rapid pitch up with a rapid rolling in one direction while the nose was violently yawing in the opposite direction. Within a few seconds the airplane appeared to flop aimlessly with a couple of complete rolls included. The recovery was initiated after a few seconds and was relatively simple in the A-7D ... just release the controls.

During this out-of-control maneuver my job was to keep the student in sight and observe. I had to be very careful because I was in formation with him and very close to stalling myself. Keeping him in sight usually required me to roll the aircraft ... concentrating on very careful coordinated use of rudder and aileron. I too would have to describe the maneuver accurately later in the debriefing so I needed to observe it throughout, even though I was probably upside down (inverted) during most of this maneuver (remaining above him).

I had instructed many, many of these departures but one that I will never forget ... I call it a memory departure ... occurred when at the instant of the student's departure I was a little too aggressive in my roll and immediately recognized that I too had just departed controlled flight. My immediate attention was riveted to my own recovery and consequently I wasn't paying much attention to the student until I recovered.

Thank God for a couple of things ... One, we both departed the same way, so we didn't interfere with each other creating a midair potential; ... and two, as I completed my recovery and looked over at the student, his recovery was identical to mine ... we were in the same relative position as we had before the departures occurred.

A perfect formation departure !! Was that cool, or what?

Not really ... test pilot instructors are not supposed to be that ham-fisted.

They're really shooting at someone

F-105 (Takhli Air Base, Thailand)

CHEVY FLIGHT (four bomb laden F-105s ... I was CHEVY 2) was staying out of the way, waiting our turn to bomb the famous Thanh Hoa railway and highway bridge (known to the Vietnamese as the "Dragons Jaw") in North Vietnam. I was about to be the 90th fighter in two days to drop bombs on that stubborn bridge.

I was really hoping the bridge would be down when we got there and we could then bomb the "alternate" target ... a huge electricity generating thermal power plant about one quarter mile from the bridge. The Washington bureaucrats would not let us bomb the power plant unless the bridge was down. Lt Colonel Robbie Risner (my personal war hero) was the mission commander and he was directing all the traffic that day ... orbiting the target in his F-105.

As we approached the bridge I noticed it was still up !! ... and then watched the flight of four F-105s in front of us drop eight 750 pound bombs each ... making thirty-two direct hits on the bridge abutment ... *"Perfect"* ... I thought. CHEVY LEAD (Captain Ted Shattuck ... my mentor and good friend) noticed the same thing and told Robbie that the bridge was obscured by billowing smoke from the previous bomb hits and we could not see it ... *"Maybe we should bomb the alternate (hint, hint)?"* Colonel Risner agreed !! ... and cleared CHEVY flight (we were the last flight that day) to bomb the power plant. Now that got my attention for sure ... the adrenaline really started flowing. We get to go for the "real" target!

I took spacing on Ted ... watched him dive toward the power plant ... and just a few seconds later began my dive bomb approach from a different heading ... to hopefully confuse all of the anti-aircraft gunners. Once one rolls over and dives on a target he is committed. And so the rule was **one pass, get out fast** ... dropping all eight 750 pound bombs at once (the same bomb load as the B-17 dropped in World War II). The anti-aircraft was severe, but I wasn't paying attention to that, concentrating intently on my delivery ... trying to achieve 550 knots, forty five degree dive angle, 5000 foot release altitude, and pipper (gunsight) placement on the precise aim point ... **all simultaneously** ... a really difficult, but with much practice, achievable task.

I pressed the pickle button ... felt all bombs come off in less than one second ... and immediately began my pullout ... trying to keep from going so low as to encounter the blast from my own bombs. My pullout put me down into range of all of the anti-aircraft, but I hoped to go fast enough to mitigate most of that (wishful thinking by all fighter pilots!). At bomb release I selected afterburner so I could be really fast (supersonic, if possible) while departing the hostile area.

As I bottomed out in my dive recovery I quickly rolled up and glanced back at the target ... and was elated at the sight !! All eight of my bombs had hit squarely in the middle of the power plant ... creating a huge eruption of flame, smoke and debris completely enveloping the power plant complex. In fact, the column of smoke and debris from my bombs obscured the power plant so much that CHEVY 3 and CHEVY 4 had to divert back to bombing the bridge ... which was still up?!

As I was "getting out of Dodge" I noticed something very unusual behind me. The real, lasting impression of that mission was unfolding ... a whole broken deck of white puffy clouds seemed to be forming just behind and slightly below me. I hadn't noticed the clouds when I was in my dive bombing pass. The cloud deck was expanding rapidly and I soon realized that it wasn't clouds ... **it was anti-aircraft fire !!** Those innocent looking "clouds" were full of deadly shrapnel !!.

It dawned on me that **they're really shooting at someone** (I think the phrase "hammering someone" came to mind). The edge of the "cloud deck" was expanding at the speed I was going and only in my direction ... staying just a short distance behind me. They were indeed "hammering someone" ... and . . . ***"Hey, I'm the only one here"*** ... all those "clouds" were just for me **!!**

All that attention was very unnerving and my jinking (rapidly moving back and forth to hopefully spoil their aim) took on a much more urgent zip-zoom fashion (probably mimicking my accelerating heartbeat). But in a few terrifying seconds, at near supersonic speed, I was out of range and they lost interest ... probably diverting their attention to CHEVY 3 and 4 ... who also happened to escape their wrath. Whew! ... that was ominous!

It took a long time to settle down in the quiet solitude of our return flight to our base in Thailand. It didn't take long, however to realize how blessed I was ... we lost four or five airplanes that day. Oh yes, the power plant was officially reported as "*seventy-five percent destroyed by well-placed 750-pounders . . . and closed for the duration*" of the war.

The Thanh Hoa bridge, on the other hand, was bombed repeatedly throughout the war, but never came down until seven years later.

Sorry boss ... that was the worst landing I have ever made

OV-10 (Cam Rahn Bay Air Base, Vietnam)

Some landings are best forgotten. The easiest "awkward impacts" to forget are those that occur when one is flying solo ... when no one else is in the airplane to observe ... and *critique!* (pilots are prone to make fun of each other's bad landings). That's one of the reasons I liked flying single seat airplanes. However, bad landings are not easily overlooked when another pilot is sharing the airplane. The worst landing I ever made was under the most humiliating of circumstances ... when the other pilot was my boss!

This memory landing occurred when I was flying an OV-10 (a two-seat, twin-engine observation airplane) out of Cam Rahn Bay, Vietnam enroute to Danang Air Base. I was in the front seat and my boss, Lt. Col. Ralph Haymaker, was in the back seat. Besides being my boss, Lt. Col. Haymaker and I had shared many fond memories, as we had gone through OV-10 training together and were assigned together at Chu Lai Air Base for several months prior to this "memory" flight. He knew me well and had a high respect for my flying skill ... at least up until this flight!

I must say the OV-10 was one of the easiest airplanes to land that I had ever flown. It was designed with a landing gear that could absorb hard landings on a rough field without much noticeable effect ... great huge shock absorbers. I often thought of the OV-10 landing gear as like great eagle legs and claws ... which would grab the ground and slowly lower the bird to a nice gentle landing.

So I wasn't too concerned as I lined up on final approach to land on the nice long concrete runway at Danang Air Base. I don't know where my mind was ... or what my eyes were looking at ... but the word "gentle" could in no way be associated with what happened next. When we 'hit' the runway the impact made a huge **whump** sound and we must have bounced at least 10 feet back into the air. The **whump** sound was magnified by the startled moan from the back cockpit. Even though my eyes were much wider after that first impact, the second landing wasn't much better ... we bounced way up in the air again ... accompanied by another guttural moan from the back seat.

I don't remember how many bounces we actually made before the airplane finally gave up and we stayed on the ground. I had just become a big fan of that over-designed landing gear. Without it something might have broken ... besides my pride.

Flying Tales

Pilots will often jazz another pilot when they make a bad landing ... <u>unless it is really bad</u> ... in which case *silence speaks louder than words*. As you might imagine, as we rolled down the runway, turned off, taxied to our parking spot, and deplaned, there was nothing but <u>stony silence</u> in the cockpit.

I wish I could forget.

Flat out in an F-4 at 100 feet

F-4 (Eglin Air Force Base, Florida)

One of the bold new missions introduced during the Vietnam war was called the Fast FAC (Forward Air Controller) ... using jet fighters in the hazardous environment of North Vietnam to locate and mark enemy targets for destruction. Our local hero and medal of honor winner Colonel Bud Day was the commander of the unit in its early days ... flying F-100 fighters.

The F-4 (Phantom II) soon replaced the F-100, but before it could do so it had to be certified to carry the seven tube rocket launcher (small, 2.75 inch diameter white phosphorous rockets were used to mark the target so the other fighters could locate and destroy it). That certification was our job at Eglin Air Force Base.

One of the last test flights when certifying a weapon on an aircraft required flying at the maximum speed the airplane might carry it ... for as long as possible ... checking it for the cumulating effects of high-speed aerodynamic vibration. We would load up the airplane with maximum fuel, allowing us to get the maximum time at the maximum dynamic pressure ... the most hostile environment for an externally carried item. We would then fly with maximum power (full afterburner) at the lowest altitude possible ... 100 feet over the water ... for as long as the fuel would last.

I was excited. I was selected to fly this last test flight and it meant going flat out in an F-4 at minimum altitude ... just push the power all the way up and let it go ... something fighter pilots chomp at the bit to do. And I got to do it solo, with no guy in the back to worry about. I was ready.

My plan was simple. I took off from Eglin ... headed straight for the Gulf of Mexico (only a few miles away) ... stayed low (100 feet) ... and once over the Gulf, with all systems go, lit both of those big afterburners and went for it ... heading due South away from the shore. The acceleration in that big beast was always awesome to experience ... a great thrill. The air speed rapidly climbed ... to 600 ... then 650 ... approaching 700 knots (nearing supersonic ... that was sure to get the attention of some of the fishing boats I flew over).

But as I got closer to the maximum speed I noticed some troubling indications in the cockpit. I had taken off with full internal fuel (nearly 2000 gallons) plus two external tanks which held 450 gallons each. An F-4 design deficiency soon reared its ugly head.

The external tanks would not deliver fuel to the internal tanks nearly as fast as the engines demanded at the high power settings required using full afterburners at very low altitude. The internal fuel, which feeds the engine, was being rapidly depleted ... and I had only been in afterburner a few minutes.

Oh, the disappointment! I so wanted to continue "pushing the envelope" ... but there was no alternative ... I had to come out of afterburner (slowing down dramatically). I then began the interminable wait for the external tanks to refuel the internal tanks ... watching the airspeed get slower and slower (still fast, but not flat out). Once the fuel had been transferred successfully, I re-selected afterburners to accelerate again, but I knew I would not have enough time to get back to those high speeds I was so keen to experience. **And** I was getting farther and farther away from Eglin ... rapidly approaching minimum fuel to return.

It was obvious, that after less than 10 minutes at maximum power at sea level, I had used up most of the available gas ... **so much for an F-4 going flat out !!**. I came out of afterburner ... reversed course ... exchanged airspeed for altitude ... and began my descent for landing back at Eglin ... a landing made with minimum fuel remaining.

7 tube rocket launchers

Oh – the engine quit!

QU-22B (Eglin Air Force Base, Florida)

It was kind of strange that the jet age Air Force would buy a small little propeller driven airplane like the QU-22. It might seem even stranger that it was assigned as a flight test project to a seasoned jet fighter test pilot like myself. However, when my boss asked if I would like to be the sole test pilot for the QU-22 test program I jumped at the chance. Getting the opportunity to design and fly the entire flight test program ... a test pilot's dream.

Lt. Vic Auterio was my able assistant ... my flight test engineer (you may remember him from *Flying Tale: "I wonder what will happen when we hit that cloud?"* page 17.

As the test program progressed from one phase to another we eventually began evaluating the climb performance. Climb tests are normally very boring. During earlier flights we had methodically determined the best climb speeds at various gross weights and altitudes. But the final climb performance test involved a "proof of the pudding" flight ... a "check climb" ... climbing at the previously determined speeds all the way from surface to as high as we could go (service ceiling ... where climb performance became less than 100 feet per minute).

An unusual problem raised its head as we approached this test. The predicted service ceiling for the QU-22 was well over 30,000 feet, but the aircraft was not pressurized. Air Force flight regulations prohibited flight above 25,000 feet in unpressurized aircraft. We would need a waiver from Air Force headquarters to conduct this flight.

Vic was a little bit apprehensive as I applied for the waiver. He knew that if the waiver was granted we would be breathing 100% oxygen under pressure ... referred to as pressure breathing ... something he had experienced only briefly (and then not favorably) when I had sent him to the altitude chamber for training earlier in the program. But I assured him that his body would not expand too dramatically at 30,000 feet ... and if it did we could laugh about it later.

The actual "check climb" technique required that we fly a straight course ... without any turns that would degrade climb rate ... on as calm a day as possible, to mitigate wind effects. The perfect day finally arrived. We took off early and commenced our check climb. My task was to hold the recommended airspeed and course precisely. Vic's task was to take notes regarding flight parameters throughout the climb.

Our climb took us into airspace controlled by Atlanta Air Traffic Control which garnered some interesting attention. I had coordinated with them earlier but their controllers were still surprised to see such

Flying Tales

a slow flying airplane on their radar screen, flying up with the jet traffic (our climb speed was just over 100 mph). The controllers kept asking me what kind of an airplane I was. I think I told them it was classified.

After a long slow climb we finally reached our service ceiling at about 31 or 32,000 feet. But our test wasn't over. Since we were already up there, we now had the opportunity to conduct a "check descent" ... evaluating glide performance from 30,000 feet down to 1000 feet. I reversed course ... pulled the throttle back to idle ... set up my best glide speed (best glide speeds are normally very slow ... ours was about 100 mph) ... and began a long boring glide back towards our base. We were paralleling Interstate 10 ... it was a beautiful, cloudless day ... and I noticed some of the cars were keeping up with us.

We eventually descended to 1000 feet, ending up several miles from our starting point. I said to Vic *"Okay, the test is over ... let's go back home and land."* The smile on his face told me he was glad it was over. So I pushed the throttle up and turned toward our base. **Whoa ... <u>there was no response from the engine</u> !!** *"Hey Vic, our engine isn't running."* Vic, wary of all the tricks I had already played on him, thought I was kidding. I didn't waste any words trying to convince him otherwise ... I had become very busy.

I sure hoped the engine would start, because we were too low to reach any suitable landing strip without power. After a flurry of activity in the cockpit the engine gradually roared back to life. My huge sigh of relief got Vic's attention ... and my anxiety level slowly restored to a more stable status.

With the engine running again, we soon made it back safely to our home base. As I pondered what had just occurred I assimilated another chapter in my book of flight knowledge: During the "check decent" the windmilling propeller, without power, rotated at the same rpm and made the same noise as it did when the engine was actually running at idle power ... making it difficult to discern actual engine performance (who knows when the engine actually quit?). Vic also learned that the wide-eyed look on my face (above the oxygen mask), the rapid movement of my hands, and the higher pitch in my voice were not normally associated with a "trick."

Don't worry ... you can't bomb that good

F-4 (Eglin Air Force Base, Florida)

It was a new experimental weapon ... we only had one of them. But we had to test it ... at least once! Time was running out. This new cluster bomb unit (CBU) was designed to destroy those pesky trucks that were hauling enemy weapons down the Ho Chi Minh Trail in Vietnam. If it worked as advertised it was urgently needed. This CBU looked like a big bomb, but was really a hollow canister that contained scores of small softball size and shape bomblets.

We would test the effectiveness of this weapon by dropping it on five old military trucks which were set up as targets on a test range west of Eglin Air Force Base. I was excited to be the test pilot scheduled to drop this one-of-a-kind weapon for its first all-up test ... releasing it in a tactical dive bomb fashion from an F-4 jet fighter.

There was only one major problem. No one knew what the size of the bomblet pattern on the ground would look like. You see, these bomblets had little ridges on them that made each one spin after they were ejected from the dispenser. The spinning armed the bomblets, but it also gave each bomblet a curved flight path, much like a pitcher throwing a curve in a baseball game. Naturally, each bomblet would curve off in a different, random direction, causing the scores of bomblets to create a doughnut shaped pattern. But nobody knew just how big the doughnut would be for this never-dropped-before bomblet. The critical element was how big was the hole of the doughnut going to be? We would soon find out.

The truck targets were spaced in a straight line 200 feet apart. The thinking was the hole in the doughnut would surely be less than 800 feet in diameter and greater than 200 feet. We only had to hit one truck with one or more bomblets to determine the CBU's effectiveness. If the pilot (me) would aim at the center truck, the bomblet pattern would undoubtedly cause one or more trucks to be hit ... so the weapon's effectiveness could be evaluated. The engineers were confident the doughnut hole would be smaller than 800 feet. My question to them at the flight briefing was *"What if the center of the hole is precisely at the aim point, and the doughnut hole is a little bigger than 800 feet?"* They confidently remarked **"Don't worry ... you can't bomb that good!"**

With that reassuring confidence in my abilities, I proceeded to my trusty F-4 ... preflighted this one-of-a-kind munition ... took off and headed for the bombing range. It was a beautiful day. The trucks were laid out in a nicely visible area. I proceeded to make a few dry runs to make sure everybody on the ground was ready (there were lots of observers as well as the photographers and other data gatherers to monitor this unique test).

The dry passes also gave me a chance to practice obtaining my test specified 450 knot, 45 degree dive angle, 5000 foot release altitude simultaneously with placing my pipper (gunsight) on the center truck. Everything looked good and we were ready for the hot drop.

The release conditions were perfect ... bombs away! After release, I pulled up straight ahead ... immediately banked to the left and began circling the target area to watch the bomblet impacts and observe their pattern unfold. When the bomblets impacted they sparkled brilliantly ... making it easy to monitor the impact pattern.

The first bomblets to hit were those that curved backwards and I watched them begin detonating about 50 feet short of the first truck. *"Oh my ... I must have missed my aim."* As the other bomblets began to hit the ground and explode I could see the doughnut shape developing. A perfect circle was forming and it was **BIG!** I'm thinking *"Oh No! The far end of the hole is going to miss the last truck!"* **Yep** ... the closest final impacts were 50 feet beyond the last truck. All the trucks were safe! ... protected by a ring of fire that completely encircled them! Not the desired test result!

So much for weapon effectiveness evaluation ... no such data was obtained ?? Not a single truck had been hit by even a single bomblet. A pretty expensive test with no benefit to show for it. EXCEPT ... we had obviously discovered the bomblet pattern for this CBU, released under these flight conditions. The doughnut hole was exactly 900 feet in diameter !! And <u>oh yes, the center of the hole was precisely over the center truck</u>!

Even without the effectiveness evaluations we desired, a most valuable lesson was learned. The pattern for this CBU was obviously <u>not</u> acceptable for combat use. The design was abandoned. This "one-of-a-kind" turned out to be a "last-of-its-kind."

My solace for the disappointment we all shared was the chuckle I got remembering the comment *"Don't worry ... you can't bomb that good."*

Check and double check

F-100 (Eglin Air Force Base, Florida)

My older brother Vincent, flying the big airplanes for TWA, had an easily remembered, but profound, saying he used when flying. Simply stated, it was ... *"Check and doublecheck."* Basically it meant to make sure all actions in the cockpit were given a second, or even a third, look ... ensuring the proper actions had indeed been made. I vividly remember an occasion when that saying saved my life.

I was flying an F-100 jet fighter at the time on a test mission out of Eglin Air Force Base ... dropping some experimental live high explosive bombs. One of the bombs did not release ... even though I had sent the release signal (hit the pickle button). A hazardous condition now existed ... called a "hung bomb." The bomb might fall off at any time.

Many questions ran through my mind: *"What's holding it on? Would it fall off at the most inappropriate time? Can I get on the ground safely?"* I alerted Eglin Tower ... called for an emergency straight-in landing ... approaching the runway from over the water of Choctawhatchee Bay, avoiding populated areas.

Eglin Tower notified the security police and they blocked the automobile traffic on the main road which passed in front of the runway ... wouldn't want any cars to get hit with a stray high explosive bomb. I had another concern as well. If it did fall off during my landing approach it would probably explode when it hit the ground ... right below me! Not a comforting thought!

With these issues on my mind I didn't really need what happened next. As I approached the runway, slowing to final approach airspeed ... something did not seem right. My attitude seemed a bit nose high for my airspeed ... similar to making a landing with my flaps up. Of course they were down! How could I make a mistake like that? Just to make sure the flaps were down I gave a quick glance at my flap indicator ... *check.* My eyes told me the landing flaps were down. They had to be. If they weren't I was soon about to stall and mush into the ground short of the runway ... too low to eject. But things still didn't feel right. So, just to make sure the flaps were down I looked out at the wings to check their position visually ... *doublecheck.* My eyes again told me the flaps were down.

But the aircraft attitude still didn't seem right and I was rapidly approaching the runway.

My eyes were now busy outside the cockpit so my hands began their own *"doublecheck"* ... by reaching for the flap handle. Boy was I surprised (actually elated!) when my fingers told me the flap switch was in the **UP** position. So that's what was wrong!

The flaps were **NOT down** !! I quickly put the flaps down, gratefully achieved the normal landing attitude my mind had been searching for, avoiding a disastrous calamity, and made an uneventful landing ... retaining the "hung bomb" throughout. **Whew !!** ... Another routine (?) test flight completed.

How could my eyes have lied to me? As I mused over that, I realized that my eyes had not lied ... my mind had just seen what it wanted to see !! Thank God I had continued to *"check and doublecheck"* ... putting new meaning to the Yellow Book phrase *"Let your fingers do the walking."* If my fingers had not continued to doublecheck for an errant flight configuration, and I had continued to slow down, the outcome might have been a big fireball just short of the runway ... in an area known as "Cobb's Overrun." Which might have been renamed "Larry's Overrun." Not a pleasant thought.

Every time I drive by that area I am reminded of that day when *"Check and doublecheck"* saved my life. Thank you brother.

Just one more pass

F-105 (Eglin Air Force Base, Florida)

"Just one more pass" ... that's all that Joe, the F-111 test pilot, was asking. But I was almost out of gas ... I was at BINGO fuel ... just enough fuel to get back to Eglin Air Force Base.

Joe was testing a new infrared warning system on the F-111 and I, in my sleek, silvery, supersonic F-105, had been making passes at him to check out this new capability against a simulated attacking fighter. He had been getting good data but he sure could use another supersonic pass from me. But we were out over the Gulf of Mexico many miles from Eglin.

I considered his request, noted that he was in between me and Eglin and that we were at 30,000 feet altitude. Going supersonic, however, meant I had to use afterburner ... drastically reducing my available fuel for a routine landing back at Eglin.

Then a wave of test pilot "innovation" lifted me up! What if I gave Joe one more pass by using supersonic speed to "toss" me back to Eglin. At the completion of the pass, as I passed adjacent to Joe, I could immediately come out of afterburner, reduce the power to idle, and zoom to a higher altitude (exchanging airspeed for altitude). Then I would just remain in idle and glide all the way to Eglin. Oh, what a "clever" idea, I thought. Confident in my analysis, I radioed to Joe *"Okay, one more pass ... let's go for it."*

As I accelerated in afterburner to supersonic speed I approached the F-111 quickly. I must say my eyes were watching the fuel gauge go down quickly also. When I passed by Joe, I immediately executed my plan. I pulled the power to idle and zoomed to over 35,000 feet ... reducing my speed to best glide speed ... about 275 mph. I then maintained my power at idle thrust to conserve fuel. Going that slow took me a little longer, but I made it to Eglin at idle power just fine ... entering the landing pattern with minimum fuel. No sweat! Chalk up another successful mission modification to astute test pilot thinking!

It wasn't long before I got another chance to revalidate that 'clever' plan. A week later I was scheduled to repeat the mission. It was the same scenario ... I would fly my F-105 as a "target" against the F-111 with its still-being-tested infrared warning system. Just like the first mission, as I reached BINGO fuel I heard the expected pleading call from Joe ... *"Just one more pass?"* Several other pilots had flown the same mission and Joe was getting the reputation for always asking for *"Just one more pass."* You see, the F-111 could stay airborne a lot longer than we could and, like any good test pilot, he wanted to get all the data he could on each flight.

Well, I had been successful the previous mission with my 'clever' plan ... why not give it a repeat? The last pass would again be heading directly towards Eglin. So, immediately and without further deliberation, I said *"Okay Joe, one more pass."*

I lit the afterburner, which typically quadruples the fuel flow, and headed directly towards the F-111. As my eyes watched the rapidly depleting fuel counter again things just didn't seem right ... the fuel consumption rate was much too high. But I had been here before and was not overly concerned. That is ... **UNTIL** ... it dawned on me that what was wrong was I was not at 30,000 feet as before. I was at **5000 feet** !! When the ramifications of that fact sunk in, I told Joe this pass was going to end ... *now !!*

I immediately came out of afterburner and gained as much altitude as I could. But this time I only got up to 10,000 feet where an idle powered glide would not get me all the way to Eglin. There was no choice ... I had to push the throttle up ... to a power setting that would give me maximum range. I pointed straight for Eglin and crossed my fingers. I couldn't help but wonder ... *had I used too much fuel by running in afterburner?* I asked Eglin Tower for a straight in approach, declaring minimum fuel so they would give me some priority. *Would I make it before the engine quit?* My eyes seemed glued to the fuel gauge ... it's amazing how much attention such a small little gauge gets when the needle gets close to zero! Thankfully my faithful F-105 came through ... touchdown came none too soon as a successful landing was eventually made. I was especially pleased to find there was even enough fuel to taxi back to the parking spot.

After walking back to squadron operations it wasn't long before I got a telephone call from the crew chief after he had refueled my aircraft. He wanted to tell me he had never before put that much fuel in an F-105. I didn't have a good comeback comment.

So much for "clever" in-flight improvisation. That wave of test pilot innovation may have worked the first time, but the second time it turned into a tsunami. No more *"Just one more pass"* for me !!

F-4 ... cattle stampede

F-4 (Eglin Air Force Base, Florida)

One never knows how animals on the ground are going to react to airplane noise above them. Inside the cockpit it is pretty quiet and non-threatening ... but outside ?!? I got a chance to find out one beautiful day flying over the farmlands of Kansas.

I was solo, flying an F-4 back from out west to Eglin Air Force Base, with a refueling stop at McConnell Air Force Base in Wichita, Kansas. I arrived there with plenty of fuel and a "great idea." I canceled my flight plan with McConnell Control Tower and told them I would be flying in the local area for about 45 minutes. That would give me enough time to proceed up to north-central Kansas where I could fly over my brother Jerry's farm ... just to say hello ... albeit, a noisy hello from a jet fighter!

The approach to my brother's farm, at low altitude of course, also took me directly over my brother-in-law Milford's farm. It was a beautiful day and I could see Milford's farm a few miles in the distance, so I just let down real low ... pushed the power up to make a big noise ... and flew directly over his farm. Didn't have time to circle and give him a good show ... just pressed on toward brother Jerry's farm, about 15 miles further. I just knew that Milford would enjoy hearing a quick, but friendly, greeting from his brother-in-law.

When I got to Jerry's farm, I circled at about 500 feet altitude looking down at the feedlot full of cattle to watch their reaction to the F-4 noise. During previous flyovers in F-100 and F-105 fighters the cattle did not seem to be affected by the jet noise, even when I lit the loud explosive afterburner both aircraft employed. The F-4's engine afterburners, however, did not make loud explosive attention-getting noises ... **but in full military power they made a horrible screeching noise.** I was curious how cattle would react to this "new" sound.

I was stunned! As I looked down at Jerry's cattle, penned in a large feedlot, I could tell they were really spooked by this strange noise overhead. They were jumping and dancing around, obviously disturbed by my "friendly" overture. I wisely decided **NOT** to make a very low pass ... even throttled back and only made a couple of circling passes over the farm, remaining at 500 feet. I didn't want to worry my brother by stampeding his cattle. I waggled my wings to signal hello to my brother, who was waving at me from the feedlot ... cut my "visit" short ... climbed up a bit and headed back to land at McConnell. A new revelation for me ... the ugly F-4 also made an ugly disturbing sound. That bit of information came in handy later on ... see *Flying Tale*: "_Hi, Carolyn_ (page 46)."

Pondering this new revelation while enroute back to McConnell I began to wonder what Milford might have thought of his brother-in-law's noisy hello, because my pass over his farm was much lower than the one over Jerry's. What I didn't know was that he was hoppin' mad ... fit to be tied ... wanted to catch that hot-shot pilot and string him up ... **etc., etc., etc.**!! I found all this out **after** I had refueled at McConnell and returned to Eglin. When I got home, my wife Carolyn told me she had heard from her sister Mary, who was trying to find out for Milford if I might know who could have caused such trouble for a nice cattle farmer like him.

It turns out that when I made my *"Hi, brother-in-law"* low, noisy pass over his farm, Milford and his boys were unloading a huge shipment of young, nervous, rambunctious feeder calves ... several dozen (maybe a hundred or so). Those calves were already upset from the long trip and were on edge, so to speak. When that "USAF *Sound of Freedom"* greeted them ... **that was enough !!** They ignored their handlers and took off running in all directions ... busting down many fences ... charging thru neighboring farm fields ... trying to escape the terror ... truly a **classic STAMPEDE !!**

Milford, who shot down a Japanese Zero during World War II, had he had his rifle with him would have gladly aimed a few choice rounds at the pesky jet fighter that caused this chaos. It took him and his boys (and many of his neighbors) the rest of the day and much of the night to round up the terrified cattle. I was mighty glad that several hundred miles separated me from Milford that night.

My wife had been discrete when she talked to Mary, telling her she didn't know if I could find out who might have caused such a ruckus. When I got home (not knowing what had happened) and told her about my wonderful "visit" to Milford and Jerry's farms, she suggested I wait a week or two to divulge that information. Wise advice! I finally got around to letting Milford know who that hot-shot fighter pilot was ... **after** he had gotten all his new calves accounted for, settled down, and used to their new feedlot. Time has a way of healing!

When he finally found out it was his brother-in-law who had done the deed he was in a more forgiving mood. Years late, though, both he and his boys usually raised their voices considerably when retelling the events - which were clearly etched in their memories.

Bucking Bronco!

OV-10 (Chu Lai Air Base, Vietnam)

The OV-10 "Bronco," an Air Force twin engine, light observation airplane, was, I had come to believe, docile and easily maneuvered ... readily responsive to a pilots every command. I flew it as a forward air controller (FAC) in Vietnam. I loved that Bronco ... it was fun to fly ... it flew like a fighter. Would a gentle airplane named "Bronco" really try to throw its rider? I found out one day in a most unexpected way.

Flying Tales

I was flying my OV-10 solo out of Chu Lai Air Base, Vietnam on a bright, clear day. I had just been replaced on my visual reconnaissance mission by another FAC and was returning to base. On the way back I was doing some simple aerobatics and decided to try out my "favorite" maneuver ... a first time for my Bronco. I had first learned this intriguing maneuver in a T-38 while flying at the Air Force Test Pilot School. After that initial experience I tried it out and enjoyed it in several other airplanes.

It was a simple maneuver. I just built up my speed and then pulled to a very steep, nearly vertical 70 to 80 degree climb ... at which point I would just put my hands in my lap and enjoy the airplane's "search for reality." That "search" normally took the form of either a zero 'g' "float" over the top (the F-4 typical response), or a more often experienced dramatic stall with an abrupt nose drop. Both forms ended up in a 70 or 80 degree dive, at which point I would then grasp the controls and recover to level flight. It was always reassuring to observe the aircraft's natural tendency to overcome the pilot's mischievous unnatural flight inducement.

The "Bronco" however, was not so amicable in its response to my spurs. It handled the pull up and release of flight controls quite well. But when it came time to recover, Bronco stubbornly decided the expected response was not to its liking. It had had enough of my "horsing around," and was not about to obediently nose over as expected. Its rider – me – was shocked when "Bronco" decided to go over the top **backwards** !!

I immediately abandoned my usual calm approach ... grabbed the stick and pushed forward. But the "Bronco" wouldn't have any of it. It was going to complete its backflip regardless of what I did to the flight controls. All I could do was hang on and ride it out. The nose flopped over backwards in a most disorienting, rolling, yawing maneuver ... with my maps and other assorted cockpit paraphernalia flying all around.

A steep dive eventually stabilized and "Bronco" finally allowed me to pull out and recover to level flight ... albeit with a very startled look on my face. To top off this belligerent behavior by my airplane, one of the turboprop engines flamed out and would not restart, requiring an attention-getting emergency landing back at Chu Lai.

"Bronco" had clearly told me, in an uncharacteristically inimical fashion, *"Don't you ever do that to me again!"* **I agreed !!**

Pilots often refer to their airplane as a "she." But this airplane was no lady !! HE had dramatically asserted HIS independence by trying to throw HIS rider ... **truly a "Bucking Bronco."**

Rudder limit

F-105 (Eglin Air Force Base, Florida)

The F-105 Thunderchief, better known as the "Thud" had an enormous vertical tail, a third of which was movable rudder. That huge rudder was really necessary for maneuvering at slow speeds. On one interesting mission I discovered it wasn't big enough.

That discovery came when Dick Strickland and I, two test pilots from Eglin, flew our F-105s to Holloman Air Force Base, New Mexico, where our mission was to drop 2000 pound bombs on a remote lava bed in the desert north of Holloman. A strange target you might ask. I thought so too ... until I found out the test involved evaluating the sensitivity of two different kinds of explosive fills by dropping non-fuzed bombs on the hardest target we could find. The objective was to see if brutal impacts would detonate either of these fills. The Air Force used a fill called tritonal in their bombs, and the Navy used a chemical explosive known as H-6. The Department of Defense was interested in eliminating one of them. We dropped several dozen of the bombs ... attempting to drop them from the slowest speed to the fastest speed.

I carried three bombs on each flight, dropping them one at a time. Dropping the bombs at the highest speeds was no problem for the F-105. I would just accelerate in the steep 45 degree dive until reaching the minimum recovery altitude ... drop the bomb and pullout ... plenty of control.

Dropping the bombs to obtain the slowest bomb impact speed was the real challenge. I would approach the target area at near stall speed, roll over into a dive and release the bomb almost immediately before gaining much speed. The release also had to be at the lowest possible altitude as the bomb would begin to accelerate on its own as soon as it was released (a 2000 pound bomb's terminal velocity is near supersonic). This meant I began the dive at the lowest altitude possible ... making sure I had just enough altitude after bomb release to gain enough speed to make a safe dive recovery.

The attention-getting aspect of this slow speed delivery occurred just after the second bomb was released. I always dropped the centerline bomb first ... leaving one bomb hanging from each wing. On the second pass, releasing one of those heavy bombs while retaining the other created quite a tendency (certainty!) to roll towards the heavy wing. In preparation for this commanding rolling moment I recalled the story of a good friend, and mentor, Jesse Locke who flew F-80s in Korea. He told me of a time when he was dropping two 500 pound bombs from his wing tips on an enemy target. Only one of the bombs came off, and before he knew it his airplane did a quick 360 degree roll !! ... before the other bomb flew off and he was able to recover ... scary !! I also remembered how my good friend, and squadron mate, Rocky Bowles had tried to drop two 3000 pound bombs from his F-105 on a target in North Vietnam and only one of them came off. The heavy wing put his airplane into a turning dive and he flew into a mountaintop ... terribly tragic! Those remembrances naturally made me very cautious as I planned my first asymmetric release.

Flying the Thud into a steep dive while at near stall speed reminded me of riding a cow when I was a youngster growing up on the farm. The cow would eventually go where I wanted to go, but it was kind of awkward.

Once I awkwardly got my Thud into the dive and pointed toward the target, I immediately released the left bomb. As expected, the right-wing (now 2000 pounds heavier than the left) began to drop ... even as I applied full left aileron to hold it up. The aerodynamic drag of the bomb, combined with all that aileron at that slow speed caused the nose to start yawing to the right (adverse yaw). In anticipation of this I had put in considerable left rudder in an attempt to counter this yawing motion.

I soon put in more rudder ... then more ... **until** ... I felt the rudder pedal bottom out ... **FULL left rudder !!** Something I had never needed before !! Yet the airplane continued its yawing motion to the right. **Full rudder ... and I needed more !!**

Fortunately, as planned, I had lit the afterburner the moment I released the bomb and I was beginning to accelerate rapidly ... Thank you Thud !! It didn't take but a few seconds of accelerating before the full left rudder application at the higher speeds began to correct the right yawing motion. As my speed increased some rudder was still required to counter the asymmetric drag ... but that was not a big problem. My efforts now concentrated on keeping the nose going straight until I had enough speed to make a reasonable pull out recovery (miss the ground!). Voila ! Success !

It all worked out. But I'll never forget the surprise I experienced when I had applied full rudder and discovered I needed more.

Oh yes ... the test results were fairly conclusive. **However ...** both the Air Force and the Navy refused to switch explosive fills in their bombs! Another flight test where the conclusions were most likely written before the test was conducted.

Now THAT'S a compressor stall!

F-100F (Eglin Air Force Base, Florida)

How does one adequately describe a jet engine compressor stall, particularly in an F-100 jet fighter?? I'll try.

A compressor stall happens when the airflow into the engine is distorted or woefully inadequate for the engine's demands. When this happens fuel is belched into the wrong places and dramatic explosions ensue. The effect is kind of like a backfire in an automobile engine ... but on a scale beyond belief.

The F-100, with its long engine air intake ... right under the pilots feet ... seemed to be the most prone to elicit this phenomenon. And a compressor stall in an F-100 was a huge jolt, an experience one never forgets. Flames shot out the nose ... and many would say out of every other slightest opening around the engine. The most attention-getting aspect was that huge explosive noise ... right under my feet, which literally flew off the floor.

The first time I experienced this shocking aircraft behavior the instructor pilot in the back seat just laughed ... told me to reduce power ... and the compressor stall immediately stopped. I was assured that this was not an uncommon experience when flying the F-100 !! No biggie ... Oh? Just disruptive to normal thought processes, that's all !!

I never really got used to it, but I did learn to laugh when it occurred (laughter has a way of obfuscating terror I'm told). F-100 pilots, in their typical fighter pilot humor, often joked about all the hair-tingling compressor stalls they had experienced or witnessed in others. I eventually learned to anticipate, and hence prevent a compressor stall in an F-100. It was most apt to happen when I was lighting the afterburner while flying at a fairly low speed.

With compressor stalls now briefly described, let me now tell you about a really memorable one that occurred while I was flying a photo chase mission at Eglin Air Force Base.

I was flying the F-100F ... the two-seat F-100 ... which had a much longer fuselage than the single-seat version and therefore more prone to compressor stalls. The mission was to accompany an F-4 on an air-to-ground missile test and photograph the results. We made several dry runs before the F-4 actually released the missile. The profile was basically a racetrack pattern climbing up to about 10,000 feet, reversing course, and then descending towards the target at the fairly slow speed needed to gather as much data as possible in the dive.

The performance difference between an F-100 and an F-4 was <u>very</u> significant. I had to use afterburner to stay with the F-4 during his climb, and then use idle power and even speed brakes to keep from passing him in his slow speed descent. During the turnaround to begin the climb again the F-4 would push his massive power up ... forcing me to light the afterburner at the beginning of every climb while still at a relatively slow speed.

Flying Tales

With that background we now come to the essence of this "tale."

You see, the airborne photographer (AP) in my back seat was <u>brand-new</u>. Brian was a young airman, just out of technical training and had <u>never flown in a jet fighter before</u>. He did have a great attitude though, and was eager to go fly. I gave him a very thorough preflight briefing on all the emergency procedures, reassuring him of the wonderful flying experience he was about to receive. But it never occurred to me to brief him on compressor stalls. Despite what I said in the previous paragraphs, compressor stalls were very rare and it had been a long time since I had last experienced one.

I think you can see where this tale is going. Without any advanced warning, Brian was about to get the surprise of a lifetime.

We were nearly through with the mission ... had flown several dry passes ... and had used the afterburner several times, with no untoward results. **And then it happened**, a huge monstrous explosive compressor stall **... kerbang ! kerbang ! kerbang !!** One of the "best" ones I had ever experienced.

"Now that's a compressor stall" I thought. But ***"OH NO ... what must my photographer be thinking?"*** ... His first jet airplane ride and the airplane blows up !! I glanced in the mirror ... saw his eyes were as big as silver dollars. I needed to quickly alert him ... it's okay, it's okay ... to reassure him ... before he could take any drastic action (like ejecting)!

But I was temporarily incapacitated ... with laughter ! Laughter so hard I could not talk !! What a time for fighter pilot humor to inject itself !! With a passenger overcome with a frightful unknown, my momentary inappropriate levity lasted much too long. After a few seconds though, I was finally able to shout ***"IT'S OKAY ... IT'S OKAY"*** He managed to utter a few squeaky words ... enough to indicate to me that his terror was under control.

I uttered a gentle "w*hew*" and then attempted to refocus his attention back on the mission at hand. I kept my eye on the mirror, and listened

245

as Brian's breathing rate gradually slowed back down. The next pass was the live missile shot. Much to his credit, Brian was able to overcome the unnerving explosion experience he had just endured and was able to get some terrific photos. **A job well done.** I was impressed.

After it was over, and we were on the ground, I told Brian *"I'm sure glad you didn't think we had blown up and then ejected yourself from a good airplane."* He told me he had thought about it ... and then said *"I didn't know what happened ... but I wasn't going to eject unless you did."*

Brian was a good man. He trusted his pilot ... and could think with his feet **off** the floor.

It's just a little thundercloud!

F-105 (Takhli Air Base, Thailand)

Oh what a relief ... finally exiting the combat zone ... I could breathe easier. Ted Shattuck, my flight lead, and I, in our two F-105s, were finally at a cruising altitude where we could engage the autopilots and settle our nerves.

It was good to be back over the friendly skies of Thailand ... heading back to land at Takhli Air Base. After the high anxiety of flying in a hostile combat environment, it was nice to sit back, relax, and enjoy the welcome thermos of ice water the crew chief had prepared for just such a moment ... (how did my mouth get so dry?). I moved back about one quarter mile behind Ted in what I called a loose route formation. We were at 30,000 feet, enjoying the vista of a beautiful day. There weren't even any thunderstorm buildups to bother us ... so common in Thailand at that time of year ... **except** for one small little thundercloud.

Just one little thundercloud in the whole area ... albeit it was tall (it went way above us), but it was so narrow (probably less than a few thousand feet in diameter). It looked like a giant white, puffy silo to this ex-farm boy. The only glitch - we were headed right for it.

Surely a little thundercloud like that would not bother our big, solid, mighty F-105 Thuds ... why should we deviate around it? Ted maintained a steady course, heading right for the center of it. As we approached the cloud he did ask me *"Two, what does your radar show?"* ... just to make sure. The F-105 had a great radar and when I trained the radar beam at this little thundercloud there was no radar return ... *"Nothing bad in that cloud"* I thought. I radioed Ted *"Nothing there."* Ted replied *"I concur ... No sweat"* and we continued on our steady course ... directly into the unknown.

Since I was behind, I watched Ted disappear into the cloud and calmly prepared to follow him. Just before I entered the cloud Ted radioed a loud *"WHOA !!"* That was probably a warning ... but it was too late.

I was only a moment away from the ride of my life.

As I entered the cloud it was like entering a popcorn machine ... only I was the popcorn! **WHAM !!** ... I was thrown to the side of the cockpit! **BAM !!** ... my helmet cracked against the canopy !! It was dark. It was violent. **WHAM !!** ... **SLAM !!** ... **BAM !!** I was being pummeled by a force much greater than my trusty Thud !! I was going through 5 or 10 of the longest seconds of my life.

Flying Tales

Flying is often humorously described as hours and hours of boredom interrupted by moments of sheer terror. This had to be one of those moments.

When I finally popped out into the clear my nose was pointed way up and I was in a pretty steep bank angle. That little innocent looking thundercloud had sucker punched me real good! When my head cleared, I began to look around for my flight lead and I couldn't find him! *"Where are you lead?"* He replied, *"I'm down here at 29,000 feet ... where are you?"* When my altimeter settled down I discovered I was at 31,000 feet. We had both entered the cloud at 30,000 feet !! Ted got tossed down 1000 feet ... I got tossed up 1000 feet !! Quite some tosses for 40,000 pound Thuds !! ... from such a little thundercloud, too! It must have been a "Rodney Dangerfield" cloud ... angrily telling us **"I don't get no respect."**

I soon rejoined with Ted ... my eyes anxiously scanning the horizon for any other "innocent" looking clouds. As I pulled up close to him I meekly transmitted *"Let's go around the next one we see."* He looked over at me and gave me a thumbs up.

Hustled by a B-58

F-105 (Eglin Air Force Base, Florida)

The B-58 "Hustler" was the only truly beautiful bomber airplane ever built ... in this fighter pilot's humble opinion. A sleek, four engine delta wing design with only one pilot !! ... and supersonic to boot. While flying fighters as a test pilot at Eglin Air Force Base I also discovered the B-58 was appropriately named the "Hustler." I got hustled flying next to this bomber one dark night.

Flying Tales

It all started when I was called in to attend a preflight briefing for a B-58 test mission to be flown that night. The briefing room was jammed ... and very rank heavy ... there were several full bird Colonels in attendance. I might have been the only Captain there. The only reason they let me in was they needed a safety chase ... someone to fly up close and observe the B-58 in the air. I was to fly a single-seat F-105 in a loose formation with the B-58 as he dropped napalm on a test range east of Eglin. *(Napalm from a bomber ?!!?* ... I think the whole objective was to conjure up a mission for Strategic Air Command (SAC) so they could send their showpiece bomber into the war in Southeast Asia).

Their test plan was to drop four 200 gallon canisters of napalm, one at a time, from 1000 feet level flight. *"1000 feet ... you've got to be kidding !!"* I mused ... *"Real napalm droppers did it at 50 feet."* ***"Ho Hum !!"*** This was going to be another routine safety chase ... but at least I would get to see the fireworks.

The briefers tried to draw me into their high level of concern by raising their voices and widening their eyes when they told me to beware of the B-58 wingtip vortices coming off its big delta wing. They emphasized the ramifications of these destructive wingtip vortices by recounting the recent loss of the magnificent delta wing XB-70 when an F-104 was sucked into it by its wingtip vortices ... causing both aircraft to crash. Okay ... I was warned. I promised them I would be careful and not run into their precious B-58.

The briefing surprises weren't quite over for me. With great pride of accomplishment one of the SAC Colonels handed me a huge four or five cell flashlight. With all that rank staring me down, I quietly accepted their kind gesture and said thank you (wondering how in the world I would use this nearly 2 foot long device in my single-seat cockpit).

With the briefing over, I waited around the squadron building while the B-58 took off ... I was to delay my take off about an hour while SAC got all their nationwide players on the same wavelength. As soon as the B-58 took off, however, I got a call to get airborne as quick as I could ... the B-58 was in trouble !!

Wow ... a real mission!! ... "Safety Chaseman" was on his way as I scrambled to my airplane ... huge flashlight in tow. Once I got the engine started I began to hear on the radio what this "terrible trouble" was. It turned out that as the B-58 took off the pilot heard a *"thump, thump"* when he raised the landing gear. My cynical fighter pilot mind smirked ... *"Oh No ... not the terrible 'thump, thump sound' emergency."* My task now was merely to join up on him and make sure his landing gear was up and locked securely.

Meanwhile the management style of SAC was rapidly becoming apparent. The B-58 pilot was frozen ... not allowed to take any action until the entire chain of command ... all the way up to SAC headquarters ... had been alerted and decided on a course of action. He was directed to <u>not</u> touch the gear handle and to proceed to the test area and establish his racetrack pattern at 1000 feet as briefed ... waiting for his safety chase (me) to join up with him and verify the status of his landing gear.

The join up was routine, but as I got closer I discovered this was not going to be easy ... <u>it was very dark</u> !! And, of course, the wingtip vortices question was lingering in the back of my mind. I gradually moved in closer and closer and determined the B-58 wingtip vortices had limited effect on my huge F-105. But ... at a cautiously safe distance I couldn't see his landing gear ... it was too dark.

"Okay" I thought *"Maybe that big flashlight wasn't such a squirrelly idea after all."* But how was I going to fly close formation ... in the dark ... with one hand on the throttle, and the other on the stick, while holding a monstrous flashlight? I got in as close as I could ... stabilized my formation ... took my left hand off the throttle ... picked up the flashlight real quick like and turned it on**. BIG SURPRISE ... FLASH !! BLINK !!** It was like being inside a giant flashbulb !! The light just ricocheted around inside my canopy.

What a pickle ... <u>my night vision was completely shot</u> ... and I was in close formation with a big bad delta wing I couldn't see any more. I dropped the flashlight (after turning it off, of course) and shoved the stick down and away from the B-58 ... thrusting me into the murky darkness. Since the B-58 was flying at a slow speed (maintaining less than landing gear operating speed) I was close to my stall speed, and it quickly dawned on me that doing this escape maneuver at night, below 1000 feet, was not the smartest thing in the world.

After I got reasonably stabilized, I "suggested" that the B-58 climb up a few thousand feet for safety. Well he *"didn't know"* ... he had to get SAC approval to deviate from the test plan. Wow ... that SAC leadership style could use some fighter pilot reasoning. Clear thinking finally prevailed as they allowed him to go up to 3000 feet !! Big deal !!

It was time to try again. This time, after I got my night vision moderately restored, I reasoned that if I put the face of the flashlight right up against the canopy I would not get that reflection/ricocheting effect of the light. I got all set ... stabilized ... let go of the throttle ... pushed the flashlight right up against the canopy ... turned it on ... AND ... **FLASH !! BLINK !!** INSIDE THE FLASHBULB ... **AGAIN !!**

After another hazardous recovery I chastised myself for not remembering about a design detail of the F-105 canopy. It was a double canopy ... two layers ... a thermopane if you will. The light went through that first layer without reflecting, but then it hit the second layer which <u>contained the light</u> quite brilliantly ... to my chagrin.

Enough of this chicanery. That flashlight was dangerous !!

I moved away from the B-58 ... let my eyes readjust to the darkness ... and decided to do this landing gear inspection the old fighter pilot way. I had been hustled enough by this "Hustler." I told the B-58 pilot to turn all his external lights on as bright as he could. I rejoined in close wing formation ... and began slowly closing the gap between my eyeballs and his landing gear ... overcoming the "dreaded" wingtip vortices. Moving in <u>real close</u>, fighter pilot style, my eye was able to determine that his landing gear was up and secure ... no problem at all.

With that call the *"thump, thump* emergency" was over and SAC gave the go-ahead and the mission proceeded as planned.

That dreaded *"thump, thump"* sound, which turned this routine mission into a drawn out thriller (for me anyway) must've been the pilot's heart beat as he realized he had just taken off with napalm on his aircraft for the first time in his life. It turned out that dropping napalm from 1000 feet was really a waste of time anyway ... inaccurate and minimum splash ... and not very impressive to this fighter pilot observer. That's why we test.

The rest of the story: The B-58 never saw combat in Southeast Asia and the B-58 I chased that night didn't land at Eglin but flew on back to its home base ... never to be seen again.

Also, after I landed that night I took that big flashlight right back to the Colonel who gave it to me and firmly told him ***"Sir, I never want to see that thing again !!"***

F-105

The 60 second pattern

F-100 (Eglin Air Force Base, Florida)

As a young curious test pilot, I was always eager to investigate new flying challenges. Sometimes those challenges were precipitated by something as innocent as a casual passing comment. That happened one evening when I was talking with an aging fighter pilot who flew F-86 Sabre jets when that airplane was king of the hill (and I was just beginning high school). He just happened to mention the "60 second pattern" implying that it was a mark of airmanship amongst the F-86 fighter pilots.

I quickly deduced that the "60 second pattern" referred to the time from Pitch-Out to Touch-Down when flying an overhead pattern. That comment really piqued my inquisitive mind. I couldn't help but ponder *"Is it possible in today's fighters?"* ... mainly thinking of the F-4 and the F-100 fighters I was currently flying.

On my very next flight, in an F-4, I timed my overhead landing pattern and found it to be way beyond one minute. I thought I had always flown a very tight pattern ... but now I knew better. Reducing my pattern time to under 60 seconds would be very difficult in an F-4. Not to be summarily undone however, as a good test pilot I began some flight tests.

But first a brief description of the overhead pattern: The overhead pattern begins by flying straight towards, and aligned with, the centerline of the runway at pattern altitude (normally 1500 feet) ... this portion of the pattern is called <u>Initial</u>. Upon arriving over the threshold of the runway a smart 180 degree level turn is made (called the <u>Pitch-out</u>), slowing from the high Initial speed (300 to 350 knots) to a slower speed on the <u>Downwind</u> leg where the landing gear and flaps are lowered. With the landing configuration established, another 180 degree descending turn (called <u>Base</u> leg) is then initiated so as to align with the runway. Once aligned with the runway (called <u>Final</u> approach) the speed is reduced and stabilized until the rate of descent and speed is reduced to accommodate <u>Touch-down</u>.

After timing my pattern while flying the F-4, I concluded that my chances were better in a different airplane. So I elected to use the F-100 in my attempt to emulate the "60 second pattern" mark of airmanship. My first attempts were well over 60 seconds. *"This was going to be tough."* As I analyzed the patterns I began to make incremental adjustments, and after several modifications I thought I was ready for the challenge.

Flying Initial at 300 knots proved optimum. At that speed I was able to make a very brisk Pitch Out and a tight turn to downwind by adding power and pulling as many 'g's as I could ... completing the 180 degree turn in minimum time ... bleeding off just enough airspeed to roll out on Downwind at gear limit speed. Power back ... gear and flaps down immediately. *"Come on landing gear ... hurry up"* I shouted. With gear and flaps finally down I began the tough part ... the maximum performance Base Leg turn. Performing such a turn while flying the 180 degree Base Leg turn in an F-100 (notorious for its adverse yaw characteristics) had ended in disaster for many an F-100 pilot. I had to be on my toes ... **literally ...** with a robust application of <u>rudder coordination</u>.

The F-100, with its full length leading edge slats, could really turn at that slow speed ... **if** I used plenty of power along with dutiful attention to rudder application. But during that turn the F-100 really talked to me ... with its burbling stall warning vibration (buffet) ... telling me that I was right on the edge ... be careful !!

Completing that maximum performance descending Base Leg turn ... rolling out lined up with the runway for the Final approach phase was indeed a relief ... the anxiety level subsided somewhat. But then the power had to be reduced dramatically and the speed brake extended to quickly slow to final approach speed ... just in time to begin the Flare to touchdown. I had shortened the Final approach phase by bringing my Base Leg in as close to the end of the runway as possible.

But now the clock ruled. Lined up with the runway I could only watch the clock tick down as I closed on the runway touchdown point. Still under one minute ... but the secondhand was moving very fast !! My task now was to be patient and not touch down at a faster than normal speed (that would be cheating!). The Flare to touch down seemed to take forever as I watched the secondhand on the clock move closer and closer to one minute.

With my finger on the clock and my eyes on the runway, I punched the secondhand stop button as the main wheels finally touched down. My concentration now was focused on completing the landing by lowering the nose, pulling the drag chute handle, and maintaining directional control. With bated breath, I was then able to glance down at the clock and evaluate my results. **59 seconds !! Success !! It was possible !!**

The "60 second pattern club" had a new member!

But was it really worth the effort? Success was not without its risk. It didn't take a steel trap mind to figure out that flying the F-100 at maximum performance in the landing pattern left little margin for error. Any flight system anomaly or failure during that one minute, particularly during the last 30 seconds, would have been very difficult to overcome.

Consequently, I was not eager to report my achievement to other fighter pilots ... and didn't ... **until now**, 40 years later. They might be tempted to be foolhardy also.

I never tried it again ... in any airplane.

F-86

My first OUTSIDE loop

MB-339 (Italian Flight Test Center)

As my flying career progressed I often wondered if I would ever get to fly an outside loop. Jimmy Doolittle is credited with flying the very first outside loop ... 10 years before I was born! But I had never flown any airplanes that were capable of sustained high negative 'g's ... so I had my doubts if I would ever do the dubious maneuver. The opportunity finally presented itself when I was Commander of the Air Force's Test Pilot School and was on a staff visit to various European flight test facilities. Those staff visits enabled us to fly various European aircraft ... a treat that we reciprocated when they visited us at Edwards Air Force Base.

When we arrived at the Italian Flight Test Center, near Rome, I was elated to find I would get a chance to fly their Aermacchi MB-339, a two-seat jet trainer that was touted to have a plus eight, <u>minus eight</u> 'g' capability ... well capable of an outside loop. During my preflight briefing I asked the instructor pilot, who would be riding in the back seat, *"Have you ever done an outside loop in the MB-339?"* He kind of grimaced and said *"Yeah, of course."* I then boldly made my proposal: *"I would like to try that during my flight."* He replied *"Okay, if you **really** want to."* Well, I surely wanted to !! He didn't seem too happy about my desire, knowing that he would also have to ride through the punishing negative eyeballs-out 'g's the maneuver required. But he couldn't very well say no without damaging his macho fighter pilot image. He did tell me I could hold it to a minus three 'g's instead of the usual four and still make it around fine.

Taxi, take off, climb and early maneuvering revealed that the MB-339 was indeed a fine flying machine. But I was eager to get to the event that I would always remember. I mentioned to the IP *"Are you ready for the outside loop?"* He responded *"Are you sure you want to do this?"* After my brisk ***"Yep"*** he merely responded *"Tighten your seatbelt and shoulder harness."* Good advice, I soon discovered.

I pushed the power up ... built up some speed in a gentle descent ... leveled off and rolled inverted (upside down). *"Here we go"* I said as I pushed vigorously forward on the control stick to obtain the desired negative three 'g's. Concentrating on keeping my wings level, up we went.

I immediately gained respect for the IP's hesitance for doing this. It was not very comfortable. My neck didn't like being pulled on by a head which weighed three times as much as normal. And the shoulder harnesses dug into my shoulder blades, while the seatbelt discovered my pelvic bone. As I went over the top I experienced the strange apparition of looking up at the top of the loop instead of looking down. Now came the *"Oh My"* part of the maneuver ... pushing the nose down towards the ground ... steeper and steeper. I knew I had to continue pushing, maintaining the same uncomfortable shoulder harness pinching. Now I knew why this was not a normal training maneuver.

As we bottomed out and completed the loop I detected not a sigh, but almost a moan of relief from the back seat. I relaxed the 'g' and rolled upright ... Ahh, back to positive 'g's !! The IP then revealed his true feelings, by saying to me *"Let's don't do any more of those."* I agreed.

My first outside loop was my last. The experience went comfortably into the renowned category of ... **"Been There, Done That."**

Formation with a bird

Glider (Tehachapi, California)

I loved flying gliders. There seemed to be a serenity ... a oneness with the air ... that only came with unpowered flight. This type of environment made for special memory moments, such as when I was flying a Schweitzer 1-26, a beautiful single-seat glider, one morning over the mountains west of Edwards Air Force Base. The serenity of soaring was magnified that morning with the awareness that I was probably the only airplane in the sky at the time after my tow plane had landed. I had been towed to about 1000 feet ... rejoicing as I released the cable that connected us ... free to soar !!

I soon began looking for vertical air currents (thermals) that would take me to a higher altitude.

I wasn't having much luck finding that perfect thermal until I looked way up above me to discover a big hawk circling overhead. I knew hawks knew thermals perfectly ... putting us soaring pilots to shame. As he circled, with his wings motionless, he was rapidly gaining altitude ... an effortless climb ... beautiful !! *"I'll just get under him and climb up too."* As soon as I got directly under him my left wing lifted up magically. I immediately began circling tightly to the left keeping my airplane inside the vertical column of wind. Up, up, up I went ... following the hawk as he climbed higher and higher. It was so exhilarating to be following the climb expert.

After climbing a few thousand feet the hawk finally exited the thermal and started gliding towards a mountain ridge several miles away ... with wings still motionless. An intriguing idea came to me *"Might I be able to climb to his altitude and follow him?"* How would he respond to a giant bird chasing after him? As I popped out of the thermal at his altitude and started heading his way, I was elated to discover my glide potential matched his fairly well. Best of all, he didn't seem to give me much concern at all.

I couldn't resist the temptation ... I had to find out how close I could get to him without disturbing his intentions. I cautiously began closing the gap. Soon I was within 100 feet ... then 50 feet ... at which point he turned his head and gave me a thorough look over and apparently decided that I was no threat ... even though I was 50 times bigger than him. This was exciting! I pressed my good fortune ... I had to give him a closer look. I closed to 20 feet ... still no reaction. That's when I noticed he had a large field mouse in his beak !! That was obviously going to work in my favor. He had worked hard to get there with that food for his family and no giant bird was going to deter him.

I got closer and closer to see at what point he might be overly disturbed by his giant escort. I put my right wing behind him and continued to close the gap. 5 feet ... then I inched closer and closer. When I got my right wing about 2 feet behind him he looked at me ... decided that was too close ... flapped his wings a couple times until he was about 3 feet in front of my wing ... and then regained his steady gliding course ... retaining a firm grip on his mouse. (I surmised he was heading for his home nest to feed his family). It didn't take too long to establish his minimum distance comfort zone ... only about 10 feet to the right of my cockpit and 3 feet in front of the wing leading edge. I was able to use my spoiler control to match his airspeed, allowing me to maintain perfect formation. In that surprisingly close proximity he didn't seem to give me any heed at all. The awesome realization of this moment began to envelop me ... **I was flying formation with a bird !! Wow !! Could flying ever get any better than this?!!**

Disregarding where I was, how far I was getting from the airfield, or any other ordinary flying concerns ... I found myself mesmerized by the experience, which lasted for several wonderful minutes. I wanted this moment to last and last. Mr. Hawk was most cooperative, giving me an occasional glance to make sure I was being a considerate wingman. I think once he looked over at me and winked !?! But I couldn't be sure, since I could only see his left eye! Maybe he was enjoying the escort as much as I was enjoying escorting.

But alas, the epic memory flight moment came to an end when he abruptly peeled off and began circling downward ... into a wooded area in the forest below, where his hungry family was undoubtedly waiting. I saluted him smartly and waggled my wings ... saying goodbye to my new friend.

As I watched him circle out of sight, it suddenly occurred to me that I hadn't been paying attention to where I was going and now didn't exactly know where the airfield was or if I had enough altitude to get back. I couldn't just follow another bird back to the airfield. Fortunately, it all worked out ... I was able to find the airfield in the distance and I had just enough altitude to glide all the way back for a safe landing. But I wasn't too concerned ... I was singing all the way back ... *"Oh what a beautiful morning !!"*

Electric and hydraulic failure

F-105 (Holloman Air Force Base, New Mexico)

Pilots train to respond to in-flight emergencies by memorizing emergency procedures (we call them BOLD FACE procedures because that's the way they are printed in our flight manuals). Such emergencies are very rare, but when they do occur they usually occur at the most inconvenient time. One of those times happened when I was on a test mission dropping 2000 pound experimental bombs from my usually very reliable single-seat F-105 jet fighter ("Thud"). I had one bomb left to drop. But it was way out on my right wing ... resulting in a very unbalanced load, commanding my full attention.

My attention was quickly diverted however, when a bunch of warning lights lit up in my cockpit. At the same time I heard (or sensed) a noisy grinding noise coming from the area forward of the cockpit. The warning lights told me that many of my electrical systems and my utility hydraulics were not functioning properly. The grinding noise told me that my real problem was with my air turbine motor (ATM) which powered my AC generator and utility hydraulic pump. The ATM was located in the nose of the fuselage right in front of me. I shut it down immediately before it had a chance to disintegrate and really cause me some problems.

My problem now was to get my Thud back on the ground in one piece ... ASAP !! I had my hands full knowing that I would be landing without normal landing gear, flap, and brake operation; without many essential electrical systems; and with a 2000 pound bomb hanging from my right wing creating a directional control problem at landing speeds. Fortunately the radio still functioned normally so I could call the Tower and declare an emergency. I told them my configuration and that I would be setting up for a straight in landing.

The memorized BOLD FACE procedures now came in handy. I lowered the landing gear using the emergency gear down procedure (the F-105 had compressed air charged bottles (accumulators) for just such a purpose). The landing gear lowered slower than normal, but perfectly as far as I was concerned. I then lowered the landing flaps using the emergency flap accumulator ... again, working just as advertised.

With gear and flaps safely down my next concern was maintaining good directional control with the heavy right wing as I slowed to landing speed. It took a lot of left aileron and left rudder to carry that big bomb through the flare to touchdown, but the Thud was up to the task.

As I touched down, I deployed the drag chute to slow me down, lowered the nose to engage nosewheel steering and got ready to apply the brakes. I couldn't help but wonder how long the brakes would last without normal hydraulic power. I mentally prepared to lower the tail hook in case my emergency brake accumulators would not bring me to a complete stop (the F-105 tail hook was built to engage the arresting barrier at the far end of the runway).

I had alerted the Tower that 30 seconds after I touched down my radio would quit operating (without AC power to cool it) and I would **not** be turning off the runway. But the Tower was way ahead of me. When I declared an emergency they scrambled all of the emergency vehicles with their brilliant, annoying, flashing lights. Several fire trucks were at the ready ... a reception that was both welcome and disconcerting. With all that attention I could not very well sneak in for an unnoticed landing.

With one steady application, the emergency brakes responded beautifully and I finally came to a stop ... right in the middle of the runway. After I stopped I opened the canopy ... wanted to get that open before the battery failed. I then just sat there with a bunch of fire truck nozzles pointed at me while the maintenance personnel inserted safety pins in my landing gear and connected a tow bar to my nose wheel.

With all the emergency vehicles escorting me (lights still flashing, of course, to proclaim to the world that they had saved another airplane in distress) I was towed to my parking place at a very slow pace ... kind of an ignominious arrival for a fighter pilot.

School's out

F-100 (Eglin Air Force Base, Florida)

Are all fighter pilots tempted to do stunts that could jeopardize their flying careers? Or was it just me?

I was ferrying an F-100 single-seat jet fighter from Florida to California ... beginning with a short hop to McConnell Air Force Base at Wichita, Kansas. I purposely planned the short leg so I could arrive at McConnell with plenty of excess fuel. That way I could fly in the local area for about an hour. The local area, incidentally (!?!) included my brother's farm ... about 135 miles north of Wichita. So began my almost mis-adventure.

I arrived over Jerry's farm unannounced ... but made my presence instantly and impressively known by lighting the afterburner right over his workshop at a very low altitude. Pulling up briskly, I did a snappy aileron roll ... and looked back to see if the noisy afterburner had scared the cattle. Nope ... they didn't mind ... **now** I could do some real fighter pilot maneuvering !! At the top of my climb I did a wifferdill (a smart wing-over like course reversal) and proceeded to make a simulated strafing pass at my brother's barn. I pulled up again, rolling of course ... did another wifferdill ... and proceeded to make a steeper simulated rocket pass. I could see my brother waving as I began making repeated passes ... up ... back down ... up ... back down ... looping and rolling between each pass. It was a beautiful clear day and I was enjoying giving my brother an **exclusive** (one doesn't do these type of things in front of a crowd), up close demonstration of all the best fighter maneuvers.

But alas, I eventually had to head back to Wichita. On the way, I thought it would be nice to just say hello to my cousin Darrell ... by flying over his farm just a few miles south of Jerry's. Not having enough fuel now to give him a real demonstration, I decided to just make one very low pass over his house ... lighting the afterburner of course **at just the right moment**. *"Hi, cousin! Are you having a good day?"*

Flying from Darrell and Jocile's house back to McConnell was a routine boring flight. All in all ... just another day at the office for a fighter pilot.

While refueling at McConnell I decided to give my brother Jerry a call on the phone to get his reaction to the wonderful display of Air Force airmanship I had just given him. He was ecstatic ... but maybe more so than I would have thought. He said the noise was incredibly loud, and the aerobatics were impressive. (Ahh ... just the response I was looking for). But best of all ... **then he let the bombshell drop** ... *his daughter Lisa's entire grade school, just a mile or so away, had been let outside just to watch the air show* !!

I was not prepared for that bit of news. Drawing that kind of public attention was not in my best interest. I now had to be concerned if my boss would ever find out ... I could just kiss my wings goodbye.

I worried about that disclosure for several days ... but it never materialized ... undeserved secrecy prevailed! Would not being caught keep me from doing it again someday? Looking back, I think I know the answer to that question ... the opening line in this flying tale.

Oh yes ... the low pass over my cousin's house caused quite a stir as well. I found this out much later when talking to Jocile. She told me she was standing at the kitchen sink, washing dishes when I flew over. The explosive noise from the afterburner could only be explained, she thought, if the house had just blown up. I feel bad that I never offered to replace all the dishes that were broken when she threw them up in the air.

Van-Williams bridge

OV-10 (Chu Lai Air Base, Vietnam)

The infamous Ho Chi Minh Trail in Southeast Asia was really a whole network of trails ... from truck-worthy roads, to bicycle paths, and finally to narrow foot paths. The enemy used this network to bring all sorts of supplies and weapons all the way from Hanoi and Haiphong, North Vietnam down into the southernmost parts of South Vietnam.

Part of that network fed right into the area that I patrolled as a forward air controller (FAC) flying OV-10 aircraft.

There was a part of that trail that really puzzled me and the rest of the FACs that worked for me. We could see a well used, narrow trail adjacent to a steep, heavily forested canyon and then resume again on the other side of the canyon ... in very mountainous terrain. The canyon was steep and deep ... there just had to be a bridge across it. But thick jungle trees covered it (and the approach to it) ... keeping it from our view.

Lt. Steve Williams and I took it as a personal challenge ... we were determined to find the exact location of that bridge ... <u>so we could destroy it.</u> The bridge was located in enemy territory well beyond the Army's artillery range so we couldn't use their big guns to go after the bridge, or even blast away the trees so we could locate it more precisely. We searched for the bridge on several occasions ... orbiting at safe altitude away from small arms fire ... scanning the area with high-powered binoculars. Steve and I gradually narrowed our search, and one day, with Steve in my back seat, we concurred that we had found the precise location. Noting the map coordinates, we passed this information on to the other FACs so when they were flying they could confirm our discovery. None of them could confirm.

With a bit of tongue in cheek, it became known as the invisible Van-Williams bridge.

Steve and I weathered the cynicism and turned our energies towards convincing higher headquarters that we had found a critical weakness in a part of the Ho Chi Minh Trail and that it should be bombed. After much pleading, we finally convinced headquarters to spare a single Australian Canberra carrying 750 pound bombs to attack our target. Steve and I were elated ... the Canberra was a great bomber ... one of the most accurate we had ever worked with ... amazing since they delivered their bombs from level flight ... a particularly difficult task, especially when bombing in the mountains.

On B-Day (bridge day) I scheduled Steve and I in the same airplane so we could direct the attack. With our binoculars (and a nice camera provided by the intelligence folks) in hand, we got airborne in our trusty, two-seat OV-10 Bronco in plenty of time to be over the target area well before the Canberra (call sign Magpie) arrived. After relocating the bridge (only a few feet of the bridge were visible through a hole in the tree canopy) we took a few pictures ... we wanted some photos of both before and after ... to convince the naysayers.

When Magpie arrived I directed them to orbit overhead while I described the target area and made sure they could see both the target area and us. They were a little bit suspicious, maybe even miffed. They had been sent to destroy a bridge and all they could see were heavily forested mountains.

When they were ready to make their bomb run I told them I would identify the exact desired bomb impact location by marking the target with a smoke rocket. With a well aimed rocket, a small white smoke cloud erupted right where I wanted them to bomb. I then uttered the words of a good FAC *"Hit my smoke."* I had directed Magpie to drop their bombs one at a time. This gave us an opportunity to clear the tree cover, exposing the bridge for final destruction. The tactic worked perfectly. The 750 pound bombs were good at clearing trees. After a couple of passes the elusive Van-Williams bridge was clearly exposed. It was easily 100 foot long and about three or 4 feet wide ... built out of wood.

The Canberra crew was now excited too. Up till then they thought they were just bombing trees. Now they could see a <u>real</u> bridge across the <u>real</u> Ho Chi Minh Trail. There was no need to put more smoke rockets on the target ... the Canberra's bombardier could now see the target clearly. I circled the bridge so Steve could get some pictorial evidence and then I cleared the bomber in for the knockout blows. With just a few passes the Van-Williams bridge collapsed a couple of hundred feet down into a pile of sticks at the bottom of the ravine. **Well done, my Aussie friends !!**

The Vietcong were not too happy about our achievement ... as many muzzle flashes from the area attested. Now they would have to carry their large supply loads on their backs down, down, down into the canyon and then up, up, up instead of just walking across a bridge ... at least until they built another one.

Australian Air Force "Canberra" bomber

Runaway Tank

F-4 (Eglin Air Force Base, Florida)

The laser guided bomb was one of the most monumental munition developments ever achieved at Eglin Air Force Base ... a bomb that would guide itself to a spot on the ground illuminated by a laser.

Simultaneously with that development was the invention of an airborne laser target designator pod, an amazing device I was intimately involved with. The pod, known as "Pave Knife," was carried on an F-4 fighter aircraft and could very accurately point a laser at a precise spot on the ground from a great distance while the airplane was maneuvering. I was the project/test pilot for Pave Knife. Both the pod and the laser guided bomb (LGB) matured at about the same time. With Pave Knife and LGB working together, a 2000 pound bomb could be dropped on a very small target while the aircraft remained at a relatively safe distance from the target area, several thousand feet in the air. There remained one question however. *Could we hit a moving target??*

The answer to that question was eagerly pursued by the test folks at Eglin, who had also just developed the capability of remotely driving an Army tank. The test plan began to take shape. Pave Knife would orbit over the tank ... pointing its laser beam on the tank turret ... the remote tank would race across the test area ... and another F-4 would release a 2000 pound LGB towards the general target area. To make the test more interesting ... and assess damage effects ... we would drop a live bomb, full of explosives. This was going to be exciting. I could hardly wait ... for I would have the best view of the entire episode.

The day of the test finally arrived ... a beautiful day, with no clouds to obscure our laser (and my view). As I looked down on the test area (range C52 ... a few miles east of Eglin, where nearly all high explosive tests were conducted) I could see the tank ... engine running and ready to roll. All of the ground cameras were set up and ready to film the event at close range. The test engineers and ground controllers were all huddled together in the range tower. I could tell by their radio calls they were very excited about this first of its kind type of test. The bomb carrying F-4 was in loose formation behind me as we orbited at 15,000 feet.

It was time for the show to begin. I entered a dive ... pointing Pave Knife at the target allowing Gene Stephens, my back seater (and very capable test navigator/weapon system operator (WSO)), to acquire and begin tracking the tank on his video display using a hand controller. As soon as Gene said *"I've got it"* I pulled up and began orbiting the target. With Pave Knife tracking the tank precisely, Gene pulled the trigger on his hand controller and began lasing the target. The lase was good ... the tracking was good ... so I gave the go-ahead for the tank to begin moving. Pave Knife was working perfectly ... tracking the 25 mph tank as if it were standing still. I immediately cleared the other F-4 to roll in and drop his bomb.

I was in a perfect position to view the entire operation. I watched as the big bomb came off the F-4 and was even able to see the LGB do its characteristic wiggle in flight ... indicating it was tracking toward the laser spot (on the center of the tank turret). The bomb sped directly towards the tank at nearly supersonic speed.

The impact was spectacular !! The bomb hit just in front of the tank ... but the huge erupting fireball completely encompassed the Army machine. I couldn't help but think *"That poor tank didn't have a chance!"* Very quickly an enormous dirt cloud (at least 100 feet in diameter) covered up both tank and fireball. I could hardly wait for the dust cloud to clear so I could observe the devastation. <u>But then</u> ... <u>to my utter amazement</u> ... **the tank came roaring out of the dust cloud** ... <u>as if nothing had happened !!</u> I was stunned !! How could anything survive the intense destructive explosion I had just witnessed ?!?

I immediately called the ground controllers and test engineer on the radio ... *"Stop that tank ... it's still moving."* But they were already on top of it. They knew it was still going ... **BUT ... they were unable to stop it !!** They soon found out they had <u>no control whatsoever</u> !! A great panic ensued, as evidenced by all the chatter on the radio. **We have a runaway tank** !! ... Where will it go?? It turned out the antenna on the tank (used to receive the remote driving commands) was designed so that if it was knocked off (destroyed) ... the tank would stop. And if the antenna was still intact the remote controllers could simply give the stop command. All those plans were foiled when the antenna was just knocked over ... so neither function could occur.

There wasn't much I could do, but I did want to stick around as long as I could ... to see what damage this runaway tank was going to inflict. I didn't want to miss the unscheduled, but now most epic grand finale.

I circled overhead and watched as it ran over a few expensive camera locations ... just missing an expensive radar site ... and clipping several other test targets. These obstacles didn't deter the determined runaway. The concern rapidly escalated however ... as the uncontrollable tank was <u>headed straight for a nearby town</u>. We all recognized the peril of this development, as the only thing between the tank and the town was a lightly wooded area ... no problem for a robust Army tank.

Fortunately, the wooded area happened to be muddy ... from a recent rain. When the tank got into the mud it slowly began digging deeper and deeper tracks until it finally came to a stop with its tracks still going round and round and round ... digging a grave-like hole deeper and deeper ... a fitting resting place for this renegade.

While the runaway tank was crossing the range and heading toward the nearby town, the range control people jumped in a helicopter ... clasping a remote-control box ... and chased the tank trying to get it to take a stop command. But that effort did not work. The runaway tank adventure was finally terminated when the helicopter landed and one of the controllers jumped out ... climbed into the now stuck-in-the-mud tank ... and shut it down.

The well thought out test plan had obviously not considered such a post-mission excursion ... and extracting a tank from the mud hole presented a whole new set of challenges.

Other than that ... we did answer the question *"Could we hit a moving target?"* But all of us learned maybe a more significant lesson ... <u>those tanks are pretty tough</u> !!

2000 pound laser guided bomb

"Pave Knife" laser target designator

Bulldozer

OV-10 (Chu Lai Air Base, Vietnam)

Whiskey-Yankee ... an innocent military designation for an area filled with enemy intentions. Whiskey-Yankee was the end of the line for enemy vehicle traffic moving weapons and other supplies down the Ho Chi Minh Trail from North Vietnam to the Vietcong troops in South Vietnam. This part of the Ho Chi Minh Trail was just across the South Vietnam border in Laos where no allied troops were allowed to go. From this point on all enemy supplies were hand carried. The enemy was pretty blatant with this part of their trail ... graded roads winding around the mountainous terrain were very visible from the air.

Whiskey-Yankee, though, was hundreds of miles from where the supply trail began ... Hanoi and Haiphong. The US Air Force was constantly attacking the entire Ho Chi Minh Trail from the air and consequently it took a long time for supplies to make it from the north of North Vietnam into the south of South Vietnam. It took a lot of slave labor to keep the trail open. Since it was in mountainous terrain a bulldozer would have been very handy. But could the Vietcong get a bulldozer all the way from Hanoi to Whiskey-Yankee?

My job was to find out.

I was flying an OV-10 Bronco aircraft out of Chu Lai Air Base, South Vietnam as a forward air controller (FAC) ... call sign Helix 11. Part of my job was to patrol over Whiskey-Yankee and identify possible targets (supplies, troops, etc.) and call in airstrikes against them. Since this was in Laos, only the U.S. Air Force operated there. The Vietcong protected this area against airstrikes so it was considered a high threat area ... I had to remain above 10,000 feet to avoid their antiaircraft fire. But with powerful binoculars I could search the roads fairly well, even though the enemy did their best to camouflage any worthwhile targets.

One day I spotted an anomaly that reminded me of something I grew up with as a farm boy in Kansas ... what looked like a **trench silo** (a rectangular shaped pit with an open top ... a dugout if you will) dug into the side of the hill adjacent to the trail (with a covering of tree limbs to disguise it). Now what would a trench silo be doing in Laos? We used them on the farm to store feed (ensilage) for the cattle. As I studied the trail in front of the trench silo I discovered tracked vehicle tracks perpendicular to the road. The enemy normally would rake or sweep away any tracks to hide them from prying eyes overhead. This time they were careless. I realized I had discovered a pearl of great price ... a bulldozer ... hidden in a trench silo covered with camouflage.

I immediately called my tactical air control party (TACP) and ordered up some fighters to attack this enemy treasure. In less than 30 minutes two F-4's out of Danang Air Base arrived overhead ... loaded with six each 500 pound snake-eye (retarded) bombs. Perfect !!

I would ask them to drop them one at a time so we would have at least 12 chances to destroy this bulldozer. Snake eyes could be delivered fairly accurately. However, I knew we would have to get one of those bombs right inside the trench silo. A short miss would only throw dirt over the bulldozer ... hunkered down in its 'trench silo' pit. I briefed the fighters (call sign Gunfighter) ... making sure they could see me and orient themselves to the general target area. I would have to mark the target for them with one of my smoke rockets, as their bomb delivery would be at low altitude and high speed ... they wouldn't be able to see the actual camouflaged bulldozer hideout. They were keen on the task ... even though they couldn't actually see the target ... knowing the importance of destroying an enemy bulldozer this far from its origin.

With eager anticipation I rolled in and fired my first white phosphorus smoke rocket. It landed just outside the 'trench silo.' Good enough, I thought ... so I called *"Hit my smoke."* Gunfighter Lead's first bomb went 50 feet over. A good bomb, but not good enough. Gunfighter 2 followed right behind with another 50 foot miss.

Now the target area was obscured a bit by dust clouds from their bombs, but a gentle breeze cleared the area revealing that the bulldozer remained unharmed. I put in another smoke rocket as Gunfighter Flight set up for their second pass. Again, near misses ... so close ... but no cigar. A third pass ... with similar results. The camouflage over the bulldozer, and the surrounding trees were being destroyed, but the bulldozer remained intact, dug in well below the surrounding terrain.

Only three more passes remained! We were all getting frustrated. When the fourth pass (bombs number seven and number eight) had the same result I decided to fire one of my H E (high explosive) rockets at the bulldozer, which was now more visible. Lo and behold, my small rocket hit the bulldozer and set it on fire. Now Gunfighter flight could see more precisely where the target was. However, this 15x30 foot hole in the ground was still mighty difficult to hit with a snake-eye

500 pound bomb. To our growing disappointment, both Gunfighter Lead's and Gunfighter 2's next-to-last bombs just missed.

Now we were down to only one bomb from each fighter. The "Gunfighters" confidence was growing though ... now that they could actually see the target. Gunfighter Lead assured me he could hit the pesky bulldozer with his last bomb. But ... Oh ... so close ... his bomb only resulted in a little more dirt on top of the bulldozer.

"Okay, Gunfighter 2 ... it's up to you" I said. As I orbited directly over the elusive target, and watched Gunfighter 2 make his approach, the pressure was on ... we needed a three point shot at the buzzer to triumph !! I could see his bomb come off ... and ... seemingly in slow motion ... sail right into the pit ... **bull's-eye !!** That bulldozer erupted into a giant fountain of flaming and smoking pieces billowing high into the air.

We were elated ... as evidenced by our congratulatory radio calls ... *"Way to go, Gunfighter Flight !!"* *"We did it, Helix !!"* **The last bomb ... on the last pass !! Wow !!**

The BDA (bomb damage assessment) would now speak volumes instead of reporting missed opportunities. Gunfighter flight was credited with a destroyed bulldozer, a feat rarely accomplished anywhere on the Ho Chi Minh Trail, let alone this far away from Hanoi. The Gunfighters would all celebrate at Danang that evening.

It would take the Vietcong a long, long time to replace the bulldozer that they tried to hide from a farm boy turned forward air controller.

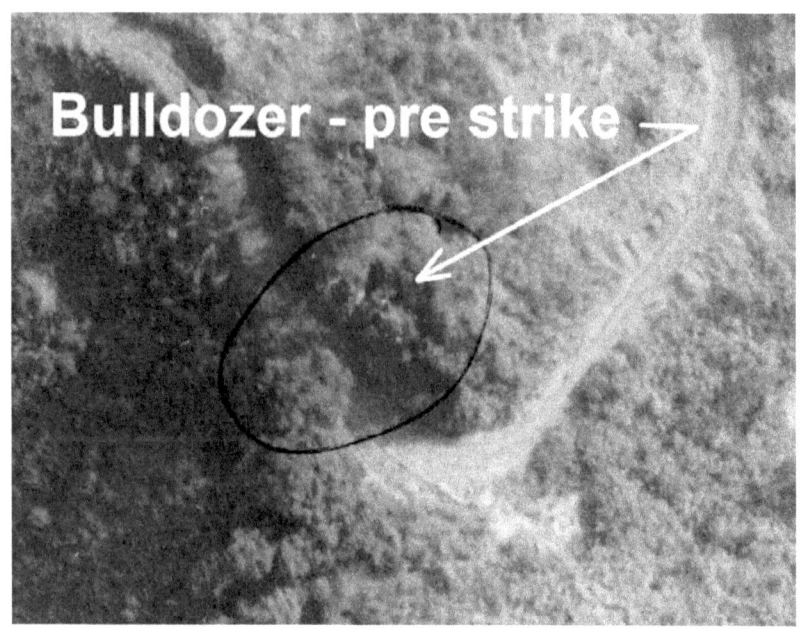

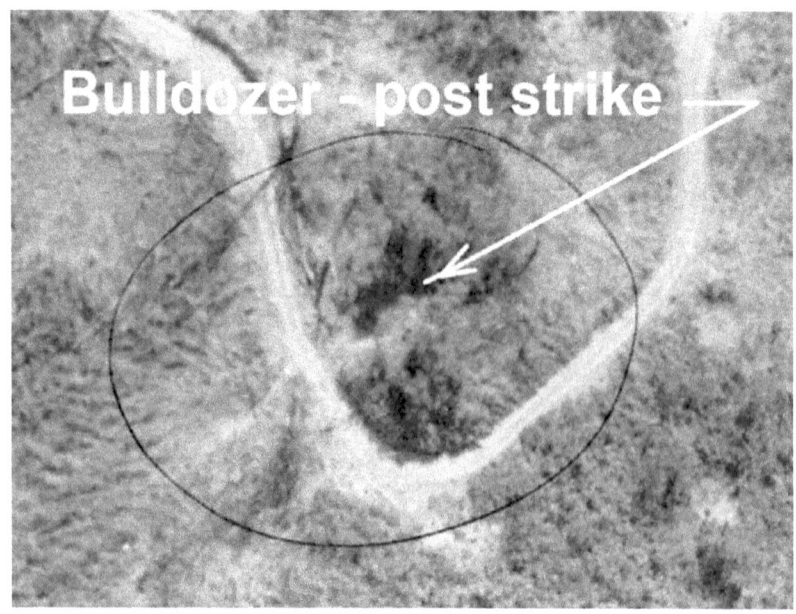

What were you doing ... strafing?

F-105 (Takhli Air Base, Thailand)

We were about to go into combat for the first time ... well-trained fighter pilots ... flying the F-105 Thunderchief (better known as the "Thud"). But none of us had ever been fired at in anger before. Aware of our apprehensions, one of the old heads, Colonel Van Etten (a Korean War combat veteran), gathered us all together and gave us an inspiring pep talk. One piece of advice I really took to heart. He said *"When you roll in to dive bomb, as soon as you get your nose pointed*

at the ground ... fire a long burst from your gun." He indicated this would make the gunners on the ground duck for cover, reducing the amount of antiaircraft fire we would encounter during the rest of the bomb run. Made sense to me at the time.

I took that advice every time I bombed the enemy. I couldn't prove if it did any good (making the enemy gunners keep their heads down) ... but it was comforting, knowing that it might. Besides, firing that Gatling gun, with its big **bbbrrrrrrrpppp** sound, was always a kick. I thought every other pilot in my squadron put into practice this same tactic ... a tactic that eventually caused our squadron commander some concern.

This concern came to a head one day when I was scheduled to fly in a four ship flight to bomb a bridge in North Vietnam. The pre-flight briefing included the normal intelligence assessment (an estimate of how many guns would be firing at us near the bridge), a detailed description of the target, our ordnance load (eight 750 pound bombs each), radio frequencies, call signs, refueling tankers available, expected weather, etc., etc. As kind of an afterthought, we were briefed that we were getting low on 20 mm ammunition ... so *"Don't use the gun."* **Strange,** I thought!

We took to the air late in the afternoon that day and when we got to the target area (in mountainous terrain) we found that low cloud cover forced us to deliver our bombs at a low angle, in a valley between two mountain ridges ... putting us closer to the antiaircraft threat dug in on the mountains around the bridge.

As I positioned myself for my bomb run I remembered the admonition *"Don't use the gun"* ... but I also remembered Colonel Van Etten's 'sage' counsel, and then said to myself **"Hey, this is war"** ... so I fired off a good long burst of the gun, pointing generally in the area where most of the anti-aircraft guns were.

With that bit of comforting relief, I then finished my bomb run dropping eight 750 pound bombs. Unfortunately, none of my bombs hit the bridge directly. As I pulled up and away, eager to get out of the high threat area, I looked back in time to see Rick's bombs hit the bridge directly and knock it down. As we all four got joined up and looked each other over (to reveal no damage to any airplane) we could breathe a sigh of relief ... and embrace a sense of group achievement ... mission accomplished ... **we** did it !!

We anticipated that the squadron commander would be as elated as we were. He met us at the airplanes as we parked near the operations area. **The bridge is down !! Thumbs up for everybody !!** We then took our good news inside to debrief the intelligence and maintenance folks ... while the crew chiefs and armament personnel readied the airplanes for the next day's flights.

I thought I had just been a part of a job well done ... until the squadron commander met me coming out of debriefing. He had just discovered that the armament personnel had to replace several hundred rounds of expended ammunition in my airplane. He did not look very pleased.

I knew enough to stand at attention while he shouted in my face *"What do you think you were doing ... strafing?"* (among other unpleasant words). I wanted to say *"Sir, we're at war"* ... but prudence told me to keep my mouth shut. A good thing too, since, as it turned out, I was the only one who fired the gun that day !!

I know one thing for sure ... I was mighty glad **we** knocked that bridge down ... diverting his attention to much more commendable things.

The Ping Pong paddle

F-100 (Eglin Air Force Base, Florida)

Eglin Air Force Base ... where nearly all USAF munitions are developed and tested ... was building a new target to test new munitions against. It was a huge, flat concrete target ... 300 feet long and 200 feet wide at its widest, over two foot thick in the middle and one foot thick elsewhere. The target was to be used to test runway defeat munitions.

All of us fighter test pilots were eager to be the first to damage and destroy this new imposing target ... that was our job! We were even more intrigued when we discovered its unique shape ... like a giant ping-pong paddle (with the paddle part a 100 foot radius, and the handle 100 feet wide and 100 feet long). Forever to be known as "The Ping-Pong Paddle" ... the target took on special meaning ... most test targets don't have names. The Air Force had acquired 24 newly designed 500 pound penetrating bombs with special fuses that needed to be tested. The new target was expensive and the test engineers had questions ... *"Was it big enough? ... Could the test pilots hit it using manual dive bombing?"*

Two fighter test pilots ... Ken Dyson and myself ... were selected to answer that question. We both felt like we had just won the lottery. ***"We get to be the first!"*** Two F-100 jet fighters were assigned to the task ... each carrying six bombs at a time. That meant Ken and I would each fly two sorties each. Now, I must admit, fighter pilots are prone to be very competitive ... so Ken and I entered into a friendly wager: 1) ... the first to miss the target would buy the other a steak dinner; and 2) ... the one with the worst average bomb score (the average distance from the center of the target of all bombs dropped ... known as the CEA, or Circular Error Average) would treat the other's entire family to a steak dinner. Besides being able to be the first to inflict our mark on the new target, we now had further incentive ... to do it well. In addition to the test pilot vs. test pilot wager, the test engineers were skeptical of our dive bombing prowess and were willing to wager a small sum of money that we would miss the target a total of at least six times ... a wager Ken and I could not resist.

The wagers made were not made out of ignorance on the part of the test engineers. They knew that manual dive bombing (releasing an unguided bomb using only pilot skills to achieve the desired release conditions ... (airspeed, dive angle, release altitude, and precise aim point ... all simultaneously) was probably the most difficult task for a fighter pilot. So difficult, in fact, that the qualifying bombing accuracy required to be a certified fighter pilot was a 140 foot CEA. In order to be successful in bombing "The Ping Pong Paddle" <u>all</u> bombs had to impact <u>on</u> the target ... a CEA significantly less than 100 feet.

When the test day arrived Ken and I thought we were ready. We had planned for optimal release conditions ... 45 degree dive angle, 450 knots release airspeed, and a release altitude of 3000 feet above the target. We eagerly manned our airplanes and were soon airborne, flying over the shiny new target a few miles east of Eglin. We both made a couple of dry passes to check wind conditions (calm !! ... perfect !!) and get warmed up.

The time had come ... I rolled in for my first dive bomb release, pickled (pressed the bomb release button), pulled up and looked back to witness the first bomb impact ... <u>the first bomb delivered against the ping-pong paddle</u>. All right !! ... about 50 feet from the center. The pressure was on Ken now. But his first bomb was better than mine. Second bomb ... similar results. My third bomb was very close to the edge but still on the target ... Ken's bomb landed short but hit the handle of the ping-pong paddle. Still no misses.

Around and around we went and when it was over Ken and I both had six hits with six bombs. The test engineers were batting zero. We both would claim our success was due to the intensity put into our effort (skill and cunning ?!?). However, the calmness of the wind was probably a much more significant contributing factor.

There were a few days before the second group of bombs were scheduled to be dropped. The Ping-Pong Paddle had to be cleared of debris and the results of the test analyzed. Ken and I, of course, were interested in the scoring of the impacts. It turned out I had a better bomb average then Ken, but not by much. The next day's test was crucial to our wager. The test engineers had mixed emotions ... they were glad that they had gotten so much data to analyze, but they realized their wager was at risk. Were they about to lose their money? ... or would the second day's bombs reward their earlier skepticism?

Day two of the test arrived and the winds were not calm anymore. Ken and I still made a couple of dry passes. It was obvious the wind would require us to offset our aim point somewhat. Ken went first this time, and I watched his bomb hit very close to the left edge of the ping-pong paddle. Noting his bomb went to the left, I moved my aim point a little farther to the right. After I released my first bomb I looked back ... and ... too much offset! I still hit the target, but very close to the right edge. This day was going to be a little touchy. Second bomb ... hit the target, but very close to the edge. Third bomb ... much better. I breathed a sigh of relief ... until I saw my fourth bomb hit close to the edge again. I had watched Ken's bombs be scattered a little bit also. My attention was focused more intensely now ... only two more bombs to go, and I needed two really good ones. As I pulled up from my fifth pass and looked back I was delighted to see an impact very close to the center of the ping-pong paddle. But Ken then dropped his last bomb right in the same spot. I needed one more good pass. Number six, my 12th (and what was to be the last bomb I ever dropped on the infamous "The Ping-Pong Paddle") ... hooray !! ... impacted very close to the center.

As I pulled up and joined up on Ken's wing for a formation flight back to Eglin, I began to think about what we had just accomplished. Ken and I had just put all 24 bombs smack dab on the new "Ping Pong Paddle" target. We could be well satisfied. And besides that, the test engineers owed us.

Ken and I would have to wait a while to see who had the best bombing average. The averages were fairly comparable ... we both claimed victory. However, the results were disputable ... craters upon craters ... exact impact points could not be precisely determined. Ken and I had to settle for a joint family night out at the steakhouse where we bought each other's family the same steak dinners. I must add that I was thankful we each had the same size family.

40 years later I flew over the infamous test target. It's old and discolored now, and there is evidence of many more impacts from test munitions. But the sight of it allowed me recollect and reminisce ... of being the first to drop bombs on "The Ping Pong Paddle."

Sidewinder vs. Searchlight

F-100 (Eglin Air Force Base, Florida)

Lieutenant Colonel Ken Coffee, one of my test pilot mentors, had been flying at night a lot. But I had no idea what he was testing ... some secret new munition I surmised. I found out about it quite by happenstance when I was told I would have to fly one of Ken's missions that night. Ken was DNIF (Duty Not Involving Flying) and I was the only F-100 test pilot available with adequate crew rest (I just happened to come in late that morning and a crew day could only be 12 hours long). The test had to be run that night. *"That's fine with me"* I said. *"What's the test?"* My eyes nearly popped out with excitement when I heard the details.

I was ushered into a small office, where I was told that Ken's test project involved evaluating modified Sidewinder air-to-air missiles to determine whether they could be used against searchlights. *Searchlights? Are you kidding? I thought those went out with World War II !!* I guess someone at higher headquarters had feared that the North Vietnamese may begin using searchlights against our night fighters. I was then told that Ken had flown instrumented Sidewinder missiles against searchlights on the range east of Eglin ... night after night ... to gather extensive data ... without firing a single missile. Pretty dull stuff, but leading up to a very exciting culminating mission ... actually firing the missiles at a searchlight ... that very night !! But Ken was DNIF and wouldn't be able to fly the mission he had been patiently anticipating. Needless to say, he was beside himself. Here a junior captain ... me ... who didn't even know this test was going on, would get to fly the real mission ... eating the pie after he had baked it.

I soon discovered there was a high level of interest in this test. So much so that the actual flight briefing was conducted in the office of the big boss ... Colonel "Dad" Risher. In addition to having a new test pilot for the "Big" test, another F-100 pilot ... from a support organization ... also uninformed about this project ... was called in to fly in my backseat (what we test pilots cynically referred to as a GIB (Guy In Back). The mission that night was to fire up to four powered, but inert (no warhead), Sidewinder missiles from an F-100F (the two-seat version of the F-100).

My task was to establish a specified dive angle towards the searchlight and fire the Sidewinder at a specified distance from the searchlight.

If the first searchlight was destroyed, a second searchlight would be turned on and I would fire the second Sidewinder from different dive angle and distance parameters, and so on (we had three searchlights). This would continue until I was out of Sidewinders or we were out of searchlights, whichever came first.

"Larry, I thought, *you really lucked into a super test mission."* I was sure glad I overslept that morning.

As the briefing went on it soon became apparent that in Colonel "Dad" Risher's mind the GIB played a major role in the safe conduct of this flight. He made it clear to Major Tom Brown that his job was to recover the airplane from the dive if I was temporarily blinded by the searchlight. He interrupted the briefing, pointed his finger right in Tom's face, and told him *"Don't you dare watch that missile ... keep your head down and your eyes on the instrument panel ... ready to recover from the dive if Larry can't see."* I had never seen our boss be so emphatic. As we finished the preflight briefing and were headed out of Colonel Risher's office, he called Major Brown over, got in his face and reiterated his point by saying *"You keep your head down and your eyes on that instrument panel ... you hear?" "Yes sir."* I heard Tom say. I kind of chuckled to myself as I wondered how Tom could possibly follow that order ... knowing how interesting this test was going to be.

When Tom and I got to the airplane to preflight before takeoff we were both met by a sight neither of us had ever seen before ... four Sidewinders loaded on an F-100. In training we had only carried one ... they were kind of expensive. The ground check-out of a Sidewinder was kind of novel ... the munitions guy just waved a flashlight in front of the Sidewinder to make sure the seeker head tracked the flashlight while I checked to see if I got a good aural tone in my cockpit headset. All four missiles checked out fine and away we went ... single ship (for some reason there was no safety chase scheduled on this mission ... I wonder if they thought he might get blinded too).

As we arrived over the test site the first searchlight was turned on. **Wow !!** ... That thing was sure easy to find in the pitch black night we were flying in. I made a couple of dry passes to make sure the test's ground radars were tracking me and I was achieving the desired release conditions. Then I set up to make the first known test firing of a Sidewinder against a searchlight. Before I rolled in though, I rebriefed Major Brown on his role, reminding him of Colonel Risher's stern admonition. Then I asked him *"Are you ready?"* His excited *"You betcha!"* kind of gave away what was to happen next.

I rolled in towards the searchlight ... got a good steady tone in my headset ... pressed the missile release button ... and **swoosh**, with a brilliant rocket flame, away went the Sidewinder, zooming directly at the searchlight As I began my recovery my headset filled with excited intercom chatter from the back seat (Tom just couldn't resist watching it!) *"Oh ... Oh ... Oh !! Look at that thing go !! Look at that thing go !! We hit it !! We hit it !!"* So much for head down in the cockpit, staring at the instrument panel !!

I couldn't criticize Tom too harshly. I was excited too. The view was spectacular !! The searchlight and the missile rocket exhaust flame were easily overlooked as I also watched that little missile streak towards and strike that searchlight like a lizard catching an insect with its tongue. That Sidewinder, without a warhead, flew right inside that 5 foot diameter searchlight ... and smashed it to smithereens.

The test engineers were excited too. They really weren't sure the missiles could guide that accurately, and thought they may have to fire four Sidewinders to get just one searchlight. They turned on the second searchlight and I set up to fire the second missile. **Swoosh ... Smash ...** another searchlight shattered !! But this time both Tom and I were hootin' and hollerin' in the cockpit. *"These Sidewinders were fun!"* As the third (and last) searchlight was turned on we were both thinking that regretfully this just might be our last shot. Sure enough ... missile three bored right into searchlight number three ... another bull's-eye ... another destroyed searchlight.

We returned to Eglin with the fourth missile unexpended ... results far exceeding the expectations of the test engineers. This turned out to be probably one of the most successful test missions I had ever flown ... especially noteworthy in the fact I had not participated in any of the hard work involved in the lengthy test planning nor had flown any of the preliminary tests ... no prior involvement whatsoever. I wasn't too excited about facing Ken ... knowing that his test program was probably over. But he took it well ... although on occasion chided me about stealing one of his most anticipated test adventures.

"Dad" Risher was waiting for us when we landed. He was glad to hear the test went well, and asked me how we handled the bright light. I told him it wasn't quite as bad as we had anticipated. Then, in an effort to negate what could have been a contentious confrontation with my GIB, I added that Major Brown did fine. I thought it best **not** to tell him his charge to Major Brown was an impossible task.

Oh, yes ... the rest of the story: To my knowledge, the North Vietnamese never did set up a searchlight, and never again was a Sidewinder ever fired at a searchlight.

Road Cave-in

OV-10 (Chu Lai Air Base, Vietnam)

The Ho Chi Minh Trail from North Vietnam through Laos into South Vietnam was a busy place. All of the supplies for the enemy Viet Cong soldiers fighting in the south came down that trail ... which began in Haiphong and Hanoi ... hundreds of miles from its final destination. The U.S. Air Force dropped untold thousands of bombs on that trail in a daily attempt to stop or slow the supplies. I got a chance one day to participate in slowing that flow by directing the destruction of several hundred feet of roadway.

I was flying an OV-10 Bronco as a forward air controller (FAC) monitoring the activity of the Trail in Laos right where it entered South Vietnam. At one point this roadway, about 10 to 15 feet wide and used by vehicles, went around the side of a relatively steep mountain. Its location made it very vulnerable to be put out of commission by bombing above the road and covering the road with a land slide. The idea caught on at higher headquarters and soon a mission was forthcoming.

I was scheduled to direct the attack which consisted of three F-100 jet fighters from Phan Rang Air Base, South Viet Nam, configured with two each 750 pound high explosive (HE) bombs and two MLU-10 750 pound land mines (a munition I had tested at Eglin Air Force Base, but had not known were available in Viet Nam). The land mines had delay fuses set to go off at random intervals. **Perfect !!** I would have the fighters cave in the mountain over the road with their HE bombs and then drop their land mines into the landslide material.

When the F-100s (call sign Tide) arrived I made sure they had me in sight and then briefed them on the task at hand ... describing the area where I would ask them to drop their bombs. I directed each fighter to drop their two high explosive bombs in a string pattern just above the road.

I marked the desired impact point (about 100 feet above the road) with a smoke rocket and then called for Tide Lead to *"Hit my smoke."* Lead's two bombs hit perfectly, creating a landslide about 200 feet long directly over the trail. I then put another smoke rocket further along and above the road and directed Tide Two to *"Hit my smoke."* Another perfect bomb drop ... caving in another 200 feet of mountain over the trail. Tide Three did equally superlative bombing. ***"Well done Tide Flight!"*** <u>I was impressed.</u>

With over 200 yards of the Trail now totally covered by the landslide, it was now time to drop the land mines that would severely hinder any road cave-in repair work. I again fired a smoke rocket to indicate right where I wanted the first two land mines to be dropped, and called for Tide Lead to drop his two about 50 feet on each side of my smoke.

With my binoculars focused on the site (I had to keep my slow-moving OV-10 at 10,000 feet altitude to avoid the anti-aircraft threat ... the enemy didn't like us messing with their supply road and protected it well), I was able to detect the land mines impact by the dirt cloud they threw up when they entered the landslide material (no explosions yet). Again Tide Lead dropped his bombs perfectly. I then called for Tide Two and Tide Three to drop their land mines in a similar fashion after I marked new aim points with smoke rockets for each of their drops. Both fighter's bomb drops were equally impressive.

These fighter pilots were good !! Actually, I had sensed this earlier just from their superb radio discipline.

Mission complete ... and extremely successful. We had just caved in over 200 yards of Ho Chi Minh Trail and had seeded the debris with six dangerous land mines. *"That should keep the enemy from using the road for some time to come."*

I congratulated the Tide's and thanked them for their exceptionally skillful bombing. I couldn't help but tell them that I was a fighter pilot too, and recognized excellence when I saw it.

It was nearing dusk when we finished the mission, so I headed for home (Chu Lai Air Base) to land. But I was eager to return the next day. I knew the enemy's slave labor would be working all night, but they had a mountain to move and I was curious to assess their progress. I arrived back on the scene very early the next morning and was I ever surprised.

Whoa !! How could this be? There was absolutely no evidence that we had bombed just a few hours before !! The road was completely clear !!

I certainly had a lot of questions. Like ... How big was their slave labor force? ... How did they move all that dirt in such a short time? ... How did they do it all in the dark? And the most intriguing question of all ... How did they handle those land mines? I now knew one thing though ... we were fighting a very tough, determined, and resilient enemy.

750 pound land mine

Grasshopper takeoff

T-38 (Eglin Air Force Base, Florida)

No, this "Tale" is not about how I once hopped and bounced off the runway ... I've repressed that memory. This is more literal, as you'll soon discover.

While flying as a fighter test pilot at Eglin Air Force Base I had the opportunity to be what we called triple current ... that is, I was current in flying three different airplanes ... the F-100, the F-4, and the T-38 Talon. The T-38 (a twinjet, supersonic trainer) was like a little sports car to those of us flying the big jet fighters. We had a saying *"Every fighter pilot ought to have one in his garage."* I was flying the T-38, with its beautiful one-piece windscreen which played a major role when this memorable "grasshopper" episode occurred.

Just prior to takeoff I taxied into the "last chance" area where maintenance personnel conducted a final inspection of the exterior of the aircraft while I completed my "before takeoff" checklist. I then taxied to the edge of the runway awaiting Tower approval for takeoff. With only minimum delay the Tower cleared me onto the runway to hold for release.

On a warm day at Eglin closing the canopy was about the last thing I did before taxiing onto the runway. With the canopy closed ... I was all sealed in ... lined up with the runway centerline ... and ready to run the engines up for takeoff. That's when the most unexpected thing happened ... a huge grasshopper (you know, the bug with wings and big legs) landed on my windscreen right in front of me. I looked at that bodacious intruder and thought *"You better get off quick while you have a chance."* But he just sat there like he had just captured a pearl of great price.

This grasshopper must have been looking for adventure. I was prepared to give it to him. I received takeoff clearance ... ran up the engines to full screaming power. That ought to scare him off ... <u>Didn't faze my new passenger one bit</u>! With a jolt I released brakes ... began rolling ... and lit both afterburners. <u>He didn't budge</u>. Now commenced a test of will and observation ... his will to hang on ... my observation to see how long he could.

He sure had my attention. The airspeed indicator really doesn't show much speed until about 40 knots ... No sweat for Mr. Grasshopper. He seemed to be enjoying the ride. But now we were accelerating ... 50 knots ... 60 knots ... 70 knots ... he was still hanging on ... apparently intent on setting a new speed record for grasshoppers. I'm thinking *"Wow, he's got some kind of strong grip on that slick canopy windscreen. I wonder how he does that?"* Now we were <u>really</u> accelerating ... 80, 90, 100 knots ... <u>Unbelievable</u> ... <u>He was still</u>

<u>hanging on</u> !! But at 110 knots his time was up ... he couldn't hack it any longer. *"Goodbye Mr. Grasshopper ... You put on quite a show ... adding an entirely new meaning to the phrase 'determined effort'"* Probably the first grasshopper to go 125 mph.

Now I could continue my takeoff without further distraction. <u>But wait</u> ... a second glance at where he had been firmly gripping the windscreen escalated the memory of his departure into the realm of the incredible ... **his legs were still attached to my windscreen** !!

Quite a sacrifice for a new speed record !! He sure was a determined critter ... refusing to let go. I was dumbfounded. I had never before witnessed such determination (stick-to-it-tive-ness ??).

His toe grip on the glass had obviously been stronger than his body grip on his legs. As I continued the take off, rotating to fly at about 150 knots, his legs remained attached to the windscreen. Finally, as I raised the gear and flaps, his legs waved goodbye. I don't know what kind of shoes he was wearing, but they had some kind of grip!

I have no remembrance of the rest of that mission. But I will always remember that grasshopper who paid a most high price for a joy ride on a jet. The whole episode kind of reminded me of when I was a little boy and some of my meaner boy friends would pull the legs off of grasshoppers. Now as an adult, I had emulated that meanness in a much more sophisticated and memorable manner.

Let it down ... Let it down

C-131 (Andrews Air Force Base, Maryland)

Why was this "old-timer" Lieutenant Colonel giving me such a hard time? I was in his office at Andrews Air Force Base, Maryland ... being interviewed to determine which airplane I would be flying after being recently assigned to duty in the Pentagon. It was his job to make that determination.

There were really only two choices ... the Lockheed T-33 jet trainer (a natural assignment for a seasoned fighter test pilot like myself) ... or the Convair C-131 (a twin engine, propeller driven passenger airplane ... a type of which I had absolutely no experience with). The choice seemed obvious to me.

However, as the interview progressed I realized there was a substantial conflict of interest. He had flown nothing but transport aircraft all his career, had experienced a lack of promotion opportunities, and seemed to have a disdain for hotshot fighter pilots ... especially those selected for promotable Pentagon assignments. He asked me what type of aircraft I had flown. With my head held high, I told him F-100, F-105, F-104, F-4, A-7, T-38 , **the T-33 (hint, hint)** and a smattering of other jet fighters (I didn't tell him about my recent experience flying the OV-10 ... I didn't want him to know I had **any** flying time in propeller aircraft). His expression didn't change much as I regaled him with my impressive flying credentials. He had apparently weathered tales like that before and was fully prepared to respond. He did mumble something about my flying background being *"interesting."* He then commenced to tell me at great length how wonderful it was flying for years and years in his wonderful cargo airplane. It didn't take a steel-trap mind for me to figure out what was coming next.

There was almost a twinkle in his eye as he sat back in his chair, crossed his arms, paused dramatically ... then slowly leaned over toward me, looked me in the face, and told me there just wasn't enough opportunities available to put me in the T-33. *"I have to put you in the C-131,"* he said ... with an unsettling finality. As he watched disappointment creep into my countenance, he accelerated the process by telling me *"There's a ground school scheduled to start in two weeks."* The interview was over.

I had been told by some of my other fighter pilot friends in the Pentagon that there was no recourse to his decision. They had kind of forewarned me about the interview I had just participated in. I meekly thanked him and left his office ... knowing that at least I had cheered somebody up ... <u>him</u>.

I could almost hear him chuckle ... <u>another hotshot fighter pilot humbled</u>. That seemed to fit his self-proclaimed job description.

The C-131 ground school was a tale in itself. There were about a half dozen of us "hotshot fighter pilots" from the Pentagon in attendance. None of us had ever flown an airplane that required a crew to fly.

Consequently, some of the comments during the school were most entertaining. I'll never forget when one fighter pilot asked (with tongue in cheek) if we had to wear an anti-g suit when flying the C-131. Before the instructor could answer another fighter pilot said *"No, you have to wear pantyhose."* We all roared with laughter, but I don't think the old-timer instructor appreciated our humor.

The actual flight check-out was fairly lengthy, as we had to schedule time away from the Pentagon to avail ourselves of the flying opportunities. We did discover that flying with a crew provided some very memorable moments ... unattainable in a single seat fighter aircraft. I described one of those in *Flying Tale:* "<u>*Get off the Brakes*</u>" (page 202).

Another memorable moment came when, after completing my check out, I was finally scheduled to fly a real mission ... a passenger carrying flight from Andrews Air Force Base to Randolph Air Force Base in Texas. I must say carrying passengers was a totally new experience for me ... the responsibility was not taken lightly ... especially since I was assigned to fly the left (aircraft commanders) seat. The same old-timer who had made my assignment to the C-131 was to fly in the copilot seat. The pressure was on.

The flight to Randolph went well. There was no undue turbulence to disturb the passengers. I had even learned how to synchronize the propellers so there was no uncomfortable noise for the passengers. The old timer seemed content. But now the real test was before me ... <u>landing</u> ... the piloting task most judged by everyone on the airplane. I was determined to please my passengers. Was I up to the task?

A visual approach to landing was made with easy gentle turns and I lined up very precisely with the centerline of the runway. As I approached the flare-to-touchdown I was really concentrating. The wind was light and the flare was smooth as I gradually reduced the rate of descent. I patiently waited for touchdown.

Contact with the runway (touchdown) can be discerned (and judged by everyone else on board !) in many ways ... from a jarring clunk ... to a bounce or two ... to the (hoped-for) just a squeak from the tires. <u>But this touchdown was different</u>. With both hands on the control wheel I could just barely feel that the main wheels had touched down ... there was no perceptible movement in the control column and no other physical evidence that we were on the ground. **A perfect landing !!** I then just held the nose at the landing attitude by slowly pulling back on the control wheel ... as we began to slow down.

Then the most memorable thing occurred. The old-timer instructor pilot (IP) was getting nervous. I could see him edge up on his seat, and he even began to move his hands towards his control column. I realized ... **he didn't know what I knew** ... **we were already on the ground**. He obviously thought we were still in the air and we were soon going to stall the airplane as our speed decreased.

Abruptly losing his calm demeanor, he shouted at me *"Let it down ... Let it down"* ... meaning, get on the ground before you mangle this landing. This outburst provided me with an opportunity I could not resist. Without saying a word, I gradually <u>lowered the nose</u> ("Let it down" now had new meaning). The nose wheel touched the runway with a gentle squeak ... making it plain to all that the main gear had been on the ground for some time. The passengers burst into applause ... the old-timer gulped. He turned stone silent. I was hoping he had just gained a new respect for hotshot fighter pilots.

That landing was obviously the best landing I had ever made. The total experience of the landing and the response to the landing was something that could never happen in a single seat jet fighter. My "humbling" at being assigned outside of my fighter aircraft comfort zone had been worth it.

Trees walking

OV-10 (Chu Lai Air Base, Vietnam)

There I was, in my trusty OV-10 Bronco, once again flying towards the Ho Chi Minh Trail in nearby Laos to look for enemy activity. But this time it was different. I had a newbie with me in the back seat of my Bronco ... someone who had never worked the Trail before. I had agreed to let one of my peers, Major Bob Smith, go with me. His tour in Vietnam was about up and he wanted to see the Ho Chi Minh trail before he left. All of his forward air control (FAC) work had been in-country (that is, exclusively in South Vietnam). His first venture over the enemy stronghold in Laos proved to be a real eye opener ... for both of us !!

When we arrived in the area, about 50 miles from any friendly ground forces, I first gave Bob a rather cursory overview of the entire trail complex that we were going to recce. We of course remained above 10,000 feet to avoid the antiaircraft threat there, forcing us to use our high powered binoculars to look for evidence of trail usage. As I was pointing out the main arteries (the trail was not just one road, but several ... something like the veins on the back of our hands) I noticed something totally new and unexpected. The enemy had placed <u>trees in the middle of the one of the main trails !!</u> This strange apparition really got my attention, and I began to study it carefully with my binoculars. I soon discovered that all the trees were small palm trees, and they were fairly equally spaced ... about 10 to 20 feet apart ... and <u>right in the center of the trail.</u> Strange place to plant trees !?! There were scores of these trees, covering several hundred feet of this part of the trail. What was the enemy up to ??

As I studied the trees further I began to focus my attention on their shadows. I then discovered that some of these trees had two trunks, like the shadow of a man with his legs apart. Closer observation revealed that a few of these trees were moving !! Trees walking?! My deductive mind began to whir ... these weren't trees at all. Well, they were in a way ... but <u>it was really enemy soldiers holding small trees</u> !! Clever camouflage ... but in the middle-of-the-road ?!

I must say they were very disciplined soldiers. As soon as they heard us flying overhead they didn't move but maintained their formation as we orbited overhead. They had apparently been marching down the trail and when we arrived the company size contingent came to a halt. But as we orbited and watched, some of the soldiers became tired. Some of the shadows turned into kneeling figures. Some of the shadows turned into sitting figures. Bob confirmed my deduction.

And boy was he excited. Finding enemy troops in the open was an extremely rare event. And here we were, probably looking at an entire enemy company ... out in the open ... on their way to enter the war against our Army troops in South Vietnam.

We continued to orbit the enemy troops, who remained stationary in the middle of the road as long as we circled overhead (they must have figured their walking tree ploy was keeping them from being detected). I immediately contacted (via radio) the Direct Air Support Center (DASC) and gave them the surprising news. Enemy troops in the open always received the highest priority and soon the DASC had located a couple of nearby F-4s loaded with 500 pound bombs and diverted them from a lower priority mission to rendezvous with us as quickly as possible. We had the right weapons coming. Now our problem was how to employ them before the enemy troops recognized their peril and dispersed.

The F-4s (call sign Gunfighter) arrived and orbited above us while I described to them the situation and the general location of the enemy troops. It would be next to impossible for them to find the exact location of the walking trees in the mountainous trail area, so I would have to put in a good smoke rocket to mark it precisely for them. I also knew that alongside the trail were many bunkers to protect personnel from air attack. I reckoned that as soon as I fired the first smoke rocket the walking trees would become running trees as the enemy soldiers scurried for those bunkers.

Consequently, I asked Gunfighter Lead if he thought he could roll in right behind me and drop his bombs in a string pattern just on the right edge of the trail (the side where the bunkers were) ... using my smoke mark as an aim point ... and have Gunfighter 2 follow right behind. That would minimize the time allowed for the enemy troops to dive into the bunkers alongside the road. He assured me they were up to the task

With FAC and fighters ready to attack, I rolled in with the fighters behind me ... fired off my white phosphorus (Willie Pete ... WP) rocket, turned hard to the left to get out from under the fighters, and glued my eyes on to the road.

There were only a few seconds left before those bombs were going to impact, but those trees began breaking ranks as soon as I fired that rocket. In fact most of those trees were just thrown down on the road, no longer having a trunk to hold them upright. Gunfighter Lead placed his six 500 pound bombs perfectly ... strung out about 50 feet apart right between the road and the bunkers. Gunfighter 2 dropped his six bombs about five seconds later just a little further down the road. The Gunfighters knew how to bomb and they knew how to work with a FAC. Our plan of attack worked. The big question remained ... had the enemy been able to avoid devastation ??

After the fighters pulled up I surveyed the trail carefully. There were no more trees walking in the middle of the road. The road was now scalloped with bomb craters which encompassed many of the bunkers. However, there was no way of knowing how effective we were at eliminating the movement of this company of enemy troops into South Vietnam. Gunfighter's bombs had been placed perfectly, and the timing couldn't have been better. The size of their force was undoubtedly reduced considerably, but by how much we would never know.

After walking all the way down the Trail from North Vietnam and then being caught in the open, the enemy soldiers that survived our Fighter/FAC teamwork attack were probably a little more reluctant to continue their mission. One thing for sure though ... Bob Smith's one and only mission over the Ho Chi Minh Trail had been a most memorable one.

Dive bombing in a Spad

A-1 (Eglin Air Force Base, Florida)

During the Vietnam War era the Air Force pulled some old World War II vintage airplanes out of the boneyard and turned them into exceptional fighting machines which did heroic work in the war. One of those airplanes was the A-1 Skyraider ... affectionately called a Spad. It was a single-engine propeller driven fighter that could carry an enormous payload and could stay airborne for hours. The Spads, using the call sign SANDY, became the primary attack escort for the JOLLY GREEN helicopters when rescuing downed pilots.

My good friend, and test pilot school classmate, Al Hale was assigned to fly a tour in the A-1 and came to Hurlburt Air Force Base, Florida for his training. I was stationed at nearby Eglin Air Force Base at the time. It was good to be able to see Al again and during many social occasions Al and I often commiserated about our daring flying exploits.

On one of those occasions Al asked me if I would like to fly with him in the A-1 on one of his training missions. Occasionally he got to fly the two-seat version of the A-1 (the A-1E) and the right seat was nearly always empty. I was ecstatic. Of course I would like to fly the "slow mover." At the time I had been flying both the F-100 and the F-4 "fast movers" doing weapons testing which involved lots of dive bombing. Al told me he would check and see if he could get me on a gunnery range mission. I thought that would be terrific ... just perfect. A few days later I got a call from Al. It was all set ... I could join him at the flight briefing ... just bring my own helmet.

It was comforting to discover that the flight briefing (four A-1s ... one instructor pilot (IP) and three student pilots ... plus a visiting copilot (me)) was just what I would have expected in any fighter briefing ... "fighter normal." Manning the aircraft ... starting engines ... radio procedures ... taxi and takeoff procedures ... were also what I would have expected in any fighter unit ... "fighter normal." The takeoffs ... the join up into a four ship formation ... and the flight to the range ... were all ... well ... "fighter normal" ... <u>except</u> we were going about one third the airspeed I was used to in a fast mover jet fighter. Sitting in the right (copilot) seat in a side-by-side cockpit was a little different. Al let me fly much of the formation and I was impressed with the good handling qualities of the A-1. The cacophonic noise of the big radial engine however, was an awesome experience by itself. *It was a good day.*

When we finally got to the gunnery range we set up for the first weapon delivery ... dive bombing. I felt right at home. There were two significant differences this time however. First of all, most of Al's flying career had been in multi-engine cargo aircraft. This was his first chance to experience weapon delivery from a small agile airplane. In fact this may have only been Al's second or third time to dive bomb.

So I was somewhat interested (concerned?) in observing Al's technique. Would he avoid the pitfalls of target fixation? Would his crosscheck de-emphasize altitude awareness? Etc. Etc. Dive bombing requires obtaining precise dive angle, airspeed, release altitude, and gun site (pipper) placement on the target ... <u>all simultaneously</u> ... a most complex and demanding task which required much experience to master.

The second significant difference arose from the fact that I had never dive bombed from an airplane that went this slow. All of my dive bombing had been at speeds well over 500 mph which required higher altitudes at release to be able to pull out of the dive with adequate ground clearance. I was about to experience diving at the ground at 200 or 250 mph. What would that be like? I wasn't prepared for the answer.

As Al rolled in from level flight into his first dive bomb pass, at a 45° dive angle I soon realized we were already below the altitude I usually **pulled out** at in an F-100 or F-4. I immediately looked at Al ... should I be overly concerned? I could tell he was concentrating and working very hard at achieving the desired bomb release parameters. He <u>seemed</u> to be in control.

But we were diving steeply at the ground and my concern level was escalating ... rapidly !! We just kept diving! ... Al kept looking through the gunsight ... I kept looking at the rapidly approaching ground. *"Come on Al,* I thought, *just release the bomb and **pull out!**"* I began to see things I had never seen before while dive bombing ... like **individual tree leaves** !!

My dive bombing experience mental warning lights began flashing ... we were too low to make a safe pull out. There was no way we could recover **... we were goners**. Now I knew what dive bombing at slow speed would be like ... I would die !!

There wasn't much I could do then except wait for the cataclysm. It was at that moment that Al hit the pickle button (releasing his practice bomb) and abruptly pulled back on the stick. The airplane responded unlike anything I had ever seen before. We kind of instantaneously recovered to level flight.

My heart could beat again ... I could stop holding my breath !! The mental warning lights turned off. The new experience light went on ... at that slow speed it only took a few hundred feet to recover from the dive ... not a few thousand !!

The remaining dive bomb passes were very similar ... low altitude, abrupt pull outs ... <u>no sweat</u>. Al really did know what he was doing ... and did it well. His technique was ... well ... "fighter normal" As my "fighter normal" breathing rate returned, I decided it best NOT to thank Al for saving my life.

Happy New Year

OV-10 (Chu Lai Air Base, Vietnam)

Why did I choose to fly the first flight of the day on New Year's Day? I kept asking that question over and over. I knew I had told everybody that it was so the Forward Air Controllers (FACs) that worked for me could sleep in and get rested after the big night of partying we had planned.

But what about me? How was I going to be rested for an early morning go? Particularly since the party was going to be in **my** small 16 x

24 foot two-man hooch !! Oh well, I thought ... the combat patrol mission scheduled for dawn should be routine with no enemy activity ... I had heard the Viet Cong (VC) also celebrate New Year's Eve. All should be "Quiet on the western Front" ... right? Boy, was I in for a surprise.

The party got kind of wild, with a dozen or more junior officers all gathered together in my now very crowded hooch. They were hootin' and hollerin' and laughing and telling loud boisterous stories about their combat bravado ... while the high-powered stereo played crazy music at max volume.

My plan was to hit the sack after all the *"Happy New Year"* shouts had ceased ... but that took a long time. Much longer than I had figured. My really big problem then surfaced. My bed was only about 10 feet from all the noise makers !!

I really tried hard to get some rest before flying off into enemy territory, but I soon discovered that earplugs and pillows around my head were very inadequate at drowning out the boisterous noise. I tried to will myself to sleep ... that sure didn't work. Tossing and turning was the order of the night. What a miserable night !! I might have caught a couple of winks before my alarm went off at 5 a.m. ... but rested I was not. Partying and lack of sleep were really not conducive to being alert for a combat patrol at first light.

I don't remember ever crawling into my OV-10 at Chu Lai Air Base, Vietnam in a more fatigued condition ... exacerbated by a 6 a.m. takeoff. But I made it ... and off I went ... hopefully for a casual and uneventful visual reconnaissance of enemy territory to the far west of our position. The radios were quiet ... except for the contact with each Army unit I flew over to exchange Happy New Year wishes. There wasn't much Army combat activity scheduled on New Year's Day ... so I could just relax and slowly reconnoiter the usual area.

Then I moseyed (do airplanes really mosey? ... I tried!) over to the territory held exclusively by the enemy ... far beyond the Army's artillery range where no US Army troops dared to venture on the ground (the Army ground patrols rarely, if ever, went beyond the range of protective artillery cover). We FACs would venture beyond that limit in efforts to discover enemy intentions.

So on this New Year's Day I found myself looking down on a foot trail used by the VC to infiltrate the friendly held territory. At one point this foot trail went through a large open cleared area ... quite visible from the air. I had never seen any activity in this clearing. The enemy could hear us coming and get back into the woods before we got close. But on this day, when I was feeling miserable and really didn't want to discover any enemy activity, I looked down in that cleared area and saw two VC soldiers just moseying down the trail (they must have felt lousy also). My presence didn't seem to faze or worry them at all. I figured if I just circled them they would get nervous and flee back into the protection of the forested area. However, it was not to be.

I was astounded. These two soldiers were pretty brazen and, instead of running, began to give me a very unexpected Happy New Year greeting. **They both raised their rifles and started firing at me ... in full automatic mode**. *"Not now guys ... I'm feeling pretty lousy."* Their effrontery, while startling me and activating what little adrenaline I had left, actually didn't concern me too much, as I figured their efforts were futile ... I was flying 1500 feet above them ... well out of small arms range. But now I had a decision to make.

The rules of engagement (ROE) specifically permitted engaging enemy soldiers in the open, and especially when being fired upon. I was carrying four 7-tube rocket pods. Firing a single, well aimed high explosive (HE) rocket would have wiped them both out. The OV-10 was also equipped with four machine guns. The two brazen VC soldiers would have been easy targets ... no match for an armed OV-10.

But I was having second thoughts ... I would have to go down into their gun range to attack. Were they worth the effort? Were they trying to draw me into an ambush? ... They were known for that. If so, I was in no condition to endure a long evasion effort if I had been shot down, for I was a long way from any friendly support and right in the middle of hostile territory. They both continued to fire at me while I circled overhead ... pondering my options. Attack or withdraw? ... Attack or withdraw?

They say that discretion is the better part of valor. I didn't feel particularly valorous, but I finally decided it was prudent to just waggle my wings at the two enemy soldiers ... acknowledging their unfriendly gesture ... and wish them a **Happy New Year**.

B-52 vs. F-4

F-4 (Eglin Air Force Base, Florida)

The Big Ugly Fat Fellow (BUFF) was in town and he wanted to duel with a Phantom. He must have known it would be futile. Why would Strategic Air Command (SAC) want to embarrass themselves by sending one of their B-52 bombers up against the Air Force's finest air-to-air fighter ... the F-4? Any F-4 pilot ... trained to shoot down enemy aircraft ... would be eager for the challenge.

At the time, with the Vietnam War in full swing ... SAC was concerned that their B-52s might be ordered to fly missions into North Vietnam where they would be apt to encounter enemy MIG fighters. They decided to test their defensive technique by coming to Eglin Air Force Base where they could fly out over the Gulf of Mexico while an F-4 made simulated attack passes ... mimicking a MIG gun attack. As an F-4 test pilot, eager to demonstrate my fighter mettle, I quickly volunteered for the test. I was thinking *"This is gonna be fun ... shooting down a big lumbering bomber that only had one defense mechanism ... a gun sticking out of the tail."* Boy, was I in for an education.

I must digress a bit and explain that fighter pilots are trained to make a gun attack from a slight offset ... pointing their noses slightly in front of the target (called pulling lead) ... using excess speed to approach within gun range ... then squeeze off a burst of lethal gunfire. This *pursuit curve* task is complicated when the target is maneuvering dramatically ... like any fighter should. But a B-52 !? ... They can't maneuver. Flying a pursuit curve against them should be a piece of cake.

With a bit of cocky fighter pilot aplomb, I went to the pre-flight mission briefing. I soon discovered that this mission was going to try to re-educate me. The SAC briefers first explained that a rear firing 20 mm Gatling gun could reach out farther than my forward firing one.

As I thought about it, that minor revelation made technical sense to me. Figuratively, I would be firing into a head wind, while they would be firing into a tail wind. Hence their maximum gun range would be greater than mine ... about 1000 feet greater. *"So what"* I thought ... I could close that gap rather quickly while they were trying to maneuver away from me in their slow lumbering aircraft.

But then the big revelation was put on me when they told me that when I came in for my attack they would **not** turn into me as a typical fighter would. They would, instead, simply turn away from me. I mused that this would place them directly in front of me rather quickly, making my task easier. But what it really did was place me in the bombers rearward facing cone of fire more quickly. I must say that kind of puzzled me. *"Kind of like fighting a skunk"* I thought. I realized I had never trained against a rearward firing defense system. Their technique made sense, but I was sure I could overcome it.

But the odds in this bomber's favor grew a little more when they told me that during this test I could **not** go supersonic !! **And** they would be flying at a very high altitude ... an altitude where at subsonic speed my maneuvering capability would be somewhat limited. My task was even further complicated when they told me I had to be visually acquired by them before closing to within a "flying safety" minimum distance. With all these constraints I was then told my rules of engagement were to make various simulated attack approaches **at my discretion**. Okay ... I could do anything I wanted as long as I was slow and they could see me ... wow, some deal.

Glad to have the pre-flight briefing over (with all its "Thou shalt not's"), and with fighter pilot confidence, I manned my high-performance Phantom and headed for high over the Gulf of Mexico to challenge the BUFF. As I joined up with the B-52, I first demonstrated some close formation wizardry for the bomber crew ... *That should impress them* ... and then I backed off about a mile and offset to the side to make my first simulated gun attack. At high subsonic speed I began my closure and turned to point my nose at the lumbering giant.

Coming in from about a 30 degree angle as I closed on him, he quickly turned his tail at me. **What a shock !!** ... I was in his gun range well before I was close enough to shoot. Embarrassed, I tried a new tactic for my second pass. I pulled line abreast to the BUFF, about a mile out, and turned smartly towards him ... for a 90 degree intercept. But half way through my turn he turned away from me ... quickly pointing his tail at me again. **This was not going well !!**

My fighter pilot ego was being bruised. I next tried attacking from way above. But not being able to go supersonic, and at the high-altitude of the B-52, this maneuver also ended up in a tail chase with me directly in his cone of fire. This subsonic limitation was a real handicap. I needed more energy. Pass after pass ended in the same result ... that big B-52 could point his tail at me before I could get into my gun range. *What was I to do?*

American innovation to the rescue. American fighter pilots are trained to be innovative. I pondered an idea ... *"What if I came in vertical ... from below?"* At the lower altitude I could have more excess energy before I began my maneuver. I could approach him from his blind belly. I backed off a couple of miles and got about one mile below ... directly behind the B-52. I accelerated directly toward him to the maximum subsonic speed ... kind of a direct tail chase position. When I got just a little bit in front of him I pulled several 'g's and headed straight up ... both afterburners going in that mighty F-4 ... and began my closure to gun range.

It was close ... but it worked !! I passed a little behind the BUFF going straight up. Must have scared the Willie out of them ... They immediately radioed ... *"Knock it off ... We couldn't see you coming!"* ... only seeing me for a second or two, as I quickly passed through their cone of danger. That was my whole idea !!

In soccer terms I had just earned a yellow flag. That kind of tactic wasn't fair, they said ... a violation of the "flying safety" minimums. There would be **no more** of those passes

I wasn't much ready for more of their tail stinging skunk like setups. Fortunately I was about out of gas and had to return to land at Eglin. The B-52 still had hours of fuel left and returned to their home base somewhere far away. Consequently there was no formal debriefing. Just as well ... our egos were substantially intact, despite the revelations. We both knew what we had learned. They must have thought that their tactics could easily handle any MIG encounter after they had defeated the mighty F-4 on multiple passes.

On the other hand, I now knew how to use a gun against a big bomber like the B-52 ... **go supersonic and come from below.** Better yet ... a long-range missile was built for this task.

Most beautiful sight

A-7D (Edwards Air Force Base, California)

How do I explain the most beautiful sight I have ever seen while flying?

Ask any aviator. Just trying to describe any flying scene to one who has never flown is tough enough. It's one of the sweet secrets pilots have in common. But painting a verbal picture of the wonderful sight that

Flying Tales

highlighted all my years of flying ... that will be most challenging. I'll try to begin by telling of the location where my most precious moment occurred.

When assigned to fly at Edwards Air Force Base the first flight (dollar ride) is used to orient the new arrival to the local flying area. At Edwards, that area includes a special topography northwest of the air base formed by the high Sierra Nevada mountains (Mt Whitney, the highest mountain in the continental US, is there). The High Sierras are a chain of rugged mountains that extend along the central spine of California for well over 100 miles. One interesting portion of this mountain range is the Kern River Canyon. This canyon has the appearance as if a giant Paul Bunyan used a giant ax to split the mountains, forming a narrow canyon with steep walls several thousand feet high. The Kern River, which begins just north of Mt Whitney, runs down this canyon.

The winding, narrow Kern River Canyon provides the perfect challenge for a fighter pilot ... **flying down the canyon** !! ... hugging the river ... with steep cliffs pressing in from both sides !! Perhaps comparable to, but much more exhilarating than, riding a motorcycle or driving a sports car on a very curvy road at a high rate of speed. It's a thrilling ride, and nearly every new pilot at Edwards experiences it on his first flight ... and then probably repeats it many times during his stay at Edwards ... as I was wont to do.

On my precious moment day I was flying a single seat A-7D jet fighter on a training sortie, which I began with another rendezvous with the Kern River Canyon. *But this time was unlike any other time.* The canyon greeted me with a special treat. It was early Spring and during the preceding winter there had been a particularly heavy snowfall in the High Sierras. The snow begins melting in the Spring, flowing down into the Kern River. However, due to the fact that unusually high temperatures had prevailed for a few preceding days, the situation was ripe on this day for a very unique event.

I was greeted by an enormous flow of water from the mountain tops into the canyon below ... far exceeding my wildest expectations. The heaviest, most rapid snow melt in years had just created the most massive, incredible collection of **_waterfalls_** *!!* ... cascading over the high canyon walls, falling dramatically into the Kern River.

As I flew down the canyon I was in total awe ... there must have been over fifty huge, and I mean **huge** waterfalls ... each dropping hundreds, some even thousands of feet to the river below. With this pelting from above, the Kern River was all white water. I was fascinated, enthralled, amazed, intrigued ... all at the same time. Waterfalls, especially long ferocious ones, always draw one's attention ... but here were over fifty of them ... from both sides of the canyon ... spread over several miles. To put it mildly, I was simply overwhelmed by the grandeur. I had never seen anything so beautiful.

I couldn't resist. I flew up and down the canyon that day, I don't know how many times ... trying desperately to soak it all in (forgive the pun) ... looking way above me as the water cascaded down on both sides of me in waterfall after waterfall. I made a point of trying to memorize that scene in my mind ... I can still see it very clearly today. I often later wished I had had a camera with me that day. But, in all candor, I don't think a camera would have been able to capture the image that I so often recall and cherish.

The next day I was anxious to fly up there and see the magnificent sight again. But when I got there, it wasn't the same. The <u>massive</u> snow melt was <u>over</u> ... perhaps only a one-day event. The snow melt was down to the normal trickle. There were only a few waterfalls ... of much diminished character.

I often wondered if I had been the only one to fly down the Kern River Canyon on that special day. No other pilot I talked to had witnessed what I had seen. I like to think of it as a scene just orchestrated for me ... a flying epiphany ?

First cluster bombs

F-105 (Takhli Air Base, Thailand)

A new and terrifying weapon was introduced into the Air Force in the 1960s. All of us fighter pilots were astounded when we were first briefed on this highly classified weapon ... a weapon guaranteed to provide a favorable outcome to any engagement between our friendly Army troops and enemy ground forces.

It was called a CBU (Cluster Bomb Unit). The CBU was basically a canister filled with hundreds of hand grenade type munitions (cluster bombs). One fighter pilot could now, on one pass, disseminate enough anti-personnel weapons to fend off a large attacking enemy force. The first cluster bombs were packed in long tubes. Air pressure entering the nose of the canister would push the cluster bombs out the rear, creating a long stream of cluster bombs.

Our mighty F-105 "Thuds" had just entered the war in Southeast Asia and my unit, the 36th Tactical Fighter Squadron was stationed at Takhli Air Base in Thailand when we received the first CBUs. We had been on alert for several days when we got the word that enemy troops were attacking the friendly Laotian troops in Laos and they desperately needed air support. We had previously loaded four F-105s with two each CBU-1 canisters in anticipation of such an event. This was our chance to employ the new CBU weapon for the very first time. Our flight of four F-105s was airborne shortly after we got the call for help. With each fighter carrying nearly 700 cluster bombs, we were confident we could turn the enemy around.

When we arrived over the scene of the ground combat we discovered it was a totally forested area ... no visible contact with the ground. How were we to identify the enemy location? We were finally able to make radio contact with an American special forces soldier who was on the ground with the friendly Laotian troops. He did his best to help us identify the area, and more importantly identify the area where the enemy soldiers were attacking from. When we told him that our bomb pattern would be several hundred feet long and maybe 100 feet wide for each airplane he suggested a course to follow over the enemy positions that would be parallel to the friendly forces frontline so we would not drop any bomblets onto the friendly troops.

The promising awesome CBU was about to be dispensed in anger for the very first time. Not sure of the enemy antiaircraft threat we elected to make passes two aircraft at a time ... in loose formation ... dispensing both canisters in one pass.

I was number two on the first delivery. We approached the target area in level flight at about 500 feet and 500 knots. At lead's command both he and I hit our pickle buttons and began dispensing hundreds of bomblets simultaneously from four of these new untried weapons, whose ominous job was to deter all future ground combat.

As I looked back the scene was rather remarkable. As each bomblet hit the trees it would explode. One after another the bomblets detonated ... leaving a sparkling path of supposed destruction. At the same time I began noticing many sparkles in the air. I could only assume we were taking fire. I radioed three and four to make sure they were aware of the threat. But as we turned and climbed ... looking back down ... it was easy to discern that the sparkles in the air were bomblets colliding with each other. But, oh my! ... It was also fairly apparent that probably none of the cluster bombs got through the foliage to the ground ... going off with impact on the trees.

If our CBU did any damage to the enemy troops it was not apparent.

The introduction of the CBU into the realm of warfare was ... well ... ho-hum! Not as ominous and terrifying as previously hyped. The noise of nearly 3000 grenades going off above them may have scared the enemy troops off. In any event, the friendly troops were able to withdraw safely ... but no damage to the enemy troops assembled below the tree canopy was reported. We probably did have an awesome impact on the monkey and bird population in the area ... but not the much ballyhooed "war ending" capability projected for the CBU. The CBU capability was obviously overblown.

Our rather deflating experience with the first CBU drop had more surprises for us too! It turned out some of the little bomblets were not forced out of their canisters by the air pressure. We discovered this when we landed back at Takhli. Upon touchdown on the runway some of the few remaining reluctant bomblets decided to dribble out, creating a very hazardous cleanup operation for armament personnel, **and** a startling hazard for the following aircraft landing.

Later flights with this now questionable munition created even more havoc as some of the bomblets when dispensed collided and exploded while still in the vicinity of the aircraft, creating unpleasant holes in the aft section of the airplane, with accompanying worrisome complications.

The history of warfare is undoubtedly replete with similar tales of overhyped expectations for a new weapon system. The CBU added to these tales. The dreams and aspirations of the munitions designers and the hopes of the fighter pilots were again tempered by the reality of the actual employment of a new munition.

Back to the drawing board!

Chopper pilot flying my jet

T-38 (Edwards Air Force Base, California)

Being an instructor at the Air Force's Test Pilot School (TPS) came with many benefits. One of those benefits was the opportunity to fly many different kinds of airplanes.

Included in the TPS curriculum was the requirement that the students fly and do a technical <u>qua</u>litative evaluation of various types of airplanes they had never flown before. The flight was simply called a

Qual. A Qual consisted of flying in the aircraft commanders seat, but with a qualified instructor pilot in the copilot seat. Of course, when a new and different type of aircraft was made available for a Qual, all of us TPS instructors were provided the opportunity to also fly the airplane, expanding our own expertise ... a real benefit.

Qual flights were the result of reciprocal agreements with other test pilot agencies, such as the Navy Test Pilot School, the Empire Test Pilot School, and various foreign flight test agencies. When we visited them we flew their airplanes and when they visited us they flew our airplanes. Flying their airplanes was great ... **but** letting them fly our airplanes often provided the more striking memories ... particularly for those of us that were called upon to be the instructor pilots in the copilot seat for a first-time flight by a budding test pilot-in-training.

One of those memorable moments occurred for me when a class from the Navy Test Pilot School visited us at Edwards Air Force Base. Now I must interject that the Navy Test Pilot School did something the USAF Test Pilot School didn't ... they trained <u>helicopter</u> as well as conventional aircraft test pilots.

Wouldn't you know it, when they visited Edwards it was my draw to have a helicopter pilot selected to fly with me in my T-38 jet trainer. I knew this could get exciting due to the significant differences between a smooth, sporty, highly maneuverable supersonic jet trainer like the T-38 and a low, slow, vibrating mixmaster called a helicopter.

I briefed the Navy Lieutenant on some of the peculiar systems in the T-38, reassuring him that I would take care of any difficulties that arose in that area. He showed me the flight card he had prepared for the Qual. It included many up and away maneuvers followed by several landing approaches. He had done his homework well. We proceeded to man the aircraft ... with me in the back seat.

The takeoff went well, despite the fact that nose wheel lift off speed was faster than his helicopter maximum speed (we were still rolling down the runway at a speed he had never seen while airborne in his helicopter). His experience with sensitive helicopter rudders gave him an advantage in maintaining directional control during the takeoff roll ... I was impressed. We did several maneuvers; some gentle turns to get himself comfortably acquainted with the airplane ... some stability and control inputs as taught by the test pilot school ... and even some acrobatics where he could experience high 'g' and rolling maneuvers. He seemed to really enjoy the nimble jet. I was beginning to smile. But then we entered the landing pattern at Edwards Air Force Base.

Just entering the traffic pattern in a jet versus a helicopter was a surprise for my chopper pilot ... not many helicopters pull high 'g's entering the traffic pattern !! ... typical in a jet trainer. His gentle turn resulted in our pattern being quite large. We did finally manage to slow down and get the gear and flaps down and then get lined up with the runway. That is when this Qual flight got very sporty.

The difference between a T-38 final approach and a helicopter final approach is a big gulp. The T-38 final approach is flown by maintaining a constant airspeed (and constant <u>attitude</u>) ... flying directly towards the runway and then gently flaring the aircraft for touchdown. Simple and straightforward. Quite different from flying final approach in a helicopter, which consists of a continuous gradual reduction in airspeed ... until zero airspeed (a hover) is attained at the touchdown point. Flying a helicopter required the adroit use of two flight controls simultaneously ... the **"cyclic"** for attitude (like a conventional airplane stick) and the **"collective"** for controlling lift. I was wondering how my chopper pilot would respond to his first jet landing. My wonder was soon magnified.

During our first landing approach I quickly recognized that helicopter flying instincts were prevalent in my front seater. <u>Most IP's</u> (instructor pilots) will tell you they will closely guard the control stick and throttles with their hands (when flying in the back seat where the student cannot see them) to observe the tendencies of the student (but mostly to guard against any untoward movements). During his first landing approach I was certainly one of those "Most IP's."

I literally had my hands full ... not just guarding the stick, but actually exerting a holding force ... pushing on the aft cockpit stick as he obviously wanted to pull his "cyclic" back as he approached landing. I'm talking to him of course ... **fast** ... but I'm still having to put a lot of force on the stick to keep him from trying to hover my T-38 while we were still several hundred feet in the air. At the same time his left hand on the T-38 throttles was also following his helicopter instincts ... treating it like a "collective" ... pulling up to maintain the proper helicopter approach. **Not good** to pull the throttles on a T-38 while on final approach while still several hundred feet in the air.

His helicopter instincts were begging for a stall in this T-38. I was forced to vigorously oppose his natural helicopter tendencies ... by pushing forward on the throttles and pushing forward on the stick. He must have thought the control forces in a T-38 were horrible.

It was obvious the first landing was not going to be a success. So I initiated a go around instead of letting him bring my airplane to a crashing halt while we were still in the sky. But I guided him right back up into the pattern where his test pilot potential was affirmed.

On the second approach to landing he made significant progress into the realm of conventional aircraft flying and I didn't have to push nearly as hard on the throttles or the control stick. We were able to make a reasonably successful landing ... hooray !! ... a touch and go. I wanted to give him several chances at mastering this new flying skill, so we did several more touch and go's ... each one a bit more successful than the previous one until finally I was hands free from the controls. I must admit, though, I never really relinquished my vigilance ... my hands remained **real close** to the stick and throttles.

When it was all over, we were both pleased. He had learned a new kind of flying ... and I had survived. I had received some wise advice early in my career ... there is something to be learned from each pilot one flies with. In this case I learned a valuable lesson about pilot instincts ... and sometimes IP's need to be **strong** !!

Swallowed gun door

F-105 (Takhli Air Base, Thailand)

My squadron of F-105 "Thud's," flying out of Takhli Air Base, Thailand, was well into the war in Southeast Asia when "Buick Flight" took off to bomb a bridge in North Vietnam. Buick Flight consisted of four F-105's, each loaded with eight 750 pound bombs plus a full load of 20 mm ammunition for our Gatling guns. We were prepared to wreck havoc on the enemy. Leading the flight (Buick lead) was the most capable and well respected Major Bruce Seeber. I was pleased to be Bruce's wing man (my call sign – Buick 2).

We proceeded to the designated target ... dropped our bombs with deadly accuracy, destroying the bridge ... with minimum exposure to the antiaircraft threat (all 32 bombs were dropped within about 15 seconds).

As we all pulled off the target and joined up in loose formation we then proceeded to do something that was very rarely approved ... <u>armed road recce</u>. We were authorized to use our Gatling guns to strafe any military vehicles we discovered in the hostile area. We had plenty of fuel remaining, so Buick lead began looking for targets, weaving back and forth over a well-used road in North Vietnam, while I flew cover above him looking out for any antiaircraft threat. Buick 3 and 4 followed a discreet distance behind doing the same thing.

Buick Lead sighted some enemy Army trucks moving down the road ... radioed for me to remain high and provide cover while he attacked. I watched as he expertly blasted a couple of enemy trucks at low altitude. As he pulled up, he radioed the dreaded message none of us wanted to hear: **"I've been hit!"** I had not seen anything shooting at lead, but now our interest in trucks instantly vanished. We had more important things to tend to.

Bruce radioed that his engine was still running but he had lost a lot of power and was slowing down. He was still at low altitude when I began closing on him as quickly as possible ... to ascertain the damage. I had to slow down considerably. He was only going about 250 knots ... barely flying speed for a "Thud." This was not an ideal environment ... right above the bad guys ... to be flying that slow. But I had to slow with him to get in close formation where I could assess his condition.

He had wisely jettisoned all of his bomb racks and external fuel tanks, but he was still barely flying ... able at the moment to maintain about 250 knots but unable to climb, maintaining level flight only a couple hundred feet above the mountains. I closed to a few yards from him on his right wing and could observe no damage ... no holes, no leaking fuel or hydraulic fluid ... no smoke ... everything looked normal. Then I moved over to his left wing. Things were different on that side, where his "problem" was most evident.

There was no evidence of battle damage. **However**, the huge 2x4 foot access door that covered his Gatling gun compartment was **completely missing !!** But why would that missing door cause such a loss of power? As I got closer I discovered that the gun bay door had not just blown away. **It was wedged in his engine intake !!** ... **completely blocking off half of the air intake to his engine.** Sucking air feverishly, that trusty J75 turbojet engine was still running ... albeit only producing enough power to barely keep Bruce's Thud airborne. How long would it continue running? The task now at hand was how to get Bruce back to a safe landing a couple of hundred miles away before the engine quit completely.

We decided that I would stay with Bruce as long as possible while Buick 3 and 4 headed back to find an airborne tanker, refuel and be ready to provide rescue support if needed.

Bruce and I headed for the nearest friendly airfield, which happened to be Udorn Air Base, Thailand. It wasn't prudent for me to stay down low and slow with Bruce since we were still over hostile enemy territory. He was barely able to maintain ground clearance ... having to repeatedly change course to avoid some of the higher mountain ridges. I moved up several hundred feet ... accelerated to about 400 knots and flew **S** turns above him so I could keep him in sight at all times and make myself into a little more difficult target. Bruce was pretty calm, considering he was flying low and slow over enemy territory. He kept giving me updates on the radio while trying to maintain sufficient altitude so that if he had to eject it could be done safely.

The minutes seemed to drag as each mountain ridge approached. Bruce was able to weave his way through ... only to find a new ridge ahead. That marvelous J75 turbojet, severely choked and starving for air, was keeping that Thud in the air. Finally there was only one last ridge to cross, but Bruce's Thud seemed to be getting lower and lower. He smoothly maneuvered his way through a saddleback in that last ridge ... and we were elated ... at last to be flying over the flat land of Thailand.

I had alerted Udorn Tower and they were ready and waiting with the fire trucks, and the runway was made clear for our emergency landing. Bruce lined up for a straight-in final approach ... wisely delayed lowering the landing gear and flaps until a landing was assured (sure didn't want that engine to give up now ... when so close). I really rejoiced when I saw Bruce touch down and the big drag chute come out ... bringing that beautiful F-105 to a halt on the runway. Bruce's flying skill and calm demeanor had saved both him and his airplane for another day.

We didn't find out till later that many pieces of the gun bay door had **not** stopped at the intake entrance, but had gone on into the engine itself, chewing up compressor blades and other important engine components!! The rugged F-105 had swallowed a big piece of aluminum and its robust J75 engine had just *taken a lickin' and kept on tickin'*.

The rest of the story: All F-105 gun bay doors were soon modified with several holes to allow dissipation of the pressure which had caused Bruce's door to blow out. On a sadder note, Bruce was later shot down and spent several years as a POW in North Vietnam ... but he returned to a hero's welcome he well deserved.

Gunsight failure

OV-10 (Chu Lai Air Base, Vietnam)

I had just climbed aboard my OV-10 "Bronco" at Chu Lai Air Base, South Vietnam and was beginning to start my engines for a rather routine visual reconnaissance mission when the emergency call came in ... *"Troops in contact ... launch ASAP!"*

For a forward air controller (FAC) the words "troops in contact" generate the most urgent attention. It meant that friendly troops were engaged ... on the ground ... at short range ... with an enemy force. In this case an Army platoon was being attacked by a much larger company size Vietcong unit. Our buddies on the ground needed help ... **pronto**. Wasting no time, I completed most of my preflight checks while taxing at a high rate of speed ... heading for the closest end of the runway ... took off downwind ... in a heavy rainstorm.

I headed directly for the coordinates given me. Enroute to the scene I was in immediate radio contact with the platoon commander and got a scary briefing on the situation. The enemy was within rifle range and was closing in. Two F-4 "Phantom" jet fighters were scrambled from nearby Danang Air Base. They would arrive on the scene just a few minutes after me. My immediate concern was to positively identify the location of the friendlies and the enemy forces. As I orbited over the combat area at a low altitude ... talking with the platoon commander ... I soon had a pretty good handle on where the friendly troops were. But to be sure, I asked him to pop a smoke (set off a smoke grenade) ... which he did.

The situation became more complicated however when **two** smokes came drifting up through the jungle canopy. The enemy was obviously listening on the radio and popped a smoke too !! I had a plan for that ... I asked the platoon commander to pop a colored smoke and not tell me what color he had popped. Up from the trees came two smokes ... one green and one orange. I then asked him what color he popped ... he said **"green."** Now I had a good handle on where both the enemy and friendly troops were, since the enemy had so graciously marked their spot with smoke also. Trying to be clever got them in trouble. I also quickly realized they were very close to each other ... much less than rifle range.

As the fighters arrived overhead, I told them this was going to be a tough mission. The weather was very marginal ... and there were mountains all around ... and the enemy was very close ... requiring precision weapon delivery. There was a ragged low cloud ceiling over the area ... with the mountains sticking up into the clouds. There was also a second layer of clouds just above the first. And to complicate matters ... it was raining. Not the optimum weather conditions ... but our friendly troops on the ground needed our help.

I climbed above the clouds and rendezvoused with the fighters, call sign Gunfighter. They had the right weapons ... Gunfighter Lead was loaded with twelve 500 pound "snake eye" bombs (retarded bombs that could be dropped at very low altitude), and Gunfighter 2 was loaded with eight 200 gallon canisters filled with napalm, also dropped at very low altitude. Gunfighter 2 was also configured with a Gatling gun ... bringing to the fight several hundred rounds of 20 mm ammunition.

I described the situation below to them and told them I would have to lead them down one at a time ... the weather and terrain would just not allow all three of us to be down there at once. I chose to take Gunfighter 2 down first because I figured that napalm would be the best weapon to initially stop the gunfight. I described the terrain to Gunfighter 2 and asked him to follow me down through the clouds as best he could (he would be going at least twice as fast as me).

I found a hole in the clouds and down we went into the valley below. As soon as we got below the lowest clouds Gunfighter 2, with limited visibility caused by the rain, was able to keep me in sight with some exceptional maneuvering. I described the firefight location, pointing out the close proximity of the friendlies and the enemy. The friendlies had helped us by setting a hooch on fire so the friendly position was more readily discernible.

Gunfighter 2 was quick to identify the target. It was going to make for a difficult napalm delivery because the enemy troops were basically in a ravine and there were mountain ridges on either side complicating a low-level deliver ... which had to be parallel to the friendlies to avoid overflight. Close air support rules require substantial situational awareness by the fighter pilot. He must positively identify the target, fully understand the desired release direction, and maintain visual contact with the FAC (to avoid a midair). Maintaining visual contact with me was particularly important in this case as I would maintain an orbit under the low clouds right above the enemy (orbiting the enemy diverted some of their firepower off the friendly troops).

Once I cleared the fighter to drop his ordnance my job was to observe him, making sure he was abiding by the rules ... heading for the proper target ... avoiding overflight of the friendly troops. I could tell Gunfighter 2 was ready, so I told him I would roll in and fire a smoke rocket to mark where I wanted him to drop his napalm. I told him to drop two napalm cans on his first pass, saving the rest for subsequent passes.

Gunfighter 2 positioned himself behind me and I rolled in to fire my first rocket. As I fine-tuned my gunsight the most surprising thing occurred. My usually reliable gunsight **came apart and fell on the floor** !! What a time for a gunsight failure !!

With no time for a "fix it" job, I reverted to my farm boy rifle shooting days and aimed and fired my first rocket <u>instinctively</u>. Fortunately, training and old habits came through and the rocket went where I wanted it to go. It had to, because before the mission was over I would have to put in eight smoke rockets, one at a time to mark the area for the fighters to drop their ordnance.

I pulled off, looked at my mark and said *"Gunfighter 2, hit my smoke"* ... which he did with amazing precision. *"Nice hit 2. Let's drop two more napalm just beyond the last drop."* He acknowledged my direction ... set up for a second pass ... made his obligatory call, *"Helix 11* (my call sign) *in sight."* I responded by giving him clearance *"Gunfighter 2 cleared in hot."* ... Two more napalm canisters precisely delivered. I put in smoke rockets to mark the desired location of the next two napalm deliveries, making sure we had covered most of the enemy territory. Our friendly platoon commander was ecstatic. The small arms fire from the enemy soldiers had diminished dramatically. It was now time to bring in the general-purpose bombs to quell the remaining resistance. I sent Gunfighter 2 above the clouds ... as I also went up to lead Gunfighter Lead back down through the cloud cover and to give him an orientation briefing. It was now much easier to locate the target area, with eight cans of napalm burning ferociously.

Gunfighter Lead oriented himself quickly and it was time for me again to mark the locations where I wanted his 500 pound bombs to impact. Without a gunsight, marking the exact location was still a challenge, but the criticality and urgency of this battle prompted me to place my smoke rockets exactly. With the enemy now fleeing the burning area I decided to have Gunfighter Lead drop his twelve 500 pound bombs in pairs ... two at a time. Prior to each pass I would put in a smoke rocket, selecting desired bomb impact points around the periphery of the burning area. Gunfighter Lead was also extremely accurate, placing his bombs precisely where I had marked, carefully aware of the near proximity of the friendly troops. His six passes, dropping two bombs at a time, effectively covered the whole enemy complex.

After being confronted with eight cans of searing napalm and twelve explosive shrapnel producing 500 pound bombs, the enemy was only able to muster sporadic gunfire. Gunfighter Flight had done good work. The enemy was in obvious disarray. But Gunfighter 2 still had a load of 20 mm ammunition. That was just perfect to ensure the remaining enemy force would retreat quickly out of the area completely.

I sent Gunfighter Lead back on top of the clouds ... went back up and escorted Gunfighter 2 back down into the battle area. Gunfighter 2's Gatling gun would provide more of a noisy threat than an actual destructive force against enemy troops in the trees below, so I asked Gunfighter 2 to spread his 20 mm impacts around ... right on the edge of the burning area closest to the friendlies ... kind of a "herding" action. Again he placed his ordnance precisely.

All ordnance on target in minimum time !! *"Well done Gunfighter Flight!"* They had worked under adverse weather and terrain conditions ... with precision and discipline ... and had done their job well.

I said farewell to Gunfighter Flight, thanking them for their excellent support, and then turned my attention back to the battle scene, discussing with the platoon commander the results of our airstrike. He immediately sent a couple of scouts towards the enemy location where they only encountered an occasional sniper. They reported the enemy had obviously retreated ... **our mission had been successful !!**. How successful we didn't know until they sent a larger patrol into the area and discovered nine dead enemy soldiers and multiple blood trails indicating many wounded enemy soldiers had been removed from the scene. A major battle won ... without the loss of any friendly soldiers !!

The satisfaction of driving off an attacking enemy force and saving friendly troops from destruction cannot be overstated. Both the FAC and the fighter pilot are trained to respond professionally in a close air support environment. When friendly troops are in contact with the enemy, mechanical failures, adverse weather, adverse terrain, etc. are no excuse for not providing the support our friendly soldiers on the ground need and deserve. It was a privilege to be a part of such an operation.

napalm delivery

www.ingramcontent.com/pod-product-compliance
Lightning Source LLC
Chambersburg PA
CBHW070717160426
43192CB00009B/1227